W9-AGU-796

Shakespeare

The poet in his world

Shakespeare

The poet in his world

M. C. Bradbrook

Columbia University Press
New York

Published in 1978 in the United States of America by
Columbia University Press and in Great Britain by
Weidenfeld and Nicolson

Printed in Great Britain

LIBRARY OF CONGRESS CATALOGING IN PUBLICATION
DATA
Bradbrook, Muriel Clara.
    Shakespeare: the poet in his world.
    Bibliography: p.
    1. Shakespeare, William, 1564–1616.
    2. Dramatists, English—Early modern, 1500–1700—
Biography.
PR2894.B69   822.3'3   78–7611
ISBN 0–231–04648–0 (cloth)
ISBN 0–231–04649–9 (paperback)

Second cloth and first paperback printing

Printed in the United States of America

Contents

Preface

'We *know* we cannot write a biography of Shakespeare; we *think* we can write one of Marlowe.'

These alarming words, pronounced a quarter of a century ago at Cambridge by Oxford's Merton Professor, have not deterred the biographers. Since those days reinforcements have come from the developing historical disciplines of social and cultural history, demography, the growth of art history and theatre research, enabling a legitimate expansion upon the documentary material of Shakespeare's personal life – less extensive than Marlowe's lawless career provided. Joel Hurstfield, Geoffrey Elton, Christopher Morris, have contributed directly as historians to Shakespearean studies – which indeed were always seen as relevant by the best teachers of the older generation, Trevelyan or my own preceptor, Helen Cam, Fellow of Girton and Professor at Harvard (America has contributed much here).

I have tried to see Shakespeare in his social context of Stratford and London; this contrast is set out in my first two chapters. Without his dual role as actor and playwright, Shakespeare's imagination could not have gained the extra dimensions of a performing art; he had to take, and constantly reshaped, what public taste and his fellows offered. Marlowe and Jonson influenced most powerfully his youth and his maturity; he set Henry VI against Tamburlaine, his final Romances against the Stuart Masque, as I have sketched out in chapters 3–4 and 11–12. The relation to his acting company, the third great influence, is the subject of chapters 5–7.

I have assumed that for him, in common with the rest of his age, family and religion were governing features of his inner as of his outer life. Neither is likely to be as powerful today;

but by many historians, from Lawrence Stone to Peter Laslett, the family is seen as the conditioning factor for Court and Country. Family tables show how close was the governing network in the Court circle of the players' patrons (there was a like pattern in the City of London). When Shakespeare had succeeded in London, his youngest brother and his eldest nephew quite naturally followed, to be introduced into his craft of the theatre, although neither achieved any fame. However, Charles Hart, the star of the Restoration stage, may have been his illegitimate great-nephew. He was Nell Gwynn's first love.

In its archæology and iconography, theatrical history has recently made great strides, but its sociology is still a comparatively unexplored field. In Shakespeare's day, religious conflicts dominated the political scenes – as in Ireland today, where the situation is inherited from those struggles which engaged and defeated Essex and Southampton at the end of the sixteenth century. Shakespeare, as a player, was exposed to special religious pressures from the left wing of the reformers and also to insults which seem to me to have left their mark in *The Merchant of Venice* and *King Lear*. Doctrine was continually at war with Charity, so that for anyone of a religious temper, the inner struggle must always have been severe. In choosing the life of the theatre, Shakespeare showed not merely courage and initiative but readiness to expose himself to the slings and arrows of outrageous fortune, not only from slander and detraction within and without the ranks but from the natural hazards of plague. It has been recently suggested that the history of epidemics is more significant than military history for Western Europe. On the most conservative estimate, seven years of Shakespeare's theatrical career were cut out by plague.

Parallel to the new tendencies to reinforce documentary biography from social history, psychological interpretation and analysis have become almost a necessity, for which any artist provides plenitude of 'evidence'. It seems to me, however, that to put Shakespeare's collected works on the analyst's couch – those triumphs of health and adjustment, so long surviving his mortal frame – is to seek the living among the dead. Though reductive diagrams have their uses, art is not material for amateur pathologists. Although modern interests are strongly drawn to the view that, for Shakespeare the artist, his prick was more important than his prayers, even the Sonnets contain a good deal of prayer.

The Sonnets also provide the largest area for biographical fancy: 'Mr W.H.', to whom the printer dedicated his unsponsored edition of 1609, would seem from the tone of that brief acknowledgment to be the printer's social equal, the procurer rather than the subject of the verses. Of the dozens of identifications which are recorded in the great Variorum edition, no single one has established itself. I have assumed that the fair youth was the Earl of Southampton, on the evidence as I read it; but of course it may be turned to fit many other candidates – a new one reached me by this morning's post. However, as I explain in Chapters 9 and 10, I think that the combined influences of Essex and Southampton on the writings of Shakespeare may be less significant than the Gunpowder Plot.

As no book on Shakespeare would be complete without the offer of a new candidate for the role of Dark Lady (or Nice Wanton), conscious that this duty has been neglected in the book itself, after much cogitation it seems to me that Mrs Winifred Burbage has the double advantage of novelty and plausibility. The lady was dark, musical and married – this is the sum of our direct information. Mrs Burbage's Christian name is Welsh; the Welsh are almost invariably dark and musical and not infrequently married. Many light o' loves in Stuart drama are named Winifred or Win; a very early story shows Shakespeare sprinting ahead of Burbage to an assignation with a citizen's wife who had fallen for the actor in his role of Richard III, and sending a triumphant message that 'William the Conqueror' was come before Richard III. Any amateur pathologist will recognize the displacement of the sonnet situation here; think too what a resonance is given to the role of Othello played by Burbage. Every ingenious reader is, of course, entitled to supply what emendations or expansions he chooses to this humble suggestion.

In conclusion, I would like to thank Professor Schoenbaum for saving me from error in the opening chapters, and the staff of Weidenfeld and Nicolson for their help.

The world he found

1 The cradle of security

> Ceres, most bounteous lady, thy rich leas
> Of wheat, rye, barley, vetches, oats and pease;
> Thy turfy mountains, where live nibbling sheep,
> And flat meads thatch'd with stover, them to keep;
> Thy banks with pioned and twilled brims,
> Which spongy April at thy hest betrims . . .
>   (*The Tempest*, 4.1.60–5)

Prospero's masque presents the country where Shakespeare was born, from which his imagination was never divided; cradled by the Malvern and Cotswold hills with their sheep-cotes, it was intensely cultivated, well stocked, richly watered. Ceres responds to the invocation with blessing:

> Earth's increase, foison plenty,
> Barns and garners never empty;
> Vines with clust'ring bunches growing,
> Plants with goodly burden bowing . . .
>   (4.1.110–13)

The poet's own imaginative opulence is epitomized in the warm fertility of the scene. His contemporaries singled out the natural wealth of his language; 'right happy and *copious* industry', praised by his fellow-poet John Webster, was termed 'easiness', 'facility' and 'fluency' by other contemporaries. The mere size of his vocabulary is increased by his facility in coining new words.[1]

In Shakespeare's day each region had its own pronunciation and its own poetic tradition. A certain continuity in the Warwickshire strain, powerful but not obtrusive, derived perhaps from the situation at the heart of England. The region was rustic without being provincial, offering the main highway between north and south (eastward, the fen country almost cut England into two).

If poetic genealogy may be regional, Shakespeare's country had provided two of the greatest masters of language in the later Middle Ages, both of whom worked in oral traditions, drawing on very old forms but blending them with more modern ones. Shakespeare, like Langland in the mid-fourteenth century and Malory in the fifteenth, composed for performance. The oral tradition allows a very easy modulation from the familiar and everyday to the heights of formal grandeur, because the spoken word can effect these transitions, where writing cannot.

Langland had made his way from the Malvern hills to London two hundred years before Shakespeare; the span and strength of execution in his *Piers Plowman* passed from waking life on the hills or in the turmoil of Cheapside or Westminster Hall to spiritual heights and depths. His words are sharp, the verse moves freely and spontaneously in the free unrhymed line that derived from *Beowulf* ('a sort of talking style', as one critic terms it), where nevertheless all his force can be put behind one phrase.

> A fair field full of folk, found I there betwyne,
> Of alle manere of men, the mene and the poor,
> Worchyng and wandryng as this world asketh,

can lead to a vision of eternity, 'For I that am lord of lyfe, love is my drink,' in a complex blend of the old alliterative form with new London ways.

Malory, who had died in a London prison about a hundred years before Shakespeare's birth, came from Warwickshire and learned from the unrhyming alliterative poets before he took to translating Arthurian tales from the French.[2] In Arthur's death scene there is a foreshadowing of *3 Henry VI*, 2.5; in both, the ultimate horror of civil war being mutual destruction of fathers and sons. The heroic tale is grave, masculine, concerned with personal relations as part of the social fellowship of the Round Table.

Both these writers re-worked and remoulded their great cyclic masterpieces, not being constrained by the artificial stability of print. Shakespeare's too was an art of performance, and so maintained continuity with the earlier times. Community of theme with his country life emerged in the rural parts of *King Henry IV*, *As You Like It* and *The Winter's Tale*.

Shakespeare's contemporary and near neighbour, Michael Drayton, invoked Ceres too in writing of Warwickshire:

> As still the year goes on, that Ceres once doth load,
> The full earth with her store, my plenteous bosom strowed
> With all abundant sweets. . . .
> (*Polyolbion*, 16th Song, 395–7)

He knows the rural legends – 'a pretty tale I of my grandam had' who, by the winter's fire, tells of 'a knight hight Cassaman', living 'far in the country of Arden', who was 'bold as Isenbras'.

The diamond-shaped wedge of Warwickshire, divided between the northern woodland of Arden and the richer southern plain of Felton, resembles the country which was to be divided by King Lear (who gave his name to Leicester, a neighbouring shire),

> With shadowy forests and with champains rich'd,
> With plenteous rivers and wide-skirted meads . . .
> (*King Lear*, 1.1.63–4)

but down in the south-westerly quarter, the comfortable little borough town of Stratford lies nearer to the Cotswolds and their hill cotes, to the apple orchards of the cider country, the gentler, warmer airs, dairy pastures and thickly planted gardens round cottages of wattle-and-daub in the Vale of Evesham than to the windier flat plains of Leicestershire. The town comes into view best where from the crest of the Evesham road it appears below, spread out beside the slowly moving Avon, with Trinity Church at the nearer end and at the farthest the great Tudor bridge of rosy brick that leads the London road across from Butts Green; while behind, along the Evesham road, lie Worcester and Bristol.

Shakespeare's town is still small, though perhaps five times the size it was in his day; yet the streets suddenly deposit the traveller in open country – the walk to Shottery and Anne Hathaway's cottage is still rural. The house in which he was born stands about five minutes' walk from the site of the one where he died, just across Chapel Lane from the school where he acquired what formal learning he chose to take: another seven minutes would bring him past the house where his elder daughter was to live, to the parish church.

He had been lucky – lucky in his birth, neither to great riches nor to great poverty, the son of a man who had moved in from one of the necklace of villages that surround the little market town. John Shakespeare, brought up a farmer's son in Snitterfield four miles to the north, where there was not even a vicar, only a poor curate, did not learn to read or write. Perhaps Shakespeare's cousin James, who farmed there after his uncle Henry died in 1596, could not read or write either. John Shakespeare was a glover and 'whitawer' by trade – that is, he cured delicate white skins for gloves for falconers and huntsmen; he was a dealer in wool (shreds were to be found between the floor boards of the eastern half of the Birthplace, which served as the shop); he also bought timber and barley; above all he bought houses and leased them. He had made a good and prudent marriage – in fact, he married his landlord's daughter, for his father Richard had been a tenant of Robert Arden of Wilmcote. Some time before 1558 John Shakespeare married the youngest daughter, Mary, who was by then an orphan possessed of comfortable property and her father's executor.

She seems to have laid claim to gentility and to have sought relationship with the very ancient family of Ardens of Park Hall; but although the Heralds' Office was later to allow a grant of arms to John Shakespeare, on his first application, in 1576, they drew and then crossed out the arms of the Ardens of Park Hall, which he wished to impale with his own. Mary Arden was *not* the daughter of Robert Arden Esquire but of Robert Arden yeoman. (The habit of claiming kinship with great families is a familiar weakness of poets; with Elizabethans it was endemic. Spenser, son of a very poor London journeyman, claimed kinship with the great Spencers of Althorp, though they were a new family, Middleton the dramatist with Sir Hugh Myddelton.) William Shakespeare reapplied, although in his father's name, renewing the earlier appeal, and arms were granted in 1597, not without some disagreement among the heralds, for gentlemen were one thing and players another. However, his fellow-players Burbage and Heminges, Phillips and Pope, all devised or simply appropriated coats-of-arms. As one of the King's Players, after 1604, Shakespeare, when deputed to wait on the Spanish Ambassador, could go suitably equipped. He hoped to found a family of country gentlefolk; his grand-daughter died as Lady Barnard; indeed, his elder daughter might have been Lady Hall, if her sensible husband had not preferred to pay a fine of £10 to evade the honour.

Just as a household was effectually represented by its head, who appeared on behalf of his family, initiated actions in court, recorded votes, so the gentry had a voice in the affairs of the county denied to lesser men. In practice, of course, communities were as important as hierarchies: a clever servant could rule his master or a shrewish wife her husband; at a dispute between lord and tenant, memories of the oldest inhabitant might prevail (in 1601 John Shakespeare, Gent., testified against the Lord of the Manor's enclosures in Stratford). But, as Sir Thomas Aston was later to say, 'The primates, the nobiles, with the minores nobiles, the gentry, consult and dispose of the rules of government; the plebeians submit to and obey them' (A Remonstrance against Presbytery, 1641). If the shape of society was changing, new men adopted old forms. Ralegh, mere Devon gentry, contrived sixteen quarterings for his coat-of-arms, while Essex (only the second earl) denounced him as an upstart.

The little country town of Stratford, which since Domesday Book had been a manor of the bishops of Worcester, at the Reformation was seized by the Crown, and suffered a period of administrative chaos. The laymen who were now lords of the manor could not, though they tried, assert rights of old custom; the town was run by its leading families, though the chief officer was still termed Bailiff, not Mayor. The old Guild of Holy Cross (suppressed in 1547), which under the bishops had administered town affairs, had built a school and almshouses, which still stand (their beautiful register, which contains 'sisters' as well as 'brethren', is also preserved). Some endowments went to the town to pay the stipend of vicars and schoolmasters, though nomination remained with the Lord of the Manor. The first town charter (1553) named fourteen Aldermen who had the right to choose fourteen other members of common council. That rapacious man John Dudley, Duke of Northumberland, the first secular Lord of the Manor, had put in Thomas Guildford as Bailiff. After Dudley was attainted of treason for his attempt to make Lady Jane Grey queen, the Crown re-granted the Lordship to Dudley's son, the Earl of Warwick, who attended court leets in 1583 and 1584.

Everyday business was carried on by the Bailiff and Aldermen – they supervised the fairs, the Court of Record, the care of the bridge and highways, school, church, chapel.

In their lists are names still to be seen today in Stratford – Whateleys and Quineys (the Quineys, vintners, into which family Shakespeare's younger daughter married, now deliver milk). These men became John Shakespeare's friends, for he must have been out of his apprenticeship before the charter put an end to administrative chaos and gave the burgesses their chance. By the next year he was a householder.

Unlike her big neighbour Coventry, Stratford had not been a town of specialists. (The famous Coventry blue thread was known all over England.) There were three markets to be supervised by the old religious guild – one at the cross, where Bridge Street leads up from the river to the High Street, running safely beyond flood level; the Rothermarket for cattle, still a market centre; with a third outside the Guild Chapel for dairy goods. Henley Street, where John Shakespeare lived, leads off from the Market Cross; excellent leather goods may still be found nearby. The town was still well wooded, with gardens, two little brooks running down to the Avon, willows along the banks. The College of Priests, founded to serve the church by John de Stratford, Archbishop of Canterbury in Chaucer's day, had been suppressed along with the guild; their building was snapped up by a leading local family, the Combes. Under the eye of such men Stratford was enjoying its new form of self-government. Of the local gentry round about, some belonged to the old faith – Catesbys and Winters, Treshams and Cloptons, some to the new – like the Grevilles, one of whom now held the Lordship of the Manor from the Earl of Warwick, and the Lucys of Charlecote; while the Throckmortons produced nationally famous specimens of both Puritans and Papists – Job Throckmorton wrote for the secret Marprelate Press in 1589, a later Throckmorton conspired in the Gunpowder Plot of 1605.

Even a little village like Snitterfield had its bailiff in 1530, it was Thomas, Lord Wriothesley, the future Earl of Southampton's grandfather, who would not disdain to collect his fee, and might stand good lord to his friends.[3] The Steward was even nobler – Charles Brandon, Duke of Suffolk, Henry VIII's brother-in-law, but doubtless he also collected his fee.

The little community at Stratford knew its neighbourly differences. Some men, like the Catholic George Badger (a draper) and Nicholas Barnhurst (another draper and a Puritan), engaged in public disputes. It was when Will Bott was expelled from the council for 'opprobrious words' that the vacancy was to be filled by John Shakespeare. The neighbours fined each other for small breaches of conduct – John Shakespeare's first appearance in the records, together with his neighbour Quiney and others, was a fine on 29 April 1552, for having an unauthorized muck-heap in the street before his house. As one of the main roads to the market cross, it should not be blocked – similar objections are made nowadays to the presence of too many motor-coaches outside that same dwelling, where, on or about 23 April 1564, William Shakespeare was born.

Throughout the first eighteen years of Elizabeth's reign, John Shakespeare continued his successful public life; the year after the birth of his eldest son, in 1565, he became an Alderman, one of the small leading group. As Chamberlain he supervised the accounts, making his mark with a pair of glover's compasses, the sign of his trade. In the year 1569, when young Will was five, John was Bailiff, and in that year the armed insurrection of the Northern Earls – the last serious armed attempt on English soil against Elizabeth's rule – meant that he had to supply the eight men the town sent to the musters with armour from the town armoury.

Not only would John Shakespeare have taken the oath to the Queen, he would also serve as JP, President of the Court of Record, clerk of the market, King's escheator, coroner and almoner. An absolute Johannes Fac Totum! (Next year, with the new Bailiff, Adrian Quiney, he went to London on business for the town.)

But in the winter, with rebellion still not quelled and the captive Mary, Queen of Scots, rushed south to Coventry, stories of the old days would be revived, days when Nevilles, Percys and Cliffords from the north fought across the length and breadth of the country in the Wars of the Roses. John Shakespeare's forebears had done valiant service for the Earl of Richmond, who became King Henry VII in 1485. Or so the heralds were told as John essayed to follow Adrian Quiney, who had already obtained a coat-of-arms and wrote himself gentleman.[4]

The sons and daughters of John and Mary Shakespeare were brought up in an illiterate household – neither parent witnessed except with a mark. In such surroundings oral memory is improved, and tales by the fire become the natural resource on winter nights, whether history, legend or romance:

a tale of an hour long ... look you, gammer, of the giant and the king's daughter and I know not what; I have seen the day, when I was a little one, you might have drawn me a mile after you with such a discourse.

(George Peele, *Life and Works*, ed. Prouty, III, 390)

This is the prelude to 'a merry winter's tale' for the early stage, but in one of Shakespeare's later romances, which is full of country lore, little Mamillius tells us 'a sad tale's best for winter' and is encouraged by his mother,

Let's have that, good sir.
Come on, sit down; come on, and do your best
To fright me with your sprites; you're pow'rful at it.

He whispers in her ear, 'There was a man dwelt by a churchyard ...' (*The Winter's Tale*, 2.1.25–30). King Richard II imagined that 'the lamentable tale of me' would send the hearers weeping to their beds; more prophetic of what was to come is the account of how he could people one little room with his thoughts 'like unto the people of the world'. The Shakespeare family would hear of the legendary local hero, Guy of Warwick, of his adventures in distant lands and how he came home at last in disguise and begged alms at his own castle gate. They would hear too the great local fairytale of the man whose family tombs filled up the old Lady Chapel of Stratford Church – Sir Hugh Clopton, who went up to London, made a fortune there and, like Dick Whittington, became Lord Mayor: how he came back and built the town's great bridge with its fourteen arches, to cross to the London road.

At the age of five William would go to petty school, where he would learn his catechism; he would have learned to say his prayers at home – Sonnet 108 implies that he continued to say them every day. He would be taught to read. Then the grammar school would receive him, and he would begin Latin with Lyly's Latin grammar. Most of the schoolboys depicted in the plays are rather unwilling scholars, hoping for holidays, but little William in *The Merry Wives of Windsor* makes a shot at declining pronouns (4.1).

After two years in the petty school and two or three in the lower school with the usher, Shakespeare would pass at ten or eleven to the upper school and the guidance of the master. From 1575 to 1579 Thomas Jenkins held the post. In spite of his name, he was from not Wales but London, the son of a poor man who was servant to Sir Thomas White. Sir Thomas had founded St John's College in Oxford and was also a great benefactor of the Merchant Taylors' School in London. If Jenkins, who had graduated from St John's College, had been a pupil at Merchant Taylors' School, he would have been taught by Richard Mulcaster, author of that great educational book the *Elementarie* and a fervent believer in teaching through play-acting to give his boys 'good pronunciation and audacity'. He trained them in pronunciation, and he believed in English – 'I love Rome, but London better, I favour Italy but England more; I honour the Latin but I worship the English.'

Mulcaster's boys often performed before Queen Elizabeth; once in their Hall they put on a 'Dream', in which they suggested that Sir Thomas White give them more scholarships to his new foundation at Oxford. Thus, Shakespeare could have been taught, and probably was, in the best tradition of English schools. Certainly all the masters in his plays (Holofernes, Evans, the pedant Prospero) like putting on plays.

Shakespeare would have begun school at six or seven in the morning and, with brief intervals, continued till five. A good schoolmaster was supposed to teach 'religion' as well as 'good letters'; learning was largely memorizing – the grind of Latin grammar, the *Sententiae Pueriles*, the *Cato* of Erasmus, Plautus, Terence and later Ovid, Vergil and Horace, with writing of themes, letters and (ultimately) orations. Study of the classics was assumed to provide against all exigencies of practical as well as spiritual life, for readiness of speech could mean life or death for a man on trial, who had to conduct his own defence – but few would contemplate that as a destined certainty. Law and the Church required eloquence, and by this means men like Sir Thomas Smith, Ambassador to Paris, or Matthew Parker, Archbishop of Canterbury, rose to eminence (Parker's father was a weaver in Norwich). But the system induced a linguistic ritualism, manifested in early Elizabethan days in stiff verbal patterns, strange theories, inkhorn terms, mad schemes for spelling reform. Spenser, one of Mulcaster's boys, worked through some preposterous experiments before he found himself.

It was well that Shakespeare had an alternative mode of education. To entertain family and neighbours, a bright lad would show his virtuosity. One of John Aubrey's legends says that the young Shakespeare would 'kill a calf' (this was a term for a dramatic monologue) in high style 'and make a speech'. Of course not all parents would approve – Ben Jonson gives his Mistress Censure some very strong views:

> They might make all their scholars play boys! Is't not a fine sight to see all our children made interluders? Do we pay our money for this? We send them to learn their grammar and their Terence and they learn their playbooks!
>
> (*The Staple of News*, conclusion to Act III)

Shakespeare would recall his school texts to guy a village schoolmaster:

Fauste, precor gelida quando pecus omne sub ombra
Ruminat –
and so forth. Ah, good old Mantuan! I may speak of thee as the traveller doth of Venice:

Venetia, Venetia
Chi non ti vede, non ti pretia.

Old Mantuan, old Mantuan! Who understandeth thee not, loves thee not. . . .

(*Love's Labour's Lost*, 4.4.89–95)

The brightest of all his young courtiers in this same play is reduced to 'russet yeas and honest kersey noes' for his wooing; the quick wit of Portia or Isabella must fall back on the Lord's Prayer to plead for mercy.

Some of the early plays might – and did – furnish examples for a school book of rhetoric –

> Was ever woman in this humour woo'd,
> Was ever woman in this humour won?
> (*Richard III*, 1.2.227–8)

which is a long way however from the wooing of earlier Tudor times in which a young scholar might ask his mistress, 'What is equipollent to your formosity?'

Though Shakespeare was pleased enough with his trope to be using it in *Richard III* for the third time, within a few lines Crookback is adding,

> And I no friends to back my suit at all
> But the plain devil and dissembling looks,
> And yet to win her, all the world to nothing!
> Ha!
> (*Richard III*, 1.2.235–8)

which throws back its own colloquial vigour on the rhetorical passages. Yet, in *Troilus and Cressida* Shakespeare was to write a whole play in specially Latinate diction. Later still he was to write, in a style that struck some of his contemporaries as remarkably naïve, of 'tales, tempests and such drolleries' but in language which is sometimes extremely intricate and elliptical.

In his darkest play, *King Lear*, reminiscences of that early training in the Bible, constant recollections of the New Testament, *Ecclesiastes* or *The Book of Job*, appear, whether in the unforgiving Goneril,

> Milk-liver'd man!
> That bear'st a cheek for blows . . .
> (*King Lear*, 4.2.50—1 ; cf *Matthew*, 5.39)

or the generous French King,

> Fairest Cordelia, that art most rich, being poor;
> Most choice, forsaken; and most lov'd, despis'd!
> *(King Lear*, 1.1.250–1; cf 2 *Corinthians*, 6.10)

Proverbs may be mocked in the mouth of the common people:

> They said they were an-hungry; sigh'd forth proverbs,
> That hunger broke stone walls, that dogs must eat,
> That meat was made for mouths ...
> *(Coriolanus*, 1.1.203–5)

but they suffice the tragic hero, in the height of his weariness
and remorse: 'It will have blood; they say blood will have blood'
(*Macbeth*, 3.4.122) though it is Macbeth who can find such a
phrase for blood as

> ... this my hand will rather
> The multitudinous seas incarnadine,
> Making the green one red.
> *(Macbeth*, 2.2.61–3)

The immense range of Shakespeare's language – his inventiveness, his facility, his power of recall to just the right level of
conscious use – was his unique endowment, but it was fostered
in the fortunate situation of good regular schooling against the
background of oral training in a not unintelligent home. (The
effects will be seen later, in considering what he was to make
of it.)

What introduction would life in Stratford have given to the
life of an actor or a playwright? Whitsun games and pageants
were not unknown: Davy Jones, who led them at Stratford in
1583, had been married to a Quiney and afterwards was to wed
a Hathaway. In that same season, three play-troupes passed
through Stratford, performing first in the Guild Hall, as had
been the custom for many years. This was the 'town's show'
before the Bailiff, who gave what reward he deemed suitable. In John Shakespeare's palmy days he too had entertained

the players in their summer visitations, and paid for their entertainment.

From the neighbouring county of Gloucester comes the record of such a performance as witnessed by a child in 1570. At the 'Mayor's play' he stood between his father's legs as he sat upon the front bench, 'where we saw and heard very well'. Seventy years later, as an old man, he was to declare, 'This sight took such impression on me, that when I came towards man's estate, it was as fresh in my memory as if I had seen it newly acted' (Robert Willis, *Mt Tabor*, 1639, 113).

The play was entitled *The Cradle of Security*, a moral mixture of show, song and lament. The chief personage, whom the child realized to be 'a king or some great prince', was enticed into a huge cradle and rocked asleep by three ladies, who suddenly transformed his face with 'a vizard like a swine's snout', cleverly manipulated into position with wire chains while they sang. Then two old men came on, the first in red with a drawn sword, the other in blue carrying a mace with which he struck a fearful blow on the cradle. The courtiers vanished, and the woeful prince, once more with a human face, started up to behold Death and Judgment and, after lamenting his condition, was carried away by wicked spirits.

Since Stratford lay on the road from Coventry to Bristol, two great provincial centres to which actors resorted in summer tours, Shakespeare could well have seen this play. In the Shakespearean *Sir Thomas More*, it heads the players' repertory (4.1.41). Perhaps he remembered as clearly as did little Robert Willis the fell Sergeant Death, 'strict in his arrest'. The two would have been much of an age in 1570.

In the year 1575, the greatest spectacle ever put on in the provinces greeted Queen Elizabeth at Kenilworth Castle. The Princely Pleasures of Kenilworth lasted eighteen days and cost the Earl of Leicester a fortune. There were shows within the moat, the Lady of the Lake appearing to do homage; there was Arion on a dolphin's back – being unable to sing through his mask, he tore it off and told the Queen that he was plain Henry Goldingham – and there were special woodland pageants on days when the Queen hunted. The men of Coventry put on a series of drill displays and mock fights, led by their muster master, a fencer, one Captain Cox, who had a whole library of romances – 'great oversight hath he in matter of story.' The townsmen took the opportunity to revive their 'storial show' which had been put down by preachers, 'too sour in preaching away their pastime'. This Hock Tuesday sport commemorated a battle between the English and Danes on St Brice's Day, 1002, but seems also to have incorporated a mock battle between men and women, a folk game for Hock Tuesday (which follows the second Sunday after Easter) when women collected money from 'captive' men, towards a feast; Coventry associated it with the life of King Edward the Confessor. Ten years earlier Mary Stuart had characteristically played the game in Edinburgh on Hock Monday 1565; the English Ambassador described how: 'On Monday, she and divers of her women apparelled themselves like bourgeois wives, went upon their feet up and down the town; of every man they met, took some pledge of money to the banquet; and in the lodging where I was accustomed to lodge, there was the dinner prepared ...' (quoted J. B. Black, *The Reign of Elizabeth*, 1936, p. 70). In 1575 Mary's statelier cousin Queen Elizabeth graciously rewarded the players with two fat buck, and five marks in money.

Since the Stratford Manor had passed to Leicester's brother, the Earl of Warwick, as the tenant-in-chief holding it from the Queen (though it was held of him by Sir Edward Greville) Stratford burgesses may have been allowed a sight of the sports or even, by favour, been allowed into the private garden, with its aviary, full of tropical birds, and the fountain, which, by turning of a hidden tap, enabled the playful courtier to drench his fellows from top to toe. Certainly the Earl of Leicester's players would be there and in fine fettle too, for they were about to open in London a playhouse built by one of their number, James Burbage, to be known as The Theatre. They were the leading troupe in the kingdom. A servant of Burghley, one Patten, wrote of the entertainment in a Letter to London which is a prime source for our knowledge of these delights.

A string of brothers and sisters joined William. In all, Mary Shakespeare bore eight children in twenty-two years, of whom half survived: William was the eldest survivor. They were named for friends and for the sisters of Mary, who lived in neighbouring villages.

In the summer of Shakespeare's birth, the plague struck Stratford, its chief victims being the very young and very old. Between one-sixth and one-seventh of the population died. Anyone who could leave such a plague-spot would do so, if they could be received elsewhere; the natural thing would have been for Mary to take her infant to Uncle Henry at Snitterfield, or to one of her own sisters, perhaps to Burton Heath, a name which stuck in Shakespeare's memory. She had already lost two girls.

Of Shakespeare's brother Richard we know nothing except that he was born ten years after the poet, died three years before him and in 1608 was summoned before the ecclesiastical court of Stratford, admitted his offence (whatever it was) and was ordered to pay twelve pence for the use of the poor. He had probably broken the sabbath, a frequent charge; nothing serious, obviously.

Gilbert Shakespeare, like his more famous brother, went to London. He became a haberdasher in St Bride's parish – near to Blackfriars. The youngest, Edmund, born when Shakespeare was sixteen, also went to London and became an actor, dying at the age of twenty-seven. He was given an expensive burial in St Mary Overy, with an hour's tolling of the great bell, paid for, presumably, by William. Shakespeare's three younger brothers all died before him, and none was married – which prompts speculation.

Their one surviving sister, Joan, married a hatter named Hart and went to live in the old home in Henley Street. (Descendants of this marriage still survive, the only collaterals of Shakespeare.) Gilbert took conveyance of a Stratford property for his brother on 1 May 1602 and was buried there four years before his elder brother, so he too retained an interest in the birthplace.

In the year of John Shakespeare's death, 1601, of an estimated Stratford population of about fifteen hundred, seven hundred were said to be 'poor'. The town council, which also acted as parish council, exercised the right of the latter to collect money for their relief.

Among the poor we must not number John Shakespeare, yet from the year 1576 (when Shakespeare at twelve would be just entered in the upper school) this active and industrious burgess suddenly and almost completely absented himself from meetings of the council. His neighbours forbore to penalize him and let him off both dues and fines. Meanwhile tell-tale bits of property, mortgaged and conveyed by leasehold, mostly within the family, reveal his decline. His wife's property in his native village of Snitterfield went in 1579 for a paltry £4. It has been suggested that this was a method of protecting property from sequestration, but the haphazard style of it, and later unsuccessful attempts to get it back, do not favour this notion.

John Shakespeare stood surety for various wrongdoers, and this was a recognized way to exploit his standing as an Alderman. He could collect a little ready money for this good office from the beneficiary – but of course he stood to lose more if the bond he gave became forfeit. William must have learned all about forfeiting of bonds in these years. Once his father went security for a neighbour who was a tinker and forfeited £10. This, and the alderman's thumb ring (which would have been used for sealing), were to crop up in the plays.[5]

Times were hard and getting harder, for the 1590s saw a big economic recession with some very disastrous harvests. In 1591 John Shakespeare, who had once processed to church in the scarlet gown of the Bailiff, dared not go for fear of being arrested for debt.

Among the Shakespearean legends is one that John Shakespeare could not continue his son's education. Sometime between twelve and fifteen was the age for proceeding to the university, if that were decided upon (Marlowe went up in 1580, at sixteen). The alternative would be to bind Shakespeare apprentice in the town, and the obvious as well as the cheapest thing would be to apprentice him to his father. An apprentice was not paid, and he served seven years, during which time he was not permitted to marry. He would expect his freedom by twenty-one.

William Shakespeare's marriage at the age of eighteen to Anne Hathaway of Stratford, maiden, was most unusual. She was eight years his senior and, at twenty-six, about the age when marriage was customary. Marriages at a younger age were common enough in great families, for the sake of securing an inheritance; and at eighteen an attractive boy would have been a strong family asset had he chosen to marry a fortune. This would have repaired John Shakespeare's circumstances and be looked on without surprise, even if the bride had been much older than Anne was:[6] but Anne Hathaway's dowry as devised by her father was only the customary ten marks (£6 13 4d). This marriage, moreover, was conducted by special licence from the Bishop; a bond was entered by Fulke Sendells and John Richardson, two friends of the bride's father (now deceased), who had been a substantial yeoman farmer in Shottery, a nearby village. It was given at the consistory court at Worcester and is dated 28 November 1582.

The fact that the clerk entered the grant of a licence in the names of William Shakespeare and Anne Whateley of Temple Grafton, has burgeoned into a whole crop of legends about a second, fictitious, lady. The most generally proffered explanation is that the licence, issued the day before the bond, has been misrecorded, the name Whateley, which occurred earlier in the records for that day, substituted by a clerical error. The record only survives – the actual document, of course, being given to the applicant.

No trace of the ceremony is to be found in any register; but the next record is quite exact: on Trinity Sunday, 26 May 1583, Susannah, daughter of the marriage, was christened at Stratford. Twenty months later, on 2 February 1585, twins, Hamnet and Judith, were also christened.

'Susannah', with its Old Testament associations, was a rare name in Stratford. The twins were named for a neighbouring baker and his wife.

Susannah was born six months after the marriage, so the presumption is that the hasty ceremony before the season of Advent meant that Anne was already pregnant. It was not at all unknown for young women to get themselves pregnant with a view to securing marriage,[7] but, as a minor, Shakespeare would have needed his father's consent, and if he had been entered as an apprentice with anyone else, he would need release from his articles.

The very prompt arrival of the twins would not have been received with any joy in the Shakespeares' household. Shakespeare's own youngest brother was still a toddler, and they were all presumably living in Henley Street.

Had Will Shakespeare been trapped, as James Joyce

suggested, by a wench that 'put to't before her troth plight' between the acres of the rye? Did he, like the hero of *A Chaste Maid in Cheapside*,[8] take his departure as the surest method of family limitation when at twenty he found himself the father of three babies? At all events, there were no more.

If William left any offspring elsewhere, there is no trace, apart from the boast of Sir William Davenant that he was more closely related to Shakespeare than a mere godson. In *The Winter's Tale* the old countryman laments:

> I would there was no age between ten and three and twenty, or that youth would sleep out the rest; for there is nothing in the between but getting wenches with child, wronging the ancientry, stealing, fighting – Hark you now! Would any but these boil'd brains of nineteen and two and twenty hunt this weather?
>
> (*The Winter's Tale*, 3.3.59 ff)

In fact, the only bastard recorded in the family belonged to Shakespeare's brother Edmund, a few months before his death at the end of December 1607. On 12 August of that year, in the church of St Giles without Cripplegate, this 'baseborn' child was buried, but his parentage was acknowledged.

John Shakespeare must have been a kindly father to countenance William's marriage in the first place, and to continue to house the family in the second; for, if Shakespeare's marriage at eighteen was unusual, his leaving of his family was equally unusual. Except for the very great, people did not maintain homes in two places. Many of Shakespeare's fellow-actors were exemplary family-men, who lived near their work. Only a married man would be able to house apprentices, who lived with the family while learning. But players on tour naturally left their families behind.

How Shakespeare spent those crucial years of his early twenties must remain unknown. Aubrey, quoting an old actor, Beeston, says he was a schoolmaster in the country. This could have given him practice in plays, if he inherited Mulcaster's tradition. Another tale puts him to service in a northern household. This was the way by which a fellow-poet, George Chapman, was enabled to write himself 'Gentleman' and to acquire learning without attendance at the university.

While dons have favoured the idea that Shakespeare was a teacher, Malone, a lawyer, thought Shakespeare worked in the office of some legal practitioner in Stratford, while Duff Cooper, a man of military interests, produced Sergeant Shaekespeare, a recruit for the forces in the Netherlands commanded by Leicester.

Of the seven blank years (1585–92), the latest at least must have been spent in the London theatres; some would give all to theatrical apprenticeship. If Shakespeare did not take up with one of the touring play-groups in need of a man, he might have turned to some of the local gentry – or someone whose family had held office, to 'stand his good lord' in London. There was the grandson of Thomas, Lord Wriothesley, lord of Snitterfield, for instance – the young Earl of Southampton – but he was still a minor and in the governaunce of Lord Burghley. It took nerve to leave Stratford for London, bettering his father's move from Snitterfield to Stratford – but there was the century-old example of Sir Hugh Clopton, Lord Mayor of London, builder of New Place. There was the nearer example of Richard Field, son of a Stratford neighbour, who at fifteen had set off for London as apprentice to a printer, married his master's widow and was to print Shakespeare's poems. 'Gallant audacity is never out of countenance,' observed Spenser's friend Gabriel Harvey.

But was the departure an adventure or a flight? Sir Thomas Lucy of Charlecote has been the local candidate for the responsibility, as the enemy of a young poacher who made ballads about him. (A taste for hunting is fully visible in Shakespeare's works; he was clearly a skilled fisherman, according to T. R. Henn, an expert in that art.) This improbable legend is based on the fact that the coat-of-arms of Mr Justice Shallow in *The Merry Wives of Windsor* is given as 'a dozen white luces' – which Evans turns into 'louses'. In *Shakespeare versus Shallow* (1931), an alternative and better explanation for this has been provided by Leslie Hotson: Shakespeare and his company were aiming at a *London* audience, and the 'lousy' coat of arms belonged to an unpopular justice of the Surrey bench of magistrates who had jurisdiction over the area round the Globe Theatre.

The desire to link some lines in a play with a local character is natural in Stratford; especially this play, which reproduces life in a small provincial town and may well bear a general likeness to that small society which Shakespeare knew at home. As to his poaching, if some grain of truth lies at the bottom of it – the deer-stealing story was current in the early seventeenth century – Sir Thomas's natural objections to depredations of his coney warren (he had no deer park) might have been increased by some deeper differences. He was a notable hunter – of papist recusants: once he literally unearthed one, starving, from a haystack. Were the Shakespeares popishly inclined?

Outwardly they conformed and, as Bailiff, John Shakespeare would have had to subscribe to the Oath of Supremacy. Moreover, he put his mark to the order which in 1564 defaced the images and the fine frescoes of the Guild Chapel with whitewash; he went to church, paid his dues, as his son was also to do. The Bible which Shakespeare knew so well was the Bishops' Bible, and later the Geneva version; he knew even better the Book of Common Prayer, particularly its Psalms. When, therefore, a case is made for secret adherence to the old faith, it rests on a document, discovered in the tiles of the Birthplace in April 1757 – the Catholic profession of faith known as the Spiritual Last Will of John Shakespeare.

This document was seen by the great scholar Edmond Malone, who first doubted it, then believed in it, but finally said he had documentary proof that it could not be genuine. The document is now lost, and Malone's proofs also remain undisclosed; they must either have proved it a forgery or established by other evidence the unshakeable reformed character of John Shakespeare's belief. Recently it has been found that many copies of this spiritual testament were distributed by the Jesuits Campion and Parsons, on their mission in 1580, when they stayed near Stratford at Clopton Hall. The formula is authentic, but we do not know how the document would stand up to inspection.

Nothing could be of more significance for Shakespeare's life as a writer than adherence to a proscribed cause. It would impose on a socially articulate figure habits of thinking and of sensibility alien to that of the majority. The Cradle of Security could never have been his. Any decision whether to adhere to the Church of England as by law established and to the government of the Queen, was the most momentous one that could be taken in the later sixteenth century.

When Elizabeth had succeeded in 1558, the country had been through such a violent series of reforms and counter-reforms that the great desire of most people was for a little peace and quiet. Stratford, as we have seen, had suffered in its local government, being left without the spiritual jurisdiction of earlier days, and only belatedly given a charter. It was not as militantly Protestant as Coventry, but it was given impeccably Protestant Lords of the Manor. None the less, some of the vicars and schoolmasters they nominated had Catholic sympathies; but everywhere the government moved very slowly and cautiously with minor offices, once the bench of bishops had been replaced entirely by trustworthy men. Warwickshire, as we have seen, had gentle families of both persuasions; at the head, of course, were the firmly Protestant Dudleys. In the little town Catholics and Protestants worked together on the Council. Only after 1570, when the Bull *Regnans in excelsis* declared Elizabeth a bastard deposed and excommunicate, did the government stiffen up its policy towards those who would not conform and alignment begin again.

Elizabeth herself, though very well equipped theologically, was prepared to have more or fewer lights in her private chapel as the need to conciliate her brother-in-law Philip of Spain waxed and waned. But this, the very latest attempt on the part of the Papacy to dictate the government of the state, could not be tolerated; so loyal Catholics were impaled on the horns of a most painful dilemma. As the conflict grew, Catholic propaganda became more vehement and emotional; the scholarly Cardinal Allen, with his appeals to doctrine, was succeeded by Father Parsons, who directed the Jesuits in a skilfully mounted campaign that did not disdain invective and emotional appeal. Echoes were heard in Stratford. George Badger the draper paid his fines and once went to jail. One of Shakespeare's schoolmates, Roger Dibdale, suffered execution as a seminary priest in 1586, at Tyburn. Another priest, executed with Edmund Campion in 1582, had been the brother of a Stratford schoolmaster, Jenkins' successor (the schoolmaster resigned his post). In 1583 a deranged Catholic from Warwickshire, John Somerville, set out from his home with the declared intention of killing the Queen. He died in Newgate prison, and a strict search of suspected houses in Warwickshire was ordered.

It is suggested today by Catholic apologists such as Father Peter Milward that John Shakespeare at this time hid his spiritual testament in the rafters; they suggest also that he never took the Oath of Supremacy (most unlikely, this), that his sale of land was a legal fiction to escape taxation.

If the document were genuine, of course it would not prove anything but that in 1580, when his son was sixteen, John Shakespeare had perhaps succumbed for the first time or sought refuge from his troubles in the old faith. Changes back and forth were not at all uncommon, since the Jesuit mission aimed at converts. As the 1580s built up towards the climax of the Armada, with all the plots that preceded it, the situation grew tenser. The difficulties of a brilliant young Catholic like John Donne are familiar; he bore the marks of the strain that his inheritance imposed long after he became a pillar of the Establishment.

Two rival queens, two identical images, faced each other on English soil; like two suns in the heavens, a dreadful portent, an unnatural and terrifying defiance of natural order, for monarchy was part of that order. God must have designed either Mary Stuart or Elizabeth Tudor to be His deputy, as every hierarchical figure was part of His design. When the claims of Mary Stuart led ultimately to her death, a young Catholic still pictured the two rival Churches as rival queens, with Una (*his* Una, not the Una of *The Faerie Queene*) challenged by Doublessa, 'Error's dreary Queen' and in outward form resembling her.

> Like ensigns she opposed to Sion's ensigns,
> Like her pretence of grace and God's high honour,
> Like grapes she did contend grew up her vines,
> And as good gold as Sion's seem'd her copper.
> (Anthony Copley, *A Fig for Fortune*, 1596)

Once, years before, Elizabeth herself had been staying at the house of a Catholic gentleman, when an image of the Queen of Heaven was accidentally uncovered, hidden in an outhouse. The country people who were dancing before her, parted to let her see 'such an image of our lady ... as for greatness, for

gayness and workmanship, I did never see a match', but which
now 'rather seemed a beast, raised from hell by conjuring'. Elizabeth commanded that it be burned, which was done by the
countryfolk, 'to the unspeakable joy of everyone but some one
or two who had suck'd of the idol's poisoned milk' (A. Jessop,
One generation of a Norfolk House, fo. 79–80).

The extraordinary wave of iconoclasm which broke over so
much of Europe destroyed irreplaceable beauty. At Ely Cath-
edral the Lady Chapel is covered with hundreds of delicate
small figures carved in stone. Every one has been brutally deca-
pitated. The mutilation of Stratford Guild Chapel was of the
same kind. But the old language of images was too closely woven
into common speech and life to be obliterated. At All Hallo-
we'en bells were rung; Christmas remained Christmas and not
Christ-tide for most. The able Whitgift, Bishop of Worcester,
left a few poor old Marian priests in office, to earn their living
as they could. The priest at Temple Grafton cured diseased
hawks: if Anne Hathaway were in service there, he may have
married her to Shakespeare. The policy was one of attrition;
horrid examples were made, but wholesale supervision was impossible. On plays and books, however, a firm censorship was
laid. Thus Shakespeare could never have expressed direct views
on religion; the consequences would have been dire.

Fortunately, as Auden observed, 'The poet is not there to
convert the world' – that was left to the eloquent preaching
which all reformed churches gave. In Geneva, where the cath-
edral is dominated by its pulpit, the congregation turned away
from the apse, former seat of idols. In London, preaching at
Paul's Cross was an attested method of putting over government policy. Preaching from the stage would have been quite
intolerable – if only because in earlier Tudor times, in the
Protestant moralities of Bale and the Catholic rejoinders later,
it had proved a two-edged weapon.

Graham Greene has remarked:

Isn't there one whole area of the Elizabethan scene that we miss
even in Shakespeare's huge world of comedy and despair? The kings
speak, the adventurers speak ... the madmen and the lovers, the
soldiers and the poets; but the martyrs are quite silent.

(Introduction to *John Gerard, the autobiography of an Elizabethan*)

The answer, of course, is to be found in the Shakespearean play on a great saint and martyr, *Sir Thomas More*.[9] His death is totally unexplained, because no explanation would have been tolerated; in this play he remains the wise, witty Londoner, and after his execution the only comment is

> A very learned worthy gentleman
> Seals error with his blood. Come, we'll to Court.
>
> (5.4.135–6)

Even so, the play was not permitted to be shown.

The Puritan opponents of the stage did not cease to call the theatre the Devil's chapel; the good woman who claimed to have been as edified at a play as at a sermon was held up to horror, so that when little choristers were used to stage plays in London, it was a large tolerance which permitted them to do so. When they were used to screen religious polemic, the Archbishop succeeded in stopping them.

On the other hand, ceremonies and vestments were equated by their Puritan detractors with play-acting; even simple finery might be denounced. 'Thou look'st like Antichrist in that lewd hat,' exclaims one of the 'persecuted brethren' in Jonson's *Bartholomew Fair*. He attacks a puppet-show with the familiar prohibition from the Bible against man's putting on the attire of the woman, to be confuted by the puppet's triumphant demonstration (by yanking up its skirt) that it is sexless.

In the course of the eighties, Elizabeth's poets and supporters appropriated for her many of the attributes of the more exalted Virgin. She was described as *Rosa sine spina*, *Virgo electa*, shown crowned with stars or standing on a map of England. The growing security of her position allowed this take-over, a more positive action than the mere destruction of images and combined also with a good deal of secular imagery. She was Gloriana, the queen; Belphoebe, the beautiful lady; Mercilla, the merciful judge; she was Pandora, Oriana, Diana, Pallas, sweet Bessy; the dramatic possibilities were endless, and sometimes they permitted her subjects to give her indirect counsel or voice criticism. The conversion of old images to the new circumstances confirmed deep endorsement of the theoretic political shift made by Henry VIII, and gave the real retort to the bull of excommunication. This new imagery coincided with the sudden appearance of great dramatic poetry.

At this moment of release and regeneration, Shakespeare, who thought in images, came to the London stage. In his English histories, by which he became famous, he transferred the religio-political conflict into acceptable political terms. The Wars of the Roses provided a mirror for the troubles of his own time. For the Red and White Rose transposed the conflict of Mary Stuart *versus* Elizabeth Tudor, or Una *versus* Duessa, into a mode where all the pain and strain could be contemplated without incurring any censorship. There was of course no one-for-one correspondence; this was not allegory but a skilful echo from the music of past time. Others had begun to re-make the new history in more primitive forms; Shakespeare gave words to what pageantry and emblem had done in the past, as for instance at Elizabeth's coronation progress through London.

The most competent of the Protestant commentators on Shakespeare observes: 'I find a rather advanced state of knowledge and understanding, though the knowledge is clearly that of a layman and not of a professional' (R. M. Frye, *Shakespeare and Christian Doctrine*, 1963, p. 113). In that age it was so easy to become a theologian and so difficult to remain religious. Shakespeare speaks only through his characters; he fitted people and situations with theology, as he fitted them with rhetoric. The ability to see different points of view had been bred in the close circle of life at Stratford. The Cradle of Security provided gentle nurture in toleration. How fortunate, for instance, was his position compared with that of his future patron Henry Wriothesley, Earl of Southampton. Born the son of an intensely embittered Catholic, orphaned at an early age, the little Harry at eight stoutly refused to go to church. His guardian was the Lord Admiral (a Catholic too), but Charles Howard took the revenues and handed the boy over to Lord Burghley, the Master of the Wards, for his upbringing. The estates were the subject of legitimate pillage by the Crown as well as the guardians.[10]

If almost any parent is universally admitted to be better than no parent, a young heir who had the misfortune to grow up as a Royal Ward was entirely at the mercy of those supposed to protect him. Burghley conscientiously kept a school at Cecil

House for the few very noble young men he took charge of himself, so the boy had an excellent education. In vacations, Burghley set him themes to write, and at Cecil House he made the acquaintance of his lifelong friend the Earl of Essex; another ward of Burghley, the Earl of Rutland, whom he met at St John's College Cambridge (Burghley's old college), made up a triumvirate.

At the same time young Southampton was undoubtedly subjected to religious pressure; it is not clear when he became a Protestant, but St John's was a most piously reformed institution. Southampton continued to give shelter to Catholic tenants and dependants; but his own circle was extremely Protestant, including Essex, his idol.

Young Southampton was so well educated that he took his MA by public disputation – most unusual for a nobleman – and went on to the Inns of Court. Later he went on a Protestant foray with Essex.

One of the chief rights of guardians was to nominate a marriage for their wards, and Burghley wanted Southampton for his grand-daughter, Lady Elizabeth Vere. But the Earl was obstinate enough to resist this plan and could not be moved. When he came of age, he was fined the crippling sum of £5,000 for his refusal; so he emerged at his majority in a state of financial stringency, which his way of life did nothing to diminish. Handsome, well educated and courted by all, whether they knew him or not, a petulance bred of thwarted energy led him to a spectacular career of folly, which in seven years left him imprisoned, ruined and under sentence of death for his part in the Essex Rebellion of 1601. Like his poet, also, he had got a wench with child and had married her, because, although poor and dowerless, Elizabeth Vernon belonged to Essex's circle. As, however, she was also a maid-of-honour to Queen Elizabeth, both had been sent to the Fleet Prison. A more spectacular ruin than the early career of Southampton would be hard to find.

The impossibly difficult economic position of the Tudor noblemen is by now sufficiently familiar. Bound to maintain a great household and to gain and keep public positions by display, they lived on grants, by indirect taxation which they farmed for the Crown; often they used the revenue instead of turning it over. Every trick of a maladjusted society in the grip of inflation was practised, in complete ignorance of any general theory underlying the situation. They worked on medieval assumptions that usury was wicked, while paying outrageous rates of interest. Only one or two managed to do well.

A few miles from Stratford lived one such who died reputed to be the richest man in England. Fulke Greville, first Lord Brooke, who in 1606 succeeded his father as Recorder of Stratford, was an important officer of the Crown, yet ready to help when the leading citizens resisted enclosure by his cousin, Edward Greville, the Lord of the Manor; to arbitrate over problems of leasing out the churchyard for grazing; and to send presents of buck for a town feast. In spite of one unreliable report that he boasted of being Shakespeare's and Jonson's master, Fulke Greville has left no record of acquaintance with the playwright, although he himself was a writer of plays and long wished to write a history of the Tudors, Lord Burghley, however, withheld the papers; and, except for a few lyrics, Fulke Greville published nothing. He destroyed one tragedy, his *Antony and Cleopatra*, lest it might be taken to reflect the story of Elizabeth and Essex. His plays, as he explained in his *Life of Sidney* (whom he had known and loved from their schooldays), are designed 'to show in the practice that the more audacity, advantage and good success such sovereignties have, the more they hasten to their own desolation and ruin' (chapter xviii). His most magnificent tragic cry belongs with the world of Hamlet:

> O wearisome condition of humanity,
> Born under one law, to another bound,
> Vainly begot, and yet forbidden vanity,
> Created sick, commanded to be sound!

This is the poetry of conflict and constraint bred by opportunity out of reflection in the greatest – in a worldly sense – of Shakespeare's neighbouring poets. Yet no one could remember a single character or event from the play from which this is taken (*Mustapha*, piratically printed in 1609). They would hear only the voice of Fulke Greville.

His writings serve to show that learning, experience of

government, high moral purpose, all that those who would
deny Shakespeare's authorship of his works consider requisite
and directly reflected there, were no substitute for the direct
knowledge of the performer's art.

The Stratford player had just produced, in 1609, his *Antony
and Cleopatra*. The early critics had insight when they praised
him for 'nature', and Nashe's advice was sound:

> Endeavour to add unto art, experience. Experience is more profit-
> able void of art than art which hath not experience. Of itself, art is
> unprofitable without experience and experience rash without art.
>
> (*Anatomy of Absurdity*, 1589; *Works*, I, 46)

Shakespeare's natural gift of retrieving relevant experience
is displayed in *Love's Labour's Lost*, where the wooing games of
a court in country retreat are studded with five recollections
of George Turberville, the gentleman Steward of the Earl of
Warwick, whom the Stratford burgesses entertained with sack
and sugar and who might have reciprocated by giving them
a glimpse of the Princely Pleasures of Kenilworth. From Turberville's technical *Book of Venerie*, where Queen Elizabeth was
shown hunting the deer, come the fine distinctions between
pricket, sorel and other deer hunted by the Princess: the ludi-
crous Russians in *Love's Labour's Lost* suggest Turberville's un-
complimentary account of that nation, where in 1569 he had
gone with an embassy. The team games of love poetry practised
by courtiers parallel those of Turberville with Gascoigne and
Googe. These three facets of Turberville's work, together with
a little joke on the absurd tags ('L'envoy') which he appended
to his *Tragical Tales* (and a glancing love-jest at Mantuan,
whom he translated), all clustered in this one pastoral of royal,
but unsuccessful wooing, suggest the significance for Shakespeare of a now forgotten courtly poet associated with his boy-
hood. They indicate too how appropriate, possibly unconscious
recall, provided deep structures for his drama.

2 A challenge to fortune

When Shakespeare came to London, the 'gorgeous playing place erected in the Fields' – James Burbage's Theatre – was about ten years old. Reluctantly, the City Fathers concluded that at least seven others existed, many within the city walls, that thousands went to the play every week. In 1583 they had started a campaign against the innovation, which had signally failed. As Stow reported in his *Annals*, the Queen herself had set up a troupe of players.

For every inhabitant of Stratford, a hundred could be found in London, a city of maybe 160,000, which dominated the country far more effectually than any other capital city in Europe. Its population constantly changed, for it was the centre of international trade as well as the seat of government. The first performances had begun in the inns which accommodated those who came up to Court, or to the law courts, or to trade to import wine and spices, or to export fine cloth. James Burbage himself had been interested in The Red Lion in Stepney, and The Boar's Head in Whitechapel had been fitted up by his brother-in-law John Brayne. The great yard, no longer used to hold wool-waggons lumbering up from East Anglia, had been fitted with a stage, and the galleries that gave on the private rooms had been extended. The players could reside there, while the carefree coming and going proper to an inn allowed all kinds of shows – fencers played their prizes, tumblers and jugglers performed in competition with dancers on the tight ropes, and with performing apes, horses, dogs and bears. Here too, as the City Fathers alleged, pickpockets flourished, city heiresses were lured to secret contracts, 'fond and simple persons' (especially apprentices) spent their masters' money – besides the allurements to sin offered in the plays themselves.

The defenders alleged *per contra* that it was better for captains waiting on the Court and gentlemen engaged in the Elizabethan sport of litigation to spend their vacant afternoons at the play rather than at a bawdy house or a gaming-table. But as late as 1597 the Lord Mayor wrote to the Privy Council: 'They are the ordinary places for vagrant persons, masterless men, thieves, horse-stealers, whoremongers, cozeners, coney-catchers, contrivers of treason and other idle and dangerous persons to meet together.'[1]

The scene on a holiday must have resembled a fairground; there was food available, at the ordinary (the *table d'hôte*), and drink at the taphouse. But The Theatre was devoted openly and entirely to entertainment, being modelled on the 'game place' of country towns, and in form resembling the bull- or bear-baiting rings of Southwark. A circular or polygonal thatched, open structure of wattle-and-daub, with three levels of galleries reached from interior stairs, and a stage backed by a tiring-house, it gave the players a settled establishment and thereby at once conferred a different status on regular performers.

James Burbage, sworn one of the Earl of Leicester's Men, who in 1575 had received Letters Patent from the Queen authorizing them to play anywhere, in 1583 had joined the Queen's own troupe; yet the next year, in flatly disobeying the City Recorder's prohibition, he sent word to that harassed officer 'that he was my Lord of Hunsdon's man and that he would not come at me, but he would in the morning ride to my lord' – presumably with a complaint. 'My Lord of Hunsdon', the Queen's first cousin, eventually as Lord Chamberlain was in control of all entertainment within the Court and so of royal players. In another ten years he would be Shakespeare's lord, too.[2]

Burbage was originally a joiner, who knew all about building wooden galleries and took to playing when 'trades served no turns'. He borrowed the necessary capital; but his greatest asset was to prove his younger son Richard, a spirited lad capable of defending the premises from interlopers with a broomstick, taunting them with 'scornful and opprobrious words', and playing disdainfully with their noses as he did so. Richard Burbage, who was to create Shakespeare's leading roles, appears in the second generation of a London theatrical family, Shakespeare's junior in years but his senior in the profession.

The players claimed, in medieval style, to be servants of the lord whose badge they wore and whose licence they carried on tour to show to Justices of the Peace. They owed nothing else to their lord, however, except the duty to come when he summoned them for some special entertainment; but they were ready to appear anywhere on command. All over the city, gardens, halls and orchards invited private performance; at one time, players even performed in Cheapside. This had been forbidden and, moreover, was not profitable. The big new money-spinner at The Theatre was not the auditorium but the box office: two narrow entrances could be even more carefully controlled than the gate of an innyard. In fact, the players proved much more efficient at extracting a penny from the apprentices who came to stand on the 'ground' than were the citizens at controlling the players.

When on tour in the provinces in 1582, the Earl of Worcester's Men lost their licence from the Master of the Revels. Forbidden by the Mayor of Leicester to perform, they defied him with 'evil and contemptuous words'. Among them was a boy of sixteen, son of a London innkeeper, who was to become one of the first two actors to reach stardom and to be known all over England. His name was Edward Alleyn. His elder, Dick Tarlton, son of another innkeeper, was already celebrated: the great Sir Philip Sidney stood godfather to his son. A singing and dancing clown, whose jokes were decidedly 'blue', he wore big shoes and baggy trousers (or 'slops') like a Tudor Charlie Chaplin. He extemporized rhymes on themes provided by the audience and was famous for his jigs and after-pieces; he was also a master in fencing, and the Queen bade them 'take away the knave' for making her laugh so excessively, as he engaged in a mock fight with her little dog. His picture was used as a sign for alehouses – and for loos.

Tarlton, London's idol, lived a merry but disreputable life and died of the plague in Armada year. Alleyn became an actor manager, made the right sort of marriage and ended, in modern terms, almost a millionaire. These two represented, as it were, the older and the newer aspects of playing, though both were full professionals.

Tarlton popped his face out between the acts and concluded a performance with a 'jig', a song-and-dance act by four clowns, two dressed as women. The humour was slapstick. This country game, adapted for a metropolitan entertainment, carried on the old carnival irresponsibility by which authority was mocked out of countenance; audience participation was provoked by questions and gaggings. At The Rose Theatre, at the end of one show, a firework display concluded with a gigantic rose that opened to shower from its petals comfits, apples, pears and fine white bread on the audience. Apples were also used in less friendly interchanges between the audience and the clowns. Guns were shot off, on one occasion with fatalities among the spectators.

Alleyn, a tragedian of magnificent presence and voice, was also capable of quick-change parts; but 'a tyrant's vein' was what the audience looked for from him. There would have been parts for both stars, written in contrasted styles, in that sturdy old favourite *The Lamentable Tragedy of Cambyses, King of Persia, mixed full of Pleasant Mirth* (about 1570), that loud-mouthed success that Shakespeare recalled more than once, and perhaps played in. Cambyses is shown as a brave soldier and a very bad man, ruled by two characters named Murder and Cruelty, and also seduced by the Vice Ambidexter, who, true to his name, played on both sides, for and against the King. He tempted an unjust judge, who was later flayed on stage 'with a false skin'. Ambidexter enthusiastically greets in the audience his cousin Cuthbert Cutpurse (a character from an earlier play, *Like will to Like* and so known to the audience already); he also fights a battle in comic armour with a gigantic snail and incites two comic countrymen to speak treason on their way to market.

Meanwhile, the wicked King has killed his heir and his wife and also an infant, to prove that even when drunk he was a perfect shot with the bow; to wind up, he enters with a sword thrust through his side, a fatality inflicted on himself as he leaped athletically on to his horse. He announces: 'A just reward for my misdeeds my death doth plain declare' – a sentiment always looked for in deaths of criminals; his lords enter and recapitulate, to enforce the point for edification – and to carry off the body.

Behold my lords, it is even so as he to us did tell:
His grace is dead upon the ground by dint of sword most fell.

The actors were, by the mid-eighties, selling their wares like any other tradesmen, forming something like a trade guild. The repertoire was changed each day; playbills announced frequent new shows, with also perhaps a procession through the town, to drums and trumpets. The flag would go up at the playing-place by two in the afternoon, the trumpets would sound and the 'two hours' traffic of the stage' would begin – its pillars painted like marble, its stage strewn with rushes and hung with coloured cloth, its penthouse star-painted.

Into this Vanity Fair walked the man from Stratford. As he came in by the west road, through Newgate, he would have, on his right, down towards the river, the superior theatre district round Ludgate. Here was the Bel Savage Inn, which belonged to the Cutlers' Company and was used sometimes by the Queen's Men. Being near to the Fleet prison, where noble prisoners were sent (if they did not deserve the Tower), it enjoyed a select but partially captive audience, swelled perhaps by young lawyers who had come up Fleet Street from the Inns of Court.

The Devil was said to have appeared in person on the stage at the Bel Savage Inn, but even a hostile witness, Stephen Gosson, had seen there two or three good comedies 'where you shall find never a word without wit, never a line without pith, never a letter placed in vain'. Nearby were the choristers of St Paul's and also of the Chapel Royal, who played in the precincts of Blackfriars. The Master of St Paul's Boys, Sebastian Westcott, had been a follower of Queen Elizabeth from her days of semi-captivity as princess, which might explain how he kept his posts as subdean, almoner, vicar choral and choir-master, in spite of being a Papist, who had been excommunicated by the Dean of St Paul's and sent to the Marshalsea prison. Perhaps, to the Puritan nostril, there was a whiff of brimstone here.

Three other players' inns stood on the arterial road that led up from London Bridge to Bishopsgate, past the church of St Botolph where the disapproving Stephen Gosson was rector. Some more were outside in Whitechapel. Outside the walls too, in the grounds of the old Priory of Holywell in Finsbury Fields,

James Burbage built his theatre, in 1577 to be joined by another small house, The Curtain. This was the neighbourhood where, in the 1520s, Rastell, brother-in-law of Thomas More, had built a theatre in his garden. Across the river, beyond the City bounds, near bear- and bull-baiting rings, a playhouse, The Rose, had been opened in 1587 by a wealthy moneylender, Philip Henslowe; in a few years his step-daughter would marry Edward Alleyn, and the two men would go into partnership.

Still further south, a mile beyond, at Newington Butts, lay another little theatre built by Jerome Savage, one of the Earl of Warwick's Men, in a garden. It was also used sometimes by the Earl of Oxford's players.

Shakespeare began as an actor, and it was by an actor's share in profits that he made his fortune. How he came to it remains unknown. The legend, originating with Davenant, that he held horses at The Theatre, is an absurdity. London was full of horse-thieves, as of every other kind of thief, and The Theatre – as the Lord Mayor observed – was a safe meeting-place for them (see note 1, above). This was the only city in England that had an underworld, eagerly described by pamphleteers; they featured freely tricks about horses. The playgoer who was not prepared to walk through the fields would bring his own attendant with him; it was risky enough to stable one's horse even in an inn, for the habits of ostlers were notorious, but no one would have entrusted him to the Tudor equivalent of a car-park.

Most of the players seem to have been the sons of tradesmen; in London, they had to compete not only with the choristers but with the occasional seasonal play by the lawyers or by the schoolboys of St Paul's, Westminster, or Merchant Taylors' schools. After the opening of The Theatre, men displaced boys in royal favour.

All would be summoned upstream or downstream to Court if their reputation stood high enough, where the old playing season, from All Hallows to Shrovetide, culminated in the Twelve Days of Christmas. However, the troupes were prepared to stay in London as long as they could, acting at the inns in winter and in the fields during the summer.

In Elizabethan England every man was expected to have a regular and settled place of work, where he could be supervised by his betters, assessed for taxes and checked for church attendance. The problems of vagrancy and beggary were being tackled for the first time by Acts of Parliament; vagrant men were treated as criminals, and without the protection of a lord, players fell into this class. Hence the importance of the London fixed base. To 'break' and go into the country, meant also the disbanding and dismemberment of a full company. In the summer, however, a tour of the principal towns was customary, for the law courts closed and the Court went on progress too. Regular playing and skill meant that the London actors outclassed all provincial efforts in a short time.

Shakespeare might have joined such a group, on its way through Stratford. For example, in 1587 the Queen's Men lost their great tragic actor, William Knell, who was killed in a quarrel with another actor at Thame, on the Stratford road. Shakespeare could not at once have stepped into Knell's shoes as an actor, but the company would be short of a man when they came to Stratford. A good musician, a good swordsman, a man of handsome appearance and of good speech would be acceptable, especially if he could pen a speech too.

If the actors encountered a quarrelsome audience their situation could be hazardous. A still older tragic actor of fame, Bentley (d. 1585), was playing with the Queen's Men at Norwich when a rioter tried to force his way in, and knocked over the day's takings. In full costume, Bentley leaped from the stage and put him to flight. Then his servant hit Bentley on the head with a stone. Fortunately it was a servant of the Paston family and not an actor who stabbed and killed the rioter. But had either of these incidents come to the ears of the City Fathers, they would have made the most of it.

The London guildsmen, like their humbler counterparts at Stratford, kept   paternalistic control, as far as the growth of the city allowed them to do so. For them the new form of social unity represented by the theatre was full of menacing possibilities, since this unity was largely created by irreverence and bawdy jests. So many of the old forms of festivity had gone that there was a deep need for some secular means of cultivating it; the theatre evolved to meet widespread desires that had no conscious formulation. The unity of the whole nation, powerfully evinced in times of danger – specifically at the time of the

Armada – found a lighter and more gratifying form in play and game. But their patterns were new, and risky.

Disorder was certainly not greater than that found in modern football crowds. If all players were classed together in irrational but highly significant hostility, the powers of enforcement were fortunately weak. Ferocious orders from the City Council about the tearing down of all playhouses produced no effect at all – and perhaps were intended only as threats. Actors were everywhere, changing their social role to fit the moment. In true medieval fashion, Leicester's Men had accompanied him overseas to war in the Netherlands in 1586; yet they also risked building enterprise based on modern credit facilities. Their enemies termed them not Comedians but Chameleons; and as early as 1578, a preacher at Paul's Cross had estimated total takings in London as amounting in all to £2,000 a year.

There were audiences other than those of the playhouses, whose attitudes were more predictable. A schoolmaster producing his pupils was a man in authority, a clerk, and he could adopt an authoritarian and admonitory tone. The Prodigal Son was a favourite theme for school plays. Not only moral truths but specific advice could be given in a polite way, without presumption, under a fictive guise and by example, even to one's betters. A humble 'offering' at least might convey a distinct warning, yet only by hints. '*Laudando praecipere*' – 'to instruct by praising' – was a recognized technique. So, listening to a contest on marriage and virginity, Elizabeth said to the Spanish ambassador, 'This is all written against *me*.' If sufficiently exasperated, as once by a students' anti-papal bit of ribaldry, she would get up and sweep out, taking the torchbearers with her.

For country people on the other hand, their play offered a chance for the relief of stifled protest. 'One that played husbandry said much against gentlemen, more than was set down in the book of the play,' was reported from Suffolk; in Norfolk, Kett's Rebellion (1549) had started at a play and produced a commune based on Robin Hood's justice, that lasted for a couple of months. In Morality plays the solemn transformation of moral views was sandwiched between lively and subversive appearances of the tempters, who in *Mankind* had all the best action and who shamelessly collected extra money from the

audience before the great devil with fireworks at his arse could
be permitted to appear.

The best London companies contrived to please everyone.
If Shakespeare had begun in a shop, he would have learned
deferential modes of persuasion, with a cry at the Market Cross
of 'What is't you lack, gentlemen?' If later he had earned his
living by sweeping it from the posteriors of little boys (as Ben
Jonson unkindly characterized the schoolmaster's lot), he
would have had parents and governors to placate.

> The proverb is, how many men, so many minds . . .
> No play, no party can all alike content.
> The grave divine calls for divinity
> The civil servant for philosophy,
> The courtier craves some rare sound history,
> The baser sort for knacks of pleasantry.
> (Prologue, *Contention between Liberality and Prodigality*, 1565)

Most mixed and volatile were the audiences of the innyards,
where the widest appeals would be those denounced by Ascham
in Malory's tales, 'Open manslaughter and bold bawdry.' The
earliest yard play of which there is notice, *A Sackful of News*,
given at The Boar's Head in 1557, was suppressed for scurrility.
From the next thirty years there survive a handful of texts –
classical tragedies like *Appius and Virginia* or *Damon and Pythias*
for the boys, Tarlton's *Famous Victories of Henry V* for the men.
Then suddenly, in the year before the Armada, the poets take
command. The unity of Elizabethan plays was secured by a
powerful and authoritarian voice, the words spoken by Alleyn,
the pen wielded by a Cambridge graduate whose style was in-
transigent, and his audacity equal to any man's in that auda-
cious age.

King Cambyses became at once outmoded, its style denounced
as 'the jigging vein of rhyming mother wits', and its morals
flouted.

Marlowe's Tamburlaine, born a shepherd, rose by war to
be Emperor of the East – this by thrusting down kings beneath
his feet and reducing them to the level of slaves: the vanquished
Emperor of the Turks was drawn about in a cage like a wild

beast; four kings with bits in their mouths were harnessed to Tamburlaine's chariot while he scourged them on;

> Holla, ye pamper'd jades of Asia,
> What can ye draw but twenty miles a day?
> (2 *Tamburlaine*, 4.3.1–2)

for 'his honour, that consists in shedding blood' demanded ever more spectacular modes of doing so, ever more prolonged humiliation of his foes. This combination of intellectual fire and primitive violence was irresistible when the white heat at which Marlowe worked welded them into an amalgam.

Because *Tamburlaine* is almost clear of religious colouring, its purely warlike spirit could appeal to the whole audience:

> I hold the Fates bound fast in iron chains,
> And with my hand turn Fortune's wheel...
> (1 *Tamburlaine*, 1.2.174–5)

introduces a play that is as secular as it is idealistic. This vaunt serves as prologue to the 'miracle' by which 'desire, lift upward and divine' has become incarnate in a human figure (in many emblems, it is *God* who holds Fortune by a chain from Heaven). In apparently defying Nature, he is actually in tune with her, since

> Nature that fram'd us of four elements...
> Doth teach us all to have aspiring minds...
> (1 *Tamburlaine*, 31.1.58–60)

and the kings who topple before him, one after another, serve only to mark his progress. The many images of a rival to God culminate in the challenge to Mahomet. The part could be realized physically by Alleyn, with his great height, his commanding voice and that audacity which in his youth led him to defy the Mayor of Leicester with 'evil and contemptuous words'. It made him as a star.

The Prologue's challenge, 'Then applaud his fortunes *as you please*', implies that the audience may well take the play in a variety of ways, and the possibility of discussion, disagreement, the continuing of the play in debate at the tavern, is of course the essence of successful drama, which is to initiate an action in each spectator. Brecht was perfectly right to see in Marlowe the originator of his kind of theatre, and the City Fathers were quite right to see in this process an element of danger. Marlowe learned from the university, as none of the other playwrights did, the art of debate. He dexterously shifted the ground by setting his drama in a remote place and taking in the larger setting continuously invoked in the poetry. It is within this frame of cosmic grandeur that the absence of conventional moral judgment occasionally gives place to provocative 'atheisms'. The paradox of the infidels calling on God to avenge them against the perfidy of Christians and entering the battle crying 'Christ!' as their signal, belongs with the outrageous and youthful aspect of Marlowe's blasphemy, like the burning of 'holy books' (supposed to be the Koran) or the aside to the captive Turk, 'Pray for us, Bajazet; we are going.' Without such a temperament, the tremendous trajectory of the double play could hardly have been plotted. The exhilaration of a new kind of iconoclasm opens up new quests.

The 'diviner Muse' of 'Kit' Marlowe led the way for a host of followers. They were never tired of playing variations on *Tamburlaine*, but as no one could match him, the results are for the most part wretched rant. To take Fortune captive became a commonplace.[3]

This challenge to cosmic authority was a rallying cry; it summarized the 'gorgeous' qualities of Marlowe, which were so well matched to the 'gorgeous playing place in the fields', and Alleyn named his second playhouse The Fortune.

Shakespeare characteristically was to take his closest borrowing not from the vaunts but from the minor mode of this play – its love poetry. In *The Merchant of Venice*, the praise of Portia uttered by the Moorish Prince of Morocco adapts Tamburlaine's lament for the death of Zenocrate to a dancing rhythm, though his choice of caskets presents him with the same end as Tamburlaine – an image of death.[4]

Another scene of Shakespeare's adapts Barabas' counsel to Ithamore to the death speech of Aaron the Moor (*Titus Andronicus*, 5.1). The effect of this, coming after a vivid four acts, is a ritualized heightening of all that has been seen, strengthened by the recall of Marlowe's play; Shakespeare is harnessing the dynamic drive for an unrepentant stand at an emotional climax.

> Even now I curse the day – and yet, I think,
> Few come within the compass of my curse –
> Wherein I did not some notorious ill . . .
> Oft have I digg'd up dead men from their graves,
> And set them upright at their dear friends' door,
> Even when their sorrows almost was forgot,
> And on their skins, as on the bark of trees,
> Have with my knife carved in Roman letters
> 'Let not your sorrow die, though I am dead.'
>
> (5.1.125 ff)

Malignancy as a principle of living is more ingenious in Aaron than Barabas': 'Sometimes I go about and poison wells . . .' (*The Jew of Malta*, 2.3.182). While the spectacular end of Barabas is to be precipitated into a burning cauldron (the traditional fate of the usurer in hell), Aaron ends with a vigorous curse that calls hell's pains upon himself, if that will bring them on his captors. Aaron is an altogether more barbaric monster than Barabas. He belongs to the woods where he plans to hide his child; Barabas to the city.

The ritual violence of *Titus Andronicus*, which is nearer to *Tamburlaine*, is combined with the grotesque vitality of *The Jew of Malta* and those qualities which were summed up by T. S. Eliot as 'savage farce'; this relates it sufficiently to the black humour of the modern stage to make it viable in performance once more. Shakespeare could have absorbed *The Jew of Malta* only in performance, for it was not printed till 1634; but he could have bought for a few pence the carefully printed text of *Tamburlaine*. This appeared in 1590, pruned of some of the stage action deemed unsuitable for the dignity of print. While Shakespeare derived theatrical material from *The Jew of Malta* and in some ways reacted against *Tamburlaine*, his sensitive ear picked up rhythms from big speeches in both. In his own more mature work, he shows upon the stage itself the effect of *Tamburlaine* upon groundlings: they heard without understanding but none the less enjoyed themselves.

Pistol talks in Marlovian vaunts:

> Shall packhorses
> And hollow pamper'd jades of Asia
> Which cannot go but thirty miles a day
> Compare with Caesars, and with Cannibals,
> And Troiant Greeks? Nay, rather damn them with
> King Cerberus; and let the welkin roar.
>
> (*2 Henry IV*, 2.4.154–)

Yet in the same audience sat intelligent young men like Donne, who was described as a 'great frequenter of plays' and who, in a verse letter written much later, during the Islands voyage of 1597, recalled 'Bajazet encag'd, the shepherd's scoff' (*The Calm*, 33), from the second part of *Tamburlaine*.

Shakespeare and Donne, in the course of the nineties, transformed and animated poetic forms, in which vivid observation and witty fancy were blended. For the creation of such complex poetry, the prerequisite was a single image in dynamic motion. Tamburlaine supplied that image. Medieval poetry had held the mirror up to nature, but the shapes in the mirror were angels or devils, Everyman or Lusty Juventus; even *The Mirror for Magistrates* subordinated the tragic occasion to a moral. To view Tamburlaine was to see a man in his native nobility, himself the architect, who imposed himself upon the entire human and natural sphere of things. This once achieved, the stage could develop complexity and conflict which were then reflected in the lyric.

Shakespeare built on Marlowe, by variation and often by counter-challenge. Their temperaments made this inevitable. Marlowe, proud and violent, 'intemperate and of a cruel heart', according to one witness, was both a scholar and a criminal.[5] Shakespeare had naturally the courtesy of a gentleman ('gentle Shakespeare'); others called him 'friendly Shakespeare', and he held something of a record in never getting himself jailed. Marlowe amazed and delighted; Shakespeare charmed. When he took to the theatre we cannot be sure, but, if *Tamburlaine* is placed in 1587, Shakespeare's first works could scarcely have been more than three years later. In five years, at all events, he was sufficiently well known to stand among the other playwrights who were serving the gorgeous playing places, now multiplying their wooden rings in a greater planetary circle round the City from east to west and from the northern fields to the southern suburbs.

A dozen years later, Hamlet was to praise the actors for a Marlovian speech about the remorseless Pyrrhus sacking Troy, at the same time as he warned them that,

If you mouth it, as many of our players do, I had as lief the town-crier spoke my lines. Nor do not saw the air too much with your hand, thus, but use all gently; for in the very torrent, tempest, and, as I may say, whirlwind of your passion, you must acquire and beget a temperance that may give it smoothness. O, it offends me to the soul to hear a robustious periwig-pated fellow tear a passion to tatters, to very rags, to split the ears of the groundlings ... I would have such a fellow whipp'd for o'erdoing Termagant; it out-herods Herod.

(*Hamlet* 3.2.3–14)

It is the actors, rather than the poet of the earlier days, who are the cause of offence; Hamlet may himself tear a passion to tatters from time to time, but he does not fail to reject his own performance. What Marlowe had rejected – the 'jigging vein of rhyming mother wits' – he had also taken up and transformed; so with Shakespeare. Once the art of acting was established, it developed more in ten years than in the previous two hundred.

The Tragedy of Hamlet itself is the re-working of an old play, which belonged to the era of *Tamburlaine*. Thomas Kyd, who, in *The Spanish Tragedy*, created the pattern of Revenge Tragedy, also wrote a lost *Hamlet*. Shakespeare's first works in all probability included his early revenge play, *Titus Andronicus*, and his classical venture, *The Comedy of Errors*. Both these plays are notable for firmness of structure, the power of redoubling effects that had been proved successful.

In *Titus Andronicus*, one of the great successes of the early stage (and which, in 1955, with Laurence Olivier and Vivien Leigh, triumphantly resumed performance), the ritual of violence is derived from Ovid's story of Philomel, from his *Metamorphoses*. Extremity of feeling will obliterate the human form; the emotion produced is one of wonder in the audience. 'Tiger' is an epithet applied to Tamora: tigers, unlike lions, the king of beasts, were devoid of the possibility of noble pity.

As for that ravenous tiger, Tamora,
No funeral rite, nor man in mourning weed,
No mournful bell shall ring her burial;
But throw her forth to beasts and birds to prey.

(5.3.195–8)

Lavinia, ravished and mutilated, becomes an emblem of all the natural world and its natural beauties destroyed and despoiled. Hence the strange artificial description of her by her uncle:

What stern ungentle hands
Hath lopp'd and hew'd and made thy body bare
Of her two branches – those sweet ornaments
Whose circling shadows kings have sought to sleep in? . . .
Alas, a crimson fountain of warm blood . . .
Doth rise and fall between thy rosed lips,
Coming and going with thy honey breath.

(2.4.16–25)

This is a metamorphosis in itself. The play shows men and women 'astonished', 'turned to stones' like Niobe or transformed to predators. Titus finally appears dressed as a cook to serve up to Tamora the cannibal banquet of her dead sons.

In *The Comedy of Errors*, Shakespeare most ingeniously duplicated a Roman plot to produce a serviceable farce which has also proved adaptable to the modern stage. It is among the shortest of his plays, but it combines the farcical and the romantic, as the story of Egeon, the merchant condemned to death, opens out into a romp of two sets of twins. Shakespeare has combined the ingredients of a medieval romance, like that of St Eustace, with a classical play of Plautus, *Menaechmi*, which he may have read at school. The tragic 'frame' for this play is further supplemented by material from *Supposes*, Ariosto's comedy, which had already been translated for acting at Gray's Inn.[6] *The Comedy of Errors* was to be associated with that same society – to which Southampton had been admitted in 1588. It was the most play-loving of the four Inns of Court, and a play of Errors, 'like to Plautus his *Menaechmus*, was performed there by the common players on 28 December 1594.

Already Shakespeare shows his unequalled skill in fitting parts together so that they reinforce each other and in the control of all the detail.[7] The main concern, as in classical comedy, is with 'errors', tricks, disguises, which he briskly duplicates and piles up. The common impression derived from *Titus Andronicus* and *The Comedy of Errors* is of a supremely competent organizer of theatrical situations, confident and in command of his material. What is lacking is the characteristic Shakespearean warmth and sympathy with human relationships, the feelings that first appear, however faintly, in *Two Gentlemen of Verona*.

3 The upstart crow

'To those Gentlemen, his Quondam acquaintance, that spend their wits in making plays, Robert Greene wisheth a better exercise. . . .'

So begins the epistle, tagged to *Greene's Groatsworth of Wit*, entered for publication at the Stationers' Hall in September 1592, about a fortnight after the author, destitute of all but moral reproof and the desire to see it printed, had died wretchedly in London. Yet, as the first English journalist, he had penned a significant notice of the players' latest enormity. 'Those puppets that spoke from our mouths, those Anticks garnished in our colours' would betray their 'benefactors', so that, as he warned his friends, to write for them was to become a wild spendthrift of wit.

Trust them not; for there is an Upstart Crow, beautified with our feathers, that with his *Tiger's heart wrapt in a player's hide*, supposes he is as well able to bombast out a blank verse as the best of you; and being an absolute *Johannes Fac Totum*, is in his own conceit the only Shakescene in a country. O that I might entreat your rare wits to be employed in more profitable courses ... whilst you may, seek you better Masters; for it is pity men of such rare wits should be subject to the pleasure of such rude grooms.

Letters urging repentance on companions in former sins were an exercise for every schoolboy; Shakespeare would have learned it out of Erasmus as had Greene.[1] Though conventional, the letter is none the less highly emotional; Greene packs a great deal of insult into these lines.

Shakespeare makes his first appearance in the world of letters in the ambiguous and precarious role of a country trader in public favour, lacking the technical (and largely irrelevant) apprenticeship to the guild of clerks at Oxford or Cambridge, who ranked as 'gentlemen' whatever their origins. Such a 'peasant', joined with other 'buckram gentlemen', in Greene's view would first 'cleave' to successful authors but in times of need or sickness forsake them.

This admonition is addressed primarily to the most notorious and newsworthy poet-playwright, who is, however, not directly named. Marlowe, 'famous gracer of tragedians', was the obvious target for a death-bed warning; Machiavelli's dreadful end might have warned him from 'pestilent Machiavellian policy' (thinks Greene) – but let him hearken to his fellow-poet who has also, like the fool, said in his heart, 'There is no God.' God has punished him through 'base' and 'wicked men': 'Defer not with me till this last point of extremity; for little knowest thou how in the end thou shalt be visited!'

All Elizabethans were firm believers in the closed shop ('Let the shoemaker meddle with his last, the cobbler with his awl'); Greene assumes that the writing even of public plays should be confined to those academic circles of privilege which had produced most mid-Tudor drama, the circles to which he himself, as a Master of Arts, with Marlowe, Tom Nashe and George Peele, who were also warned, belonged.

Shakespeare stepped in and appealed not to the publisher but to the editor and printer of Greene, Henry Chettle, who made a handsome apology, admitting that the warning was 'offensively by one or two of them taken' to whom it was addressed.

With neither of them that take offence was I acquainted and with one of them I care not if I never be; the other, whom at that time I did not so much spare, as since I wish I had, for that as I have moderated the heat of living writers, and might have used my own discretion (especially in such a case) the author being dead, that I did not, I am as sorry as if the original fault had been my fault, because my self have seen his demeanour no less civil than he excellent in the quality he professes; besides, divers of worship have reported his uprightness of dealing, which argues his honesty and his facetious grace in writing, that approves his art.

Shakespeare had taken offence, but in a civil, gentlemanly fashion; far from ranking with 'country Anticks' (dumb players disguised as animals or birds) or with the puppets of the fairground, he excelled in the player's 'quality'. 'Divers of worship' – that is, men of substance who were not nobles (they would be 'divers of honour') – have vouched for his probity, which argues a good general character, and also for the elegance of his witty writing, which gives proof of his good education ('art' means the seven liberal arts, not literature in the modern sense, which would be 'letters').

Shakespeare, by implication, is bracketed with Marlowe as playwright and congratulated on his comedy, which was Greene's speciality. Chettle, who had copied Greene's manuscript ('his hand being none of the best'), adds that he had suppressed charges against Marlowe such 'as to publish had been intolerable' – these may be assumed to be further 'atheisms', or blasphemy.

Nashe, who had been suspected of having a hand in this, denied all connection with the 'scald lying pamphlet'; he in fact had also been warned to learn to 'reprove all and name none ... tread on a worm and it will turn'.

In a society based on codes of public shame and honour, the power of Ill Fame blowing a Black Trumpet was deeply dreaded;[2] and the Black Trumpet had been very recently loudly blown over Greene by one of the leading members of his own university in return for defamation of his family. This was Gabriel Harvey, Fellow of Trinity Hall and University Praelector in Rhetoric.

Greene was, in fact, so vulnerable that a spectacular repentance was the only course open to him. A saddler's son from Norwich, Greene had entered St John's College Cambridge as a sizar; that is, a poor scholar, with menial duties. Like Shakespeare, he had left a wife at home when he came to London; but he had spent her fortune first. Under the name of 'Robin Goodfellow', he was known in the revelry of taverns; after a success as writer of pamphlets and romances – he could 'yark up a pamphlet ... in a day and a night as well as in seven year' – his spendthrift ways allowed wealthy actors to attract him into writing comedies.[3]

Greene had lived with a prostitute who brought him a

bastard son named Fortunatus, or perhaps Infortunatus, and whose brother had been hanged at Tyburn for murder. He was known in such brothels as The Red Lattice in Turnbull Street and also at the pawnshops. He adds that the player who seduced him had been a 'country author' but, uneducated as he was, he had assured Greene that his share in playing apparel could not now be bought for £200. This sounds as if it could be Shakespeare; the Burbages and Alleyn were not countrymen.

Greene's miserable end was made the most of by himself, by his enemy Gabriel Harvey and perhaps by others who added to the stream of posthumous 'repentances'. His last letter to his wife exists in several forms, the most poignant dated the day before his death: 'Sweet wife, as ever there was any good will or friendship between thee and me, see this bearer (my Host) satisfied of his debt. I owe him ten pounds, and but for him I had perished in the streets.' At his wish, his hostess, a shoe-maker's wife, crowned his dead brow with bays, the victor's prize in poetry; he was taken to be buried in the 'New Churchyard' at Bedlam near The Theatre.[4]

Shakespeare had tactfully but firmly defended himself, and the modest assurance of his approach is reflected in the friendly response of Chettle, so notably absent in his reference to Mar-lowe. It would have been gallant to have issued bloodthirsty threats, as perhaps Marlowe did. ('Let him use me no worse than I deserve,' said Chettle defensively.) It would have been easy to have started a pamphlet war – Nashe attacked and worsted Gabriel Harvey – but Shakespeare pursued the modern line, by producing sound and steady third-party evidence – pre-sumably from an alderman or vicar or the head of one of the big London schools, which was a notable exercise of reason and self-control. Yet it must be assumed, from the pains he took to counter it, that the attack cut deep. Years after, Polonius remembered that 'beautified' is a vile word.

Greene had used two conventional weapons. Country 'anticks' were used to present grotesque derisory mimes against objects of social contempt, reducing their victims to animal level. Queen Elizabeth was disgusted when Cambridge tried to entertain her with an anti-papal show of this kind, although at her first Twelfth Night, cardinals, bishops and abbots appeared in the likeness of crows, asses and wolves. Such grotesque beast-shows were found in plays – as in Robert Wilson's *Cobbler's Prophecy* – and dumb-shows of scorn were especially popular in 'country' farce like *John à Kent and John à Cumber*.[5]

In real life, such rituals of public humiliation as riding through the City, dressed in 'papers' setting out the victim's crime (a punishment for perjury), could precede the worse humiliation of the pillory or the stocks. Shakespeare, as 'the Upstart Crow', is wearing a feather costume of black, which was what the Devil wore in the old craft plays (he 'pomped in feathers'); he has become part of Greene's private beast fable, at once an 'antick' in a disgraceful show, and also the victim of it – in Greene's own terms.

As a group, players were the destined victims of social denigration; one of the methods of attack was to accuse them of precisely that same 'contempt' which was practised on them by the accuser – by the noisy groundlings who hurled rotten fruit, or the noisy clerics who hurled anathema.

However, seen through Envy's distorting glass, this not-so-dumb player had been condemned out of his own insolent mouth. By parodying a line from *3 Henry VI*, 'O tiger's heart wrapt in a woman's hide', Greene had turned his own success against him. This was the regular form of academic dispute, where it was essential to take the opponent's proposition and turn it round to confute him by his own words, thus making his case the instrument of its own demolition. Such rhetorical device is to be found in Shakespeare's own quarrel scenes, as when Lady Anne spits at Richard Crookback, wishing it were poison, and he replies, 'Never came poison from so sweet a place.' She responds, 'Never hung poison on so foul a toad.'

The crime that Greene imputes – that of being the strange monster, an actor-playwright, the most ridiculous fabulous hybrid of mixed form – gave Shakespeare his very special advantages, which only Jonson and Heywood, among the later playwrights, were to share with him. The actor could get inside the roles as they were composed, could feel the whole dramatic conflict not only in a writer's or debater's terms but with his muscles, his stance, in images of action or grouping. The 'dumb language' of the stage when joined with the power of words gave intuitive grasp of a fuller complexity, made up of many kinds of 'language', to be realized in performance.

Shakespeare's language is that of 'spoken words which have strayed on to the page'; his dramatic imagination powerfully developed this extra dimension from the beginning; whereas Greene, an autobiographical writer, achieved success only in a limited dramatic field.

Its basis in stage experience gave Shakespeare's imagination a range of sheer inventiveness which modified whatever he fed into the plays; and since he remained a dramatist, this extra dimension was always part of his imaginative life. The most important and the most ironic definition of the poet's eye is given by Duke Theseus before the full parody of *Pyramus and Thisbe* grotesquely underlines it (*A Midsummer Night's Dream*, 5.1.2-22). Within their 'seething' brains, poets apprehend more than reason can ever identify; begotten in imagination, 'things unknown' gain a 'shape' (which was the technical term for an actor's costume), a 'habitation' (or 'locus' on the stage) and a 'name' (which early actors, who doubled many parts, wore pinned to their breasts on a scroll). This enlargement is shared with the lunatic and the lover:

> Such tricks hath strong imagination . . .
> . . . in the night, imagining some fear,
> How easy is a bush suppos'd a bear?
> (5.1.18-22)

Such a stirring of imagination was what the actors strove to wake in the audience. 'Think when we talk of horses that you see them,' pleaded the prologue to *King Henry V*.

By the autumn of 1592, Shakespeare had already achieved just this kind of success, for a month earlier than Greene's attack, Nashe had written of the success of *1 Henry VI* as a novelty (it seems he did not trouble about the author but gave the success to the actors).

How would it have joyed brave Talbot (the terror of the French) to think that after he had lain two hundred years in his Tomb, he should triumph again on the stage, and have his bones new embalmed with the tears of ten thousand spectators at least (at several times) who, in the Tragedian that represents his person, imagine they behold him fresh bleeding? (*Pierce Penniless his Supplication: Works*, ed. McKerrow, I, 212)

The author's feat was to combine imaginative participation with strict control; the discipline of the stage meant that Shakespeare entered imaginatively into all the parts. In this way he created the wider Elizabethan drama, displacing other forms.

By 1592, Shakespeare had produced, in what order we do not know, a comedy and a tragedy on classical lines, *The Comedy of Errors* and *Titus Andronicus*, with an elegant little comedy of love, *Two Gentlemen of Verona*, which in spite of flaws is so far ahead of Greene's best that he did well not to mention it. As a writer of comedies, Greene naturally did not advertise his rival in his own field but indicated that the Upstart Crow had produced tragedy and history. Here Greene's instinct was right, for Shakespeare's main achievement at this time was in English history, where he harmonized the most varied traditions, challenged the power of his greatest rival and produced a form that immediately opened out possibilities for himself and for others. In the years before 1600 he was to write nine histories, about the same number of comedies and three tragedies. History had been brought back to a living form so that the public 'tableau with speeches', the 'speaking picture' of the great London shows, had been animated. This new kind of history was to remain impressed so long on his generation that as late as 1627 Drayton was still plugging away at poems on 'The Miseries of Queen Margaret'.

English history plays had until then been confined to circles of privilege, as when courtiers or lawyers performed before the Queen, or a Cambridge scholar presented *Ricardus Tertius* in the decent obscurity of a learned language. Tarlton's 'merriments' on the famous victories of Henry v were not much more historical than Greene's own *Scottish History of James IV slain at Flodden*, upon the title page of which a historically-minded Master of the Revels was to write in exasperation, 'The Scottish History or rather Fiction of English and Scottish matters historical'.

Henry VI, in its three parts, shows the increasing breakdown of order in the Wars of the Roses, a historical process known to the people of London by its triumphant conclusion. For Elizabeth's coronation, her grandparents Henry vii and his queen had been presented in a rose bower. Poets wrote:

> Under a throne I saw a virgin sit,
> The red and white rose quartered in her face . . .

Tourneys and Accession Day tiltings presented tableaux accompanied by speeches and songs on this theme. Shakespeare relied on Holinshed's chronicle – a costly investment, if he had not borrowed it from some great man's library – but Holinshed's orderly division into happy and troublesome times is far from the dynamic horrors generated in this play, which are Shakespeare's own.

As he developed the struggle, the various characters emerged, deeply enmeshed in action, until at the end one gigantic, demonic figure, compounded of much that had gone before, yet entirely new in his vitality, became the centre of the oldest drama that has survived in performance continuously from that day to this. It took three plays to reach the creation of King Richard III.

> I have't. It is engender'd. Hell and night
> Must bring this monstrous birth to the world's light.

Or so the charming, friendly young writer might have observed to himself as he put down the part which is the final cause, the whole reason of the histories in the actors' terms.

Henry VI is the opposite of Tamburlaine in that, born to inherit conquests, he lost his foreign dominions through the misfortune of a long minority when his kingdom was torn by faction;[6] then, as his culpable innocence connived at his own destruction, he grew at best a 'fool of God' while his land sank deeper into unnatural brutalities bred of civil war. Anarchy has issued from innocence, and order is regained only through atrocity.

As the son of a conqueror, Henry is overshadowed from the beginning (this was stressed in the Stratford productions of 1977), but he is not idle like Tamburlaine's foolish opponents or his gamesome son. The Marlovian opening of *1 Henry VI* none the less shows Shakespeare in Marlovian mood, with its theatrical pun on the black-hung 'heavens' of The Theatre:

> Hung be the heavens with black, yield day to night!
> Comets, importing change of times and states,
> Brandish your crystal tresses in the sky
> And with them scourge the bad revolting stars

That have consented unto Henry's death!
King Henry the Fifth, too famous to live long!
(*1 Henry VI*, 1.1.1-6)

'O tiger's heart, wrapt in a woman's hide' (singled out by
Greene) is indeed a key: part two, opening with Henry's fatal
wedding, brings in Margaret of Anjou, 'England's bloody
scourge', rejoicing not only in battle but in what for Shakespeare was the ultimate atrocity, the murder of a child. At the
end of *Richard III*, she has become a spirit of Revenge or
Nemesis; she appears and vanishes almost like the witches of
Macbeth, and is far more akin to the dark powers than is Joan
of Arc, who is presented as a witch; the two fatal women are
captured together (*1 Henry VI*, 5.3).

No transformation in the history of Shakespeare is more start-
ling than the rehabilitation, during the last quarter-century,
of the three parts of *Henry VI*. First acted in sequence in 1953
and many times since, they have vindicated the actors who put
them into the Collected Works. Fifty years ago, historians of
ideas began to treat the history plays as documents of Tudor
England's social attitudes, 'mirrors of policy'. We are now prepared to look at myths and imagination as part of history, interpretations being as 'factual' as events. Early Elizabethan
'Mirrors for Magistrates' could be dreary; but since stage re-
vivals have shown the thew and sinew of these plays, the old
idea that Shakespeare was revising Greene has been extin-
guished. What Greene wrote at his best comes nowhere near
these plays.

The mood of these plays is more understandable in the
present age of social instability, and modern critics have noted
parallels between their scenes of violence and those of modern
times. In the late 1580s, disquiet had followed on the triumphant mood which greeted the defeat of the Armada. In 1589 a
counter-Armada set out from Plymouth to the enthusiastic
'Farewell' of George Peele and others. Drake and Norris took
twenty-two thousand men to intercept the Spanish treasure-
fleet, restore the Portuguese claimant to his throne and annex
the Azores. Two months later they limped home, having failed
in all three objectives and suffered a heavy toll of sickness.[7] In
1591, the Earl of Essex led what Dover Wilson termed 'a smart

little expeditionary force' to aid Henry of Navarre in the French civil war, but the attempt to relieve the siege of Rouen was a costly failure. Rouen held the tomb of John Talbot, hero of *1 Henry VI*.

Of course Shakespeare designed the plays as art; Talbot's death ends the era of military glory and foreign power; in part two, the murder of Gloucester marks the collapse of law and order; in part three, civil war brings anarchy. Joan of Arc, burnt in 1431, gloats over the body of Talbot killed in 1433; Somerset is slain by Richard Crookback, then aged eight; Queen Margaret gloats over the fall of Gloucester's wife, who was disgraced three years before her arrival. Shakespeare's best invention is the scene in Temple Gardens where the contending factions first pluck the red and white roses (*1 Henry VI*, 2.4). Faction breaking out in the home of the law could be paralleled in the sometimes deadly feuds at Elizabeth's Court, when one faction wore blue, another yellow; or in the street fights which humbler members of the audience would have seen. The last lines of the scene are given to the Earl of Warwick, the Kingmaker, who was to dominate the conflict:

> Here I prophesy this brawl today,
> Grown to this faction in the Temple Garden,
> Shall send between the Red Rose and the White
> A thousand souls to death and deadly night.
>
> (*1 Henry VI*, 2.4.124-7)

Here was a scene to bring the play home to the young gentlemen of the Inns of Court, the most intelligent part of the audience. Perhaps Shakespeare picked up from them some tradition of an after-dinner dispute in the garden they knew so well; if so, we never learn what the legal point at issue had been.

'In order that a drama may be properly historical,' as Coleridge thought, 'it is necessary that it should be the history of the people to whom it is addressed.'[8] Shakespeare began the story for the Londoners, but he ended it in his own countryside, with his own local myths, perhaps even some family history, incorporated. He was in some respects still the country author that Greene had thought him, though his personal responses blended with and kindled his social art.

The Earl of Warwick who made and unmade kings was a Neville, but the Dudley Earls of Warwick of Shakespeare's day still used their old badge of the Bear and Ragged Staff; a Catesby from the local family, Crookback's right-hand man, was executed after Bosworth. Even more intimately close is John Shakespeare's claim in applying for a coat-of-arms that his 'late grandfather for his faithful and valiant service was advanced and rewarded by the most prudent prince King Henry the Seventh of famous memory'. 'Valiant service' can mean only service under arms; John Shakespeare's grandfather would have been of an age to serve at the Battle of Bosworth, fought some thirty miles from Stratford, which concluded the Wars of the Roses and was the most considerable engagement of Henry's reign. Presumably he joined the forces of the Earl of Richmond (as Henry then was) which, having advanced through Wales, and numbering about five thousand men, on 25 August 1485 confronted about twice as many mustered (under dire threats for non-appearance) by Richard III. Was an earlier Shakespeare one of the little group of yeomen archers who, under the Earl of Oxford, valiantly held the centre against the charge of the Duke of Norfolk's men?

As one wearing Stanley's badge Shakespeare would have a further interest. To the left of Richmond's little army, between the two forces, stood an uncommitted power of four thousand men under the banners of the Stanleys – Cheshire men in their red and white coats, men from Lancashire and the Pennines. These were the followers of Richmond's step-father, the Earl of Derby, whose heir, George, was held hostage in Richard's camp. They did not stir. As the hand-to-hand fighting whittled down his small power, Richmond, desperately hard-pressed, broke out towards the Stanleys to implore their aid, supported by only fifty knights. As he exposed himself, his banner displayed, Richard from his hilltop vantage saw his chance and put in a cavalry charge of great weight, himself riding straight forward to impale Richmond's standard-bearer on his lance. This, however, was the moment of truth for the wavering allies; to the cry 'A Stanley! A Stanley!' the four thousand advanced and caught the King's charging troop squarely on the flank. His horse killed under him, Richard remounted and bravely resumed the charge, to be cut down and, in the words of the chronicler,

> naked and despoiled to his skin and nothing left above him, not so much as a clout to cover his privy members, and was trussed behind a pursuivant of arms called Blanche Sanglier or white boar, like a hog or a calf, the head and arms hanging on one side of the horse and the legs on the other, and all besprinkled with mire and blood. (G. Bullough, *Narrative and Dramatic Sources of Shakespeare*, III, 209–300; from Holinshed)

So, under his personal cognizance, he was brought to his obscure burial in Leicester. Shakespeare would have read all this in the chronicle; but he might also have heard an obscure soldier's version at his own fireside as a family legend. 'If you do free your children from the sword / Your children's children quit it in your age' (5.3.261–2). 'The Battle of Bosworth' may have developed into a family game, for mock fights were the most popular form of May Games, and the most famous local game, the Coventry Hocktide Play, commemorated the Battle of St Brice's Day between English and Danes.

In these plays the passionate relations are those of descent and dynasty – of the elder and younger Talbots in their hopeless stand; the younger Clifford transformed by his father's death into 'Butcher Clifford', killer of little Rutland; of the murder of Henry's son, the Prince of Wales, avenged by the murder of the little Yorkist Princes in the Tower. At the battle of Towton, where Henry is confronted by a father who has killed his son and a son who has killed his father, the image itself is as old as *Gorboduc*, the first blank verse drama, 1561:

> The father shall unwitting slay the son,
> The son shall slay the sire and know it not
> (5.2.375–6)

but here it is given the full stage life in a battle as yet undecided. Henry sees the red and white roses transformed to the blood and waxy corpse flesh of his subjects; but 'the saintly yet dangerously ineffectual Henry is only dimly aware that but for

him and his despairing goodness these cruelties would not be.'⁹
In the hard light of history, of course Henry could not be held
responsible, for he suffered long periods of total mental in-
capacity.

Shakespeare is singular in using his humble characters not
merely for comedy but to reinforce the tragic pattern; and not
merely by stage spectacle but in vivid and pungent verse. This
begins with Joan of Arc. As a herald comes reciting the many
honours of dead Talbot, she curtly deflates the funeral pomp:

> Him that thou magnifi'st with all these titles,
> Stinking and fly-blown lies here at our feet.
>
> (*1 Henry VI*, 4.7.75–6)

Two wretched peasants who later stage a false miracle at St
Albans are unmasked with mirth, but as their savage punish-
ment is decreed by the good Protector, Shakespeare allows the
woman one line: 'Alas, sir, we did it for pure need' (*2 Henry
VI*, 2.1.153). No one but Shakespeare would have added that.
Yet at the same time his immense images range from the end
of the world down to intimate inner changes, invoked by young
Clifford over his father's body.

> Fear frames disorder, and disorder wounds
> Where it should guard . . .
>   O, let the vile world end
> And the premised flames of the last day
> Knit heaven and earth together!
> Now let the general trumpet blow his blast . . .
>   Even at this sight
> My heart is turn'd to stone; and while 'tis mine,
> It shall be stony. . . .
>
> (*2 Henry VI*, 5.2.32–51)¹⁰

Already, in the previous scene, the 'frame of disorder' had produced its own counter-order in the diabolic wit with which
Richard Crookback challenged old Clifford.

> RICHARD   Fie! charity, for shame! Speak not in spite,
>   For you shall sup with Jesu Christ tonight.

CLIFFORD Foul stigmatic, that's more than thou canst tell.
RICHARD If not in heaven, you'll surely sup in hell.

(2 Henry VI, 5.1.213–16)

With as long a pedigree in literature as in life, Richard III is the reason for the survival of the play that bears his name. (In the eighteenth century the play was to be altered by Cibber to make him even more dominant, with memorable lines like, 'Off with his head! so much for Buckingham!') Although he is compared to a devil many times and compares himself to 'the Vice, Iniquity', Richard resists the moral condemnation so plentifully heaped on him, for the old Vice was 'by origin a kind of clown who attracted to himself the attributes of anti-Christ bent on the mocking destruction of accepted virtues; a singularly welcome figure whenever virtue becomes tedious or oppressive'.[11] From Ambidexter or Haphazard he inherits his rapport with the audience, his ironic interpretation of events which he shares with the spectators; inside the play he is an ironic actor, a witty chameleon who plays the honest simple soldier, the pious student of divinity supported by clerical tutors (the role of Henry, whom he murdered) sharing with the audience all the pleasures of alienation, until that final moment of truth when his nerves register the total isolation which he had proclaimed from the beginning.

> What do I fear? Myself? There's none else by.
> Richard loves Richard; that is, I am I.
> Is there a murderer here? No – yes I am . . .
> I am a villain; yet I lie, I am not.
> Fool, of thyself speak well. Fool, do not flatter.

(5.3.182–92)

Stricken, not cowed, his words mark the distance from that opening prologue in which he had 'determined to prove a villain' and from its grotesque comedy. The role was perfectly suited to Richard Burbage, a 'Protean' actor who 'never put off his part, not so much as in the tiring house' till the play was done.[12] Bishop Corbet describes an old innkeeper at Bosworth who, in showing travellers round the battlefield,

> telling how King Richard died,
> cried, 'A horse, a horse' – he, 'Burbage' cried.

Where did Shakespeare get the backbone for his plays, the structural strength, the sheer craftsmanship? Partly from Holinshed, partly from the old interludes where the action was often ironically plotted, partly from another craftsman, Thomas Kyd.

Kyd's 'English Seneca', his dark Stygian underworld, presents itself in the dream of Richard's first victim, his brother Clarence:

> I pass'd, methought, the melancholy flood
> With that sour ferryman which poets write of,
> Unto the kingdom of perpetual night.
> *(Richard III*, 1.4.45–7)

This imagery of night and hell, the presence of avenging powers, the encounter with the Shades, belong to Kyd's *Spanish Tragedy* and presumably also to his lost *Hamlet*. If only a minor writer compared with Marlowe, Kyd 'in a strange inspiration shapes the future by producing something new',[13] and his name is linked with Marlowe's as Shakespeare's precursor by Ben Jonson in the lines prefixed to the First Folio. The architecture of Revenge Tragedy, where so many writers were to better their own best, originated with Kyd; he showed the younger men how to knit act and consequence in the detail of the verse:

> First in his hand he brandished a sword,
> And with that sword he fiercely waged war
> And in that war he gave me dangerous wounds,
> And by those wounds he forced me to yield,
> And by my yielding I became his slave.
> *(The Spanish Tragedy*, 2.1.121–5)

In later years Shakespeare was to parody the famous opening lines of this same scene – which Kyd had lifted from his friend Watson in the first place.

> In time the savage bull sustains the yoke,
> In time all haggard hawks will stoop to lure ...
> *(The Spanish Tragedy*, 2.1.3–4)

was quoted by the Prince in *Much Ado* (1.1.226) and controverted by Benedick; but in spite of parodies and general derision, with Alleyn in the lead, the old play still held the stage. Ben Jonson, who had also played lead (in the country), did not disdain to write some new scenes, and the Jacobeans still called for it. 'Kyd has left a blank where the moral dramatist would have set his seal of Christian approval or disapproval or his presumptuous indication of the hand of heaven. And he has therefore written a tragedy and not a tract.'[14]

This ironic variety is richer in Shakespeare and sustained by richer language. The unequalled success of his plays is attested by the fact that there are four in the series. This registers the equivalent of three encores. They could not have been planned in advance, as so many critics have asserted, for the players were the controlling power in this matter, and they were led by the taste of their audience. The author could not choose according to his own fancy; the prologue to the second part of *Tamburlaine*, by a notably independent writer, makes this clear. Many plays began by hopefully saying that a second part would follow, for which in fact there proved to be no public demand.[15]

Shakespeare found out his success in the traffic of the stage; 'all the images of Nature were still present to him, and he drew them not laboriously but luckily; when he describes anything, you more than see it, you feel it too.'[16] If for 'luck' we substitute 'intuition', the judgment stands.

The usual recipe for history plays was lots of fighting; in a prologue, disputing with History and Tragedy, History is distinguished by her emblems of drum and ensign. The death of the chief character is also the natural end. It seems possible, therefore, that *Henry VI* was composed backwards. Jack Cade in *2 Henry VI* is indebted to an earlier rebel, Wat Tyler; on St Simon's and St Jude's Day 1590, the story of Wat Tyler was revived in the Lord Mayor's Pageant. The verse is wretched, but no doubt the tableau was gorgeously presented:

> Jack Straw the rebel I present, Wat Tyler was my aid,
> Hob Carter and Tom Miller too, we all were not afraid
> For to deprive our rightful king, Richard the second named,
> Yet for our bad ambitious minds by Walworth we were tamed....

Compare this with the vigorous movement of Shakespeare's

'Up Fish Street! down St Magnus' Corner! Kill and knock down! Throw them into Thames!' (*2 Henry VI*, 4.8.1–2), and Nashe's enthusiasm for the 'life' of the plays is much reinforced.

The implicit claim in these plays is a very large one. It is the claim to give a voice and a presence to the whole land. In the fourteenth century, somewhere in the West Midlands, William Langland saw 'a fair field full of folk' – kings and knights and bishops and beggars. A desperate state of disunity fell upon them; they withdrew to defend themselves into the great barn of Unity, Holy Church.

William Langland came to London and dwelt on Cornhill; more than two hundred years later, William Shakespeare, having encountered a London much greater, a disunity much deeper, spoke in a clearer voice and put his own mark on history.

Marlowe's response to Greene's insults was an even stronger refutation than Chettle's. He wrote *Edward II*. The dependence of this play on *Richard III* is shown in the way Mortimer, as 'protector' of the young Edward III, is indebted to Crookback.[17] A weak king as the centre was a new departure for Marlowe, which he countered by making homosexuality the main motive and drive. Edward, standing in the filth of the castle dungeon, is made to enact his shame, and he appeals to what is and what has been:

> Tell Isabel the Queen I looked not thus,
> When for her sake I ran at tilt in France,
> And there unhors'd the Duke of Cleremont.

The medieval Wheel of Fortune has spun him downwards; after his even more shameful death, his murderer is dispatched with equal ferocity, and finally the adulterous pair, Mortimer and the Queen, meet justice at the hands of the young King.

Although he has telescoped events in Shakespeare's fashion, Marlowe has none of Shakespeare's feeling for the land itself, the 'common mother of us all', or for its people. He is concerned with a passion absolute and yet outlawed, in a man who is neither gentle nor trustworthy but despairingly and totally fixated. After Edward's forced abdication, everyone else becomes absolute, issues orders; Mortimer boasts that, like Tamburlaine, he can 'make Fortune's wheel turn as he pleases', but finally he too feels her power, and all that remains to him is the strength to despise his Fate:

> Base Fortune, now I see that in thy wheel
> There is a point to which, when men aspire,
>   They tumble headlong down; that point I touch'd.
>   (5.6.59–61)

The central moment, Edward's abdication, was to be Shakespeare's study when in turn he came to write *Richard II*; for *Edward II*, the greatest history play outside Shakespeare, is both the best tribute to him and the one from which he himself learned most (see p. 103).

4 The poet of the plague years

In contrast with the blankness in his biography of the years when Shakespeare was in some way serving his apprenticeship, the years 1592 to 1594 are full of significant events in the world at large and of glimpses into Shakespeare's inner life which his narrative poetry affords.

Throughout the spring of 1592 Lord Strange's Men were playing 'Harey the vi' – as Henslowe termed it in his diary – to large crowds at The Rose. Record takings of forty shillings were entered; but the entries cease at midsummer. On 7 September, when players would be thinking of returning from their summer tours, the City Council put into effect its dreaded plague orders. All performances were forbidden. The worst outbreak for many years of bubonic and pneumonic plague together had hit the capital; not till the summer of 1594 were players to be allowed more than very brief appearances even in the suburbs of London.

It is estimated that one in six of the population perished.

The effect of plague was more devastating than war; physically and mentally, everyone lived under stress. Ignorance led some to terror, others to bravado. Grass grew in Cheapside, while on the doors in red appeared the T-shaped cross and the inscription, 'Lord have mercy on us', to warn of infection within. At night the corpse-bearers went their rounds, and, roughly wrapped in a winding sheet, the dead were thrown into vast pits. The 'watchers' and nurses would at times rob the dead and dying, while criminals fleeing from London for fear of contagion would be shunned by officers of the law in the country. All who could betook themselves to the roads, and many died miserably in fields and ditches or under haystacks. Others died in the streets, for the city had no pesthouse: 'A poor boy that died under St John's wall', 'a poor wench died in the Cage', 'a poor child found at Mistress Bake's door', are entered in the burial records. A girl of twenty-one sickened and died on her wedding-day in the parish of St Peter's, Cornhill, where too a man died at the door of the house where he had been born. Most pitiful of all was the lot of the prisoners, whose jails were always full of disease. There was little relief from alms in such times, and many were starved. John Donne's younger brother, Henry, thrown into Newgate for harbouring a proscribed secular priest, died of either plague or jail fever in 1593.

The onset was sudden; in a later visitation, as a joint service was being held in St Clement's Danes, one cleric fell sick as he gave the sacrament, went home and was buried the following Thursday; a second fell sick before he had finished and was thirteen weeks in recovering; only the third escaped, 'not only then, but all the contagion following without any sickness at all' – and he was much given to drink.[1]

Much earlier it had been noted in one small town that, while the plague was undoubtedly a visitation of God for sin, the state of the town ditch might be held contributory. The stench of the ditch round London Wall was known to be noxious (for more died in its vicinity than in three parishes), and nowhere was it worse than at Moorgate, as Shakespeare knew too well, for this adjoined The Theatre (*1 Henry IV*, 1.2.87–90). Remedies for the plague ranged from rue and herb of grace (which Edward Alleyn, on tour in the provinces, urged upon his wife and father-in-law at home), rosemary and onions, to the exotic unicorn's horn. Bubonic plague was carried by rats, pneumonic plague was highly contagious, but the distinction was not made; every kind of quack remedy found its ready purchasers. Yet in the fierce upsurge of the will to survive, recklessness would lead some to dance defiantly on the very brink of the plague pits. The whorehouses of Southwark did a brisk trade, never better; but the nearby Rose was dark. The players had continued on the road; Edward Alleyn got as far as Newcastle and Bristol, although his family stayed in town. Other companies collapsed, joined together or simply melted away, and the playwrights, like the players, were scattered. Greene had died, theatrically cursing plays and repenting his sins, for, as one preacher was to remark: the cause of plague is sin; the

cause of sin is plays; therefore the cause of plague is plays. Peele
sank into illness; Lyly, his career ruined, went to his wife's
people in the country; Thomas Lodge shipped off to sea with
Cavendish – in the next visitation, as a qualified physician, he
would stay at his post and write a treatise on what he saw in
London.[2] Marlowe went to Chislehurst, to the house of Sir
Thomas Walsingham, a good friend to poets, cousin to the
founder of the Queen's Men; Nashe found refuge first, it would
seem, at the palace of the Archbishop of Canterbury in Croydon,[3] then with Sir George Carey's family in the Isle of Wight.

Nashe was a satirist and not a poet; but the plague made
a poet of him. He was to write to the Earl of Southampton
in 1594: 'A dear lover and cherisher you are, as well of the lovers
of Poets as of Poets themselves. Amongst their sacred number
I dare not inscribe myself, though now and then I speak English'
(Dedication to *The Unfortunate Traveller*, 1694). Yet London's
threnody for this disastrous summer came from his pen, and
if a man were to write one poem only, he could not do better
than 'Adieu, farewell earth's bliss'. As a poet of our own day
has said,

> There is a tree native in Turkestan . . .
> Will ripen only in a forest fire.
> (William Empson, 'Note on Local Flora')

The plague ripened the talents of Nashe – and of Shakespeare
– as it destroyed those of other men.

> Rich men, trust not in wealth,
> Gold cannot buy you health;
> Physick himself must fade
> All things to end are made
> The plague full swift goes by,
>   I am sick, I must die;
>   Lord have mercy upon us.
>
> Beauty is but a flower,
> Which wrinkles will devour,
> Brightness falls from the air,
> Queens have died young and fair,

> Dust hath clos'd Helen's eye.
> I am sick, I must die;
> Lord have mercy upon us.
>
> Strength stoops unto the grave,
> Worms feed on Hector brave,
> Swords may not fight with fate,
> Earth still holds ope her gate
> Come, come, the bells do cry,
> I am sick, I must die,
> Lord have mercy upon us.
>
> (ll. 1581–1601)

This is the note of late medieval poetry, the full, grave *memento mori* with the weight of tradition behind it.

If Nashe ends by vaunting that

> Heaven is our heritage,
> Earth but a player's stage

yet he brings back the lament, and in the final song he comes near home with another litany:

> London doth mourn, Lambeth is quite forlorn,
> Trades cry woe worth that ever they were born . . .
> From winter, plague and pestilence, good Lord, deliver us.
>
> (ll. 1179 ff)

These songs are part of *Summer's Last Will and Testament*, performed at Croydon by members of the Archbishop of Canterbury's household – and perhaps the little choristers of St Paul's – which, in its natural festivity, as of a traditional harvest play, contrives to make death part of the cycle of the turning year. We meet the exquisite song 'Spring, the sweet spring is the year's pleasant king'. Summer has called on Spring because, as he says in his opening words,

> What pleasure always lasts? No joy endures:
> Summer I was, I am not as I was:
> Harvest and age have whitened my green head . . .
>
> (ll. 123–5)

a note that was to be found in Shakespeare also:

> When lofty trees I see barren of leaves,
> Which erst from heat did canopy the herd,
> And summer's green all girded up with sheaves
> Borne on the bier with white and bristly beard ...
> (Sonnet 12, 5–8)

and which sounds, throughout the early part of his sonnet sequence, as though it were an autumnal composition.

Nashe is pent up at Croydon; the Law Term has been prorogued: 'The want of Term is town and city's harm', and he must shiver in a summer hall (probably lightly built of wood):

> Close chambers do we want, to keep us warm,
> Long banished must we live from our friends ...
> (1882–3)

In the Isle of Wight, Nashe's note grew more pious and penitential, as he penned *Christ's Tears over Jerusalem*, dedicated to Lady Elizabeth Carey.[4] St Paul's steeple had been struck by lightning. The plague-struck 'feel a sensible blow given them, as it were with the hand of some stander by', and the print of a hand is seen on them. Yet London does not repent: 'God hath forsaken us, but we have not sorrowed; of the heaviest correction we make a jest ... London, thou art the seeded garden of sin' (*Works*, ed. McKerrow, II, pp. 158 ff). And indeed a year later, in his novel Nashe was to revert to just such a tone, in describing 'the sweating sickness' in London, which sent his Unfortunate Traveller out of town as fast he could run.

> Then happy was he, that was an ass, for nothing will kill an ass but cold, and none died but with extreme heat. The fishes called sea stars that burn one another by excessive heat, were not so contagious as one man that had the sweat was to another. Masons paid nothing for hair to mix their lime, nor Glovers to stuff their balls with, for they had it for nothing; it dropped off men's heads and beards faster than any barber could shave it. O, if hair breeches had then been in fashion, what a fine world had it been for tailors.
> (*Works*, II, p. 229)

This note of desperate gaiety is comparable to that with which soldiers under stress maintain their morale. Defensive ribaldry was one of Nashe's specialities.

If the shock of disaster on such a scale could turn Nashe momentarily from his jesting and could ripen him into poetry, it is hardly possible to estimate its effect on the brilliant and sensitive poet who had just won the acclamations of the town with his *Henry VI*. At the very moment of victory, the ground was suddenly cut from under his feet. What were the players to do when their livelihood vanished overnight?

In the provinces they might not be welcome; and they did not thrive. By September 1593 Henslowe wrote to Alleyn: 'As for my lord a Pembroke's which you desire to know where they be, they are all at home and has been this five or six weeks, for they can not save their charges (i.e. cover their expenses) with travel as I hear and were fain to pawn their 'parel for their charge.' One of their plays, *The True Tragedy of Richard, Duke of York* (Shakespeare's *Henry VI Part 3*), came out in 1595 as 'sundry times acted by the Right Honourable the Earl of Pembroke his servants' and a quarto of *Titus Andronicus* in 1594 mentioned the servants of the Earls of Derby, Pembroke and Sussex as having played it. So they had also sold their playbooks.

In time of stress the companies changed their titles very quickly. Shakespeare apparently worked with Lord Strange's troupe, and so did Alleyn, who, however, remained a personal servant of the Lord Admiral (Lord Charles Howard). Anyone who really knew his lord would not lose the connection. The crumbs of sustenance that fell to troupes not supported by an Alleyn may be estimated from Joan Alleyn's letters to her husband (they had been married only on 22 October 1592), which were signed 'your poor mouse for ever'. On a later plague visitation she wrote: 'Though you have worn your apparel to rags, the best is you know where to have better, and as welcome to me shall you be in your rags as if you were in cloth of gold or velvet, try and see' (*Henslowe Papers*, p. 60).

Shakespeare could presumably have gone back to Stratford, but the happiest alternative would be some country house. As a physician, Thomas Lodge was to counsel wisely: 'Briefly, to live in repose of spirit, in all joy, pleasure, sport and contentation amongst a man's friends, comforteth heart and vital spirits, and is in this time more requisite than any other things' (*A Treatise on the Plague*, 1603).

The Court kept away from London; most extraordinary precautions were taken to prevent infection reaching it, but disease was rife among the servants in their tents and outhouses and made the perambulating army of royal followers a menace. Savage penalties were imposed on any infected persons who resorted there.

The only evidence of where Shakespeare might have been is his two dedications to the Earl of Southampton of his poems *Venus and Adonis* and *The Rape of Lucrece*, in 1593 and 1594. The first is distantly respectful, without the excesses of Nashe's dedication to the same nobleman in *The Unfortunate Traveller*. Shakespeare writes:

I know not how I shall offend in dedicating my unpolished lines to your Lordship, nor how the world will censure me for choosing so strong a prop to support so weak a burden, only, if your Honour seem but pleased, I account myself highly praised, and vow to take advantage of all idle hours, till I have honoured you with some graver labour. But if the first heir of my invention prove deformed, I shall be sorry it had so noble a godfather; and never after ear so barren a land, for fear it yield me still so bad a harvest. I leave it to your Honourable survey, and your Honour to your heart's content; which I wish may always answer your own wish and the world's hopeful expectation.

Your Honour's in all duty, William Shakespeare.

This may be compared with Nashe's hyperboles:

My reverent dutiful thoughts (even from their infancy) have been retainers to your glory.... Incomprehensible is the height of your spirit both in heroical resolution and matters of conceit. Unreprievably perisheth that book whatsoever to waste paper, which on the diamond rock of your judgment chanceth to be shipwreckt. A dear lover and cherisher you are, as well of the lovers of Poets as of Poets themselves.

Nashe was certainly well known (he was of the same college as Southampton), but he was not given any encouragement to acquire 'a new brain and a new wit', whereas in the same year

Shakespeare brought forward his 'graver labour', *The Rape of Lucrece*.

> The love I dedicate to your Lordship is without end; whereof this pamphlet, without beginning, is but a superfluous moiety. The warrant I have of your Honourable disposition, not the worth of my untutored Lines, makes it assured of acceptance. What I have done is yours, what I have to do is yours, being part in all I have, devoted yours. Were my worth greater, my duty would show greater; meantime, as it is, it is bound to your Lordship; to whom I wish long life, still lengthened with all happiness.
>
> Your lordship's in all duty, William Shakespeare.

The confidence of acceptance is here very strong, though the nature of its 'warrant' is unexplained; the repetition of 'duty', and the duty being 'bound', would certainly authorize, though of course it does not absolutely infer, some form of recognized attachment as sworn servant or follower. It is a very positive word for Shakespeare: when the soldiers leave Hamlet with 'Our duty to your honour', he replies 'Your loves, as mine to you' (1.2.252–3); Cordelia and Kent use it of and to Lear; Macbeth to Duncan in response to his thanks:

> The service and the loyalty I owe,
> In doing it, pays itself. Your Highness' part
> Is to receive our duties; and our duties
> Are to your throne and state children and servants,
> Which do but what they should by doing everything
> Safe toward your love and honour.
>
> *(Macbeth, 1.4.22–7)*

It is also used to define the relation of wives to husbands.

That the relation of master and servant could be one not only of love but of a depth that goes beyond the familial bond is perhaps difficult to grasp in an age when contracts and money wages were replacing older feudal ties; but the gentlemanly profession of serving-man could still receive such praise at this time.[5] A part that was reputedly played by Shakespeare himself shows such 'duty':

> O good old man, how well in thee appears
> The constant service of the antique world,

When service sweat for duty, not for meed!
Thou art not for the fashion of these times,
Where none will sweat but for promotion ...
                        (*As You Like It*, 2.3.56–60)

For poet and patron, the Renaissance strengthened the ties.
Tasso 'confided in him [his patron] not as we trust in man, but
as we trust in God. It appeared to me that, so long as I was
under his protection, fortune and death had no power over me
... I became almost an idolator.' A servant could, however,
be subject to humiliating whims. The Earl of Southampton's
cousin forbad his servants to turn their back on the roast that
was cooking on the spit for his dinner,[6] and those with the ill
fortune of a mistress rather than a master might be brutally
exploited by some cunning widow, who dangled prospects of
matrimony before the hopeful aspirant.[7] The ideal of noble service had to contend with harsh practice (as in Shakespeare's
Sonnets 57 and 58).

The insecurity of great men's fortunes made for insecurity
among household dependants too, yet social prejudice still
lingered against some forms of publication. Not, however,
against all. With the publication of *Venus and Adonis*, Shakespeare was at once attempting to compete with the other poets
addressing the Earl of Southampton and to make for himself
a second reputation, in which he certainly succeeded. The
author at once received recognition and respectful notice, even
among those who despised, or affected to despise, the work of
the common stages. In a few years, the students of Cambridge
would commend in a play the poet Shakespeare ('Who loves
not Adon's love or Lucrece rape?') while they gave a pulveriz-
ing defence of Shakespeare the playwright to Kempe the ignor-
ant clown: 'Few of the university pen plays well, they smell
too much of that writer Ovid and that writer Metamorphoses.
Why here's our fellow Shakespeare puts them all down ...'
(Second Part of *The Return from Parnassus*, 4.3). The noble realm
of the gods set this author far above the beasts where Greene
had placed him; this is a literary equivalent of the application
to the Herald's College for a coat-of-arms.

The poem was carefully printed by Richard Field, of the
Stratford family; it had been 'entered' to him on 18 April 1593

and was certainly in print by June, having been licensed by no less a personage than Whitgift, the Archbishop of Canterbury (did he read it or merely read the dedication?).

This is perhaps a signal that it had noble approval – that of Southampton's mother, or even his guardian, the great Lord Burghley.

In 1593, Southampton at nineteen had been two years at Court, and before that at Gray's Inn; his obstinate refusal to marry his guardian's grand-daughter had provoked a Latin poem entitled *Narcissus*, written by one of Burghley's secretaries, John Clapham, published with a dedication to the young Earl in 1591.[8] This work of admonition shows Narcissus (who resides in England) visiting the Temple of Love; later, mounted on an untameable horse named 'Lust', he drinks of the Fountain of Self-Love, into which his horse (after it has bolted with its rider) has hurled him. In the end he is drowned, and Venus transforms him into a flower.

No doubt Burghley rewarded his secretary for this piece of advice to the youth, whose main recoil may have been due not so much to a dislike of the lady as to the prospect of having Lord Burghley as a grandfather, perpetually in charge of him.

Shakespeare may already have written a few of the early sonnets (some of them were published in a volume named *The Passionate Pilgrim*) where the wooing of Adonis by Venus is treated comically:

> Ah, that I had my lady at this bay,
> To kiss and clip me till I run away!
> (Sonnet xi)

There is still plenty of comedy in his *Venus and Adonis*, which both praises and warns – as we have seen, this was quite customary (see p. 38 above). On the title page, *Venus* is printed small *AND ADONIS* very large, directing emphasis to the youth. By making the goddess a wooer, the internal struggle is shown as the attack of a higher force from beyond the self; the bolting horse is made an example of the kind of animal instinct that is being roused – to be set against that other animal instinct of hunting which is Adonis' ruling passion. It is all so much more tactful than Clapham; but the message is the same.

Venus' attentions are overwhelming; as many have ruefully

observed, she is both larger and stronger than the lovely boy, whom she tucks under one arm while she deals with the courser's reins, and then inflames the horse with a young wild mare. Beautiful Venus Genetrix, celebrated by Chaucer in the great Poem to the third book of *Troilus and Criseyde*, is Nature herself in one aspect:

> In heaven and hell, in earth and salte sea
> Is felt the might, if that I well discern:
> As man, bird, beast, fish, herb and grene tree . . .

The boar that kills Adonis, besides being an emblem of nature's destructive forces and of sexual ferocity (nuzzling Adonis with his tusks) may be a direct symbol of the plague, for the wound is in the flank or groin, where the dreaded plague spots, the 'bubos', appeared – under the armpits and at the crotch.

Ovid's *Metamorphoses* presented a world of change, of Protean transformations, while his *Heroic Epistles* provided stories of human passion in its strength and frailty. Shakespeare was to be identified as Ovidian by Francis Meres: 'As the soul of Euphorbus was thought to live in Pythagoras; so the sweet witty soul of Ovid lives in mellifluous and honey-tongued Shakespeare, witness his *Venus and Adonis*, his *Lucrece*, his sugred Sonnets among his private friends etc' (*Palladis Tamia: Wits Treasury*, 1598).

Ovid represented natural man in revolt against custom: 'Ovid's tales presented a virginal world without history or morality. It was inhabited by figures who were creatures of impulse embodying divine or natural forces . . .' (J. W. Lever, 'Shakespeare's Narrative Poems', in *A New Companion to Shakespeare Studies*, 1971, p. 117). The flow of impulse is arrested by the set speeches of Venus and Adonis, and often at the height of action, a simile will remove the reader to a considerable psychic distance. While the beauty of the flesh, its texture and warmth, its sweat and quivering, is directly apprehended, it may suddenly be transformed into what Yeats would have called a 'Byzantine' piece of art:

> Full gently now she takes him by the hand,
> A lily prison'd in a gaol of snow,

> Or ivory in an alabaster band;
> So white a friend engirts so white a foe.
>
> (*Venus and Adonis*, 361–4)

Venus herself is a bird of prey – an eagle, vulture or falcon; and the wooing is itself a kind of hunt, with Venus 'foraging' and, after Adonis' death, confessing,

> Had I been tooth'd like him [the Boar], I must confess,
> With kissing him I should have kill'd him first.
>
> (1, 117–18)

Adonis rejects love because 'I have heard it is a life in death' (413); Venus on the other hand fears that the Destinies are hostile.

> As burning fevers, agues pale and faint,
> Life-poisoning pestilence, and frenzies wood,
> The marrow-eating sickness . . .
> And not the least of all these maladies
> But in one minute's fight brings beauty under.
>
> (739–46)

Venus' fear is physically realized in the discovery of the corpse – the end of her desperate quest with all its self-deceiving alternations of hope and despair:

> She looks upon his lips, and they are pale;
> She takes him by the hand, and that is cold;
> She whispers in his ears a heavy tale,
> As if they heard the woeful words she told;
> She lifts the coffer-lids that close his eyes,
> Where, lo, two lamps burnt out in darkness lies.
>
> (1,123–8)

Death is then the undersong to this celebration of the flesh and the delights of country pursuits. The hunted hare, described by Venus herself, the landscape which her body extended offers Adonis ('I'll be a park and thou shalt be my deer'), the woods through which she struggles, held back by briars, with such detail as the snail shrinking backwards in his shelly cave with pain, the divedapper peering through a wave, are natural to this half-pastoral kind of poetry. All this suggests renewed contact by the poet with the countryside if not that from which he had been exiled. His taste for hare coursing may have been acquired in Warwickshire, but the pastoral setting is now the counter-assertion of life against the threats that provide the 'undersong'. The hare in this poem is both realistic and symbolic.

Was Shakespeare then at Titchfield where a few years before the Queen had been entertained? If so, was he a guest or a member of Southampton's household?

The natural hope of any aspiring writer was to join a noble household, as tutor or secretary or in some part of the administration that looked after the thousand and one concerns of great estates. Daniel was William Herbert's tutor; Spenser, in the previous generation, had aspired to intimacy with the household of Leicester, whom he calls 'my lord'. His career showed the dangers inherent in the position, for, over-zealous in his patron's cause, he committed the incredible folly of attacking Burghley in *Mother Hubbard's Tale*, so that Leicester, who possessed the most acute sense of what was acceptable to the Queen, dropped the poet very suddenly.[9] Instead of being sent on some foreign embassy, Spenser found himself dismissed and exiled to Ireland. The offending poem itself contains the bitterest indictment of the servant's fate:

> Full little knowest thou, that hast not tried,
> What hell it is, in suing long to bide ...
> To speed today, to be put back tomorrow,
> To feed on hope, to pine with fear and sorrow ...
> To fawn, to crouch, to wait, to ride, to run,
> To spend, to give, to want, to be undone ...
> That curse God send unto mine enemy.

(p. 895 ff)

Certainly the natural thing for a poet who had become not only a follower but a trusted one would be some form of household attachment. Early tradition asserts that Southampton gave Shakespeare a sum of money 'to enable him to go through with a purchase that he had a mind to'.[10]

If Shakespeare was residing at Titchfield during the plague years, he would have had access both to country pursuits and to the intimate ways of a noble household. It is one thing to learn the manners of the great from courtesy books and another to take a close part in the wit-combats, the flirtations and the sudden enmities of the life of privilege. This was in itself an education. Chapman, as we saw, does not seem to have attended the university but resided in the great household of Sir Ralph Sadler (see below, p. 201). He gives a memorable picture in *The Gentleman Usher* of the folly that expectation of favour will create in a servant. The Gentleman Usher, exploited by the noble young Vincentio in order to gain access to his mistress, fondly imagines himself beloved, calls the nobleman 'Vince' and is fooled to the top of his bent. It is a cruel picture. In *Colin Clout's Come Home Again*, Spenser, after revisiting the royal Court, returns to his exile.

Was Southampton, then, the fair youth of the *Sonnets*? The rival candidate favoured by some scholars is William Herbert, heir to the Earl of Pembroke.[11] He received the dedication of the First Folio (with his brother) but, as he was born in 1580, it would mean that the sonnets must be put considerably after *Venus and Adonis*. When the folio was published, he was the Lord Chamberlain and the obvious person for the company to choose as sponsor. It would be an astonishing coincidence if Shakespeare knew two young noblemen in the same predicament and used the same methods of persuasion for both.

The first sonnets are close to *Venus and Adonis* in style as well as theme; they are decorative and heraldic. Throughout the series the youth is called 'beauty's rose', 'my rose',[12] which is the epithet of Adonis ('rose cheek'd') and may carry a pun on Wriothesley (pronounced Roseley). All through the series the images of the bounty of the earth, the connection of love with tillage, the beloved as Nature's rich treasury, persist as something more than the common language of lovers. But while the Flesh is almost overpoweringly present in the poem, in the sonnets addressed to the youth, Eros has become Agape. (Even in the sonnets of betrayal with the Dark Wanton, it is the betrayal itself that is unendurable.) Although sometimes there is total submissiveness, at other times frank plain-speaking appears. The very inconsistency makes up a most convincing picture of love's changeable moods; sometimes the poet thinks his verses worthless, at others he affirms that they will bring immortality and preserve the beauty of his beloved for ever, and so on, veering and contradicting himself, yet always able, in this one relationship, it seems, to digest any experience to the nature of love. Far from being weak, this is an immensely strong attitude. There is little to be learned about the youth, nor, except for his betrayal with the dark lady and his adoption of the rival poet, does he ever do anything except simply to be what he is. In the later poems it is sometimes the poet who deserts his friend and who therefore begs forgiveness, in something very near the language of prayer (more often he is conscious of unworthiness than of downright guilt[13]). The relationship depicted at the end is one of complete equality, which could arise only after a period of years; at least three years are mentioned.

The sonnets themselves are of most uneven achievement; there are some trivial and some fanciful exercises, some that are a weaker rendering of stronger versions. But it is not at all necessary to assume that these different sonnets represent a correspondingly wide range of time. In such a concentrated form, and in the context of intense personal relationship, it is to be expected that Shakespeare's dramatic imagination should sometimes bring him to a level which he could not maintain except very briefly.

In all this variety of accomplishment, there is no variation in that capacity for a transfer of the whole centre of being into the life of another, which is the mark linking these sonnets to dramatic art. They are not idolatry (Shakespeare anticipates this charge, in Sonnet 105), although the mood is always a mood of love. 'Fair, kind and true' may not be equally present, but one or other is always there – whether it be 'lascivious grace', 'tears [of] pearl', a fair flower with 'an ill savour', 'Eve's apple' or the 'cankered' rose.

The early pleas to marry and beget an heir have good precedent. There was one exalted personage in England who had been consistently besought not to let beauty's rose wither unpropagated, whose incomparable perfections, though in themselves immortal, should not be suffered to live and die in single blessedness. Queen Elizabeth provided the exception, but for any other great heir the duty to transmit an inheritance was inevitable. Southampton had only too good reason to know the perils that an orphan encountered, the need to father a son in youth. In this time of plague the argument became doubly strong, and the force of it is behind Sonnet 9:

> Is it for fear to wet a widow's eye
> That thou consum'st thyself in single life?
>
> (1–2)

– otherwise hardly an argument to apply to a youth.

It could be argued that fierce and consuming passion for the Dark Wanton was also strengthened by the ever-present sense of death. In such times of stress and danger the impulse to live fully in the senses can flame up with uncontrollable violence. Into that relationship goes all the dark aspect of Venus, anger, wit and ruthless dissection of deceit and self-deceit. The poet, older than both, accepts from the woman that measure of mutual deceit which in the youth's relation is the source of deepest pain.

Compare

> When my love swears that she is made of truth,
> I do believe her, though I know she lies,
> That she might think me some untutor'd youth . . .
>
> (Sonnet 138, 1–3)

with

> How like Eve's apple doth thy beauty grow,
> If thy sweet virtue answer not thy show!
>
> (Sonnet 93, 13–14)

In spite of the insight and sympathy, it is not at all clear, except in their relation to the poet, what sort of people these were. It is impossible to conceive of their replies, to see them as independent figures in the sense that a drama could be built on the sonnets, dramatic as they are, for the mesh of relationships constitutes an *internal* drama, where the reader responds with the poet's responses. This deep self-exploration may have conferred the power of dramatic detachment, which appeared only later in the plays. It may be possible to see something of the Earl of Southampton later in Bassanio, and in Bertram of *All's Well*.

The miniature of the youthful Earl, by Hilliard, shows a mingling of beauty and obstinacy; the girlish quality of the long lovelocks and the small mouth combine with a hard expression. Southampton could be loyal to friends (as we shall see), and in his later life he became a reformed character, in every sense, attending church with King James.

The experience with the dark beauty was important, but how important was the person herself, when, as Shakespeare knew, his 'doting' conferred the attraction, and all was self-generated? Perhaps, although he is nominally addressing the woman, his real audience was other men who had felt the same about women (*Troilus and Cressida* is the dramatic projection of this lacerative self-knowledge). The savagery, kept out of his relationship with the youth, burst out here in compensation.

Perhaps the decision for lover and beloved to go their separate ways was the poet's. In more than one sonnet he feels that he should withdraw himself; he writes from a distance that he awaits better times 'to put apparel on my tatter'd loving' (Sonnet 26); he laments the miles that separate them (Sonnet 50) but envisages return (Sonnet 52). Thinking of his own death, he would not wish so much as to be remembered (Sonnets 71, 72). Following some insult and betrayal (Sonnets 33, 34, 35), there is implicit a decision to stay in his humble role, even though to some it seems infamous ('if *you* have behaved badly, I am no fit companion for you'):

> Let me confess that we two must be twain,
> Although our undivided loves are one;
> So shall those blots that do with me remain,
> Without thy help, by me be borne alone . . .
> I may not evermore acknowledge thee,
> Lest my bewailed guilt should do thee shame;
> Nor thou with public kindness honour me,
> Unless thou take that honour from thy name.
>
> (Sonnet 36, 1–4, 9–12)

It would not have been an indelible shame for Shakespeare to be made Southampton's gentleman usher or secretary. Somewhere deep down perhaps did not Shakespeare find that the pull of his art was the stronger of the two impulses? It is true that he took no pains to publish his plays; he did not continue his non-dramatic poetry (or if he did, it has all perished). His was an art of performance, 'the perfume and suppliance of a minute' – but this was what he had tried to fix for ever in the sonnets, catching the transient beauty of youth as it was sensed in direct, momentary experience. Immediacy of impression is caught by skill in practice of his art. All Court poetry was an art of performance; the most successful was Ralegh's. His great poem to the Queen put her into a cosmic setting; she was the Moon Goddess Cynthia, he the Ocean – and *he* was certainly seeking to make his fortunes from the bounty of his lady. It did not prevent his writing very great poetry:

> From fruitful trees I gather wither'd leaves
> And glean the broken ears with miser's hands . . .

From a material point of view Shakespeare did better than this, according to tradition. If Southampton gave Shakespeare a gift to go through with a purchase, probably a share in a company of players, that must have been to some extent Shakespeare's own choice, as it was Spenser's choice to return to his Irish estate and exile.

By his poems Shakespeare had established himself. He would do as much for his profession, would help to raise it, as Alleyn was doing, to a level where the Crown itself might resume the role of patron.

This, in ten years, was achieved.

Other poets varied in the perseverance of poetic praise. Michael Drayton spent his whole life in the worship of his 'Idea' – a noblewoman – modestly, respectfully. Samuel Daniel could equally modestly give over after fifty sonnets, addressed to the Countess of Pembroke – 'I say no more, I fear I said too much'; but he published them as 'monuments of your honourable favour' with a proper dedication. This was a year after the appearance of the only sonnets really comparable with Shakespeare's, and, like his, published without authorization – Sidney's *Astrophel and Stella* (1591). Philip Sidney was the revered model for all the young men of Essex's and Southampton's circle – and of course they were all closely linked by family ties.

Daniel has the heraldic prettiness of Shakespeare's first sonnets: 'Now, while thy May hath fill'd thy lap with flowers', Sidney the passion of a complex and self-critical personality, very courtly but very human. He did not cease to be a craftsman, by becoming a lover; his poems were used as examples for rhetoricians, yet he breaks away from convention very dramatically. We meet Sidney the soldier, the tilter, the artist, who finds himself unable to discuss politics because he is absorbed in Stella, who is impatient with friends:

> Be your words made (good sir) of Indian ware
> That you allow them me by so small rate ...
> You say, forsooth, you left her well of late.
> O God, think you that satisfied my care?
>
> (Sonnet 92)

It is all much more worldly than Shakespeare's verses, where the two external figures, the dark wanton and the rival poet, alone bring up some sense of the external world.

Sidney's love is part of his social life; it belongs to his courtly circle, the in-group, almost as much as Ralegh's praise of the Queen; they had their audience, though certainly not a public audience. Immediacy and poignancy and self-mockery were brought into the English sonnet by Sidney; at its most artificial, the sonnet need not be about anybody at all ('She may be some College', wrote Giles Fletcher of his insubstantial Licia). Stella was known to everyone; yet memorial verses about Astrophel and his love could, after Sidney's death, be dedicated to his widow, Frances Walsingham, with no sense of embarrassment. Shakespeare's sonnets are much more private because he is not distant like Daniel and Drayton; he is not writing as an equal, like Sidney. His sonnets to the dark wanton are full of the kind of sexual nausea that Donne expressed in such poems as 'The Apparition' or his *Elegies*. Love, when lightly seen, was a kind of hunt, undertaken for pleasure; but rarefied sentiments, such as those of Petrarch's pupils, were contrasted with franker classical descriptions. Shakespeare was associated with these when he was termed a witty 'Ovidian' in his sonnets (this is Meres' epithet). In *Amores*, Ovid had written of how he tore out his mistress's hair and beat her black and blue; Catullus described the alternations of love and hatred. That very moral Elizabethan, George Gascoigne, had drawn a devastating picture of an unfaithful mistress in *The Adventures of Master F.J.* (1573), which was autobiographical. ('And if I did, what then?' is the woman's response to accusation.) Nashe had written for the Earl of Southampton a poem of such erotic crudity that it had to be copied out in cypher (*The Choice of Valentines or Nashe's Dildo*) and William Burton had produced for him a salacious story with homosexual episodes. By the mid nineties, erotic themes were fashionable.[14]

Shakespeare's sonnets are still those of a craftsman, though the pain and anger revealing themselves in bawdy jests may start with a simple proverb: 'Whoever hath her wish, thou hast thy Will' (Sonnet 135). At no point does any affection for this woman appear; the whole series of poems are an attack on her; if she could read, it would certainly have been needful to send somebody to counteract the unbroken series of insults and innuendos. This is a totally self-centred feeling, 'lust in action', obsessive and as involuntary as 'my gross body's treason', so wittily and devastatingly shown when flesh stays no further reason,

> But, rising at thy name, doth point out thee
> As his triumphant prize.
>
> (Sonnet 151, 9–10)

To praise by dispraising was a paradox that would not surprise; 'My mistress' eyes are nothing like the sun' merely inverts the old worn phrases. Adultery, if it produced a stable relationship, would not be insulting. But accusation of promiscuity, to be 'the bay where all men ride', was a rare form of insult; it put the woman on a bad level with the prostitution of talent implied in

> Alas, 'tis true I have gone here and there
> And made myself a motley to the view,
> Gor'd my own thoughts, sold cheap what is most dear...
>
> (Sonnet 110, 1–3)

Nowhere is there the generous exchange of forgiveness that makes the reciprocal relationship with the youth:

> That you were once unkind befriends me now ...
> But that your trespass now becomes a fee;
> Mine ransoms yours, and yours must ransom me.
> (Sonnet 120, 1, 13–14)

Here, and in the agonized sonnet on Lust (129) the poet's state of mind is described as 'hell' – a state of mind so dark that it does not seem to belong to time, though felt in time.

With the introduction of the rival poet, a more alarming rival than the woman, the play of fancy bounds from self-confidence to utter dejection, culminating in two sonnets (85 and 86) where the poets appear as rivals in verse competition (one thinks of Wagner's *Mastersingers*). The relation of *Hero and Leander* to *Venus and Adonis* makes it possible that the rival was Marlowe, and 'the proud full sail of his great verse / Bound for the prize of all too precious you' fits both his style and his temperament. Shakespeare associated Marlowe's verse, rather exceptionally, with love and the countryside (see p. 41), and if they both took part in some country-house interlude, the association would be explained.[15]

The relations of Shakespeare and Southampton are supposedly discussed in a cryptic little work by Henry Willoughby, *Willoughby his Avisa* (1594), which was immensely popular, although now it is impossible to decide what exactly H.W. and the 'old player' W.S. are supposed to be doing. In 1597 Southampton was to quarrel violently with Ambrose Willoughby, a member of the Queen's household, who had evicted him from the Presence Chamber because the Queen had retired. Outside, Southampton struck Willoughby, who in turn pulled out a handful of Southampton's long hair. The Queen supported him against the Earl.[16] This, however, was later, and in 1594, when Shakespeare offered his 'graver labour', Southampton was just coming of age, escaping from Burghley.

In this poem we meet Lust in its most violent form, more violent even than in *Narcissus*. *The Rape of Lucrece* was regarded by everyone as a moral work, written to please the wise. It might be regarded as too much of a warning to be a self-sufficient work of art. Southampton's family motto is cunningly worked into the admonition:

> The aim of all is but to nurse the life
> With honour, wealth, and ease in waning age;
> And in this aim there is such thwarting strife
> That one for all or all for one we gage . . .
>
> (141–4)

'*Ung pour tout et tout pour ung*' appears also in Sonnet 105.

The poem is nearly twice as long as *Venus and Adonis*; the first half is vivid in its account of Tarquin's inner conflict between honour and lust, but here there is little of the fair world of the countryside, for the scene is set within doors and at night, in Lucrece's chamber. Her hand on the green coverlet, 'like to an April daisy on the grass', is the one glimpse of that sacramental universe which unites humanity with the breathing, organic form of the earth. The very beasts of this poem are characterized morally as lambs and wolves, eagles and hinds, predator and prey.

The act of rape has to be seen in Elizabethan terms as making any further physical relation with her husband impossible to Lucrece. It is as if (in modern terms) Tarquin had not only raped her but taken her off in a fast car and smashed it, leaving her paralysed or crippled. Her body is no longer tolerable to her, and her knife re-enacts his violence.

> He, he, fair lords, 'tis he,
> That guides this hand to give this wound to me.
>
> (1, 721–2)

Tarquin's account of his shame gives an explicitly Christian dimension to the conflict of body and soul (ll. 717–28); by her suicide, unsheathing her soul from its 'polluted prison', for Lucrece the black event is 'cancelled' from destiny.

The 'freezing' of people by some atrocity too vast to be comprehended has been seen in *Titus Andronicus*; Tarquin foreshadows other night prowlers – Macbeth, Iachimo – and all this suggests some catastrophe too vast to be brought fully to light. As in *Hamlet*, it is something that resists the poet, that 'into words no virtue can digest', although he tries too many words here, in Lucrece's long laments.[17] At the end of all the fluent eloquence, we can catch only an overtone, something like the whisper that in Joseph Conrad's story came at the heart of darkness: 'The horror! the horror!'

Yet, on the other hand, it is also a highly self-conscious study of the relation of art to life. When the ravished Lucrece studies the painting of Troy, she sees powerful feelings presented obliquely; here she finds Hecuba, the image of her own grief, and Sinon, the image of deceitful Tarquin, which so transports her that she attacks the painting. Shakespeare had used before and was to use again the image of Troy as the ultimate secular disaster; he would have learned the story in his schooldays from the second book of the *Aeneid*.

The world he made

5 The poet of love

In 1604 Dekker wrote *The Wonderful Year*, celebrating the splendours and miseries of King James's happy succession to the English throne in 1603, the new outburst of plague, and many other marvels. Shakespeare's wonderful year had come exactly a decade earlier, in 1594. His art had leaped into another dimension, and the life of the poet is henceforth the life of his art. His love poetry celebrated that happy state in which the beloved constitutes the whole world, and in that presence all things become harmonized.

'You are my all the world' or 'the better part of me' (Sonnets 112, 39) so that 'What is it but mine own when I praise thee?' 'Incapable of more, replete with you' (Sonnet 113), he does not need love tokens. Perhaps in the end he does not need the bodily presence, for the vision has been made fully part of himself. 'Those who belong together don't need to stick together,' said Freud to one of his colleagues; and Ibsen went so far as to suggest that *for the artist* some act of separation was necessary (later he came to think the price too high). The beloved is the best and only record of his own nature.

> Who is it that says most which can say more
> Than this rich praise – that you alone are you?
> (Sonnet 84, 1–2)

Eloquent praise becomes 'a tomb'. The opposite is also true. The friend of the sonnets has been reincarnated in an 'eternal summer' of beauty and goodness. Out of this exclusive devotion came a new world that the poet made; he might say with Donne,

> Let sea-discoverers to new world have gone,
> Let maps to others, world on world have shown,
> Let us possess one world, each hath one and is one.
> (*The Good Morrow*)

Gradually the initiating experience faded – the friend, the rival poet, the dark beauty, provided energies for actions on the public stage and were not merely transplanted there.

On 5 June 1594 Henslowe began to record performances at the little theatre in Newington Butts by 'my Lord Admiral's men and my Lord Chamberlain's Men' – the two troupes that were to dominate for the next thirty years. They played *Titus Andronicus* and *The Taming of a Shrew* – which may not be Shakespeare's *Taming of the Shrew* – with a *Hamlet* that cannot be his (though Peter Alexander thought it could[1]). After 15 June the players went on tour, but on 8 October the Lord Chamberlain was negotiating with the Lord Mayor for the use by 'my new company' of the Cross Keys Inn in the coming winter. This had been Burbage's headquarters in the old days. Five men from the company of the deceased Earl of Derby (formerly Lord Strange) came over – Will Kempe, Thomas Pope, John Heminges, Augustin Phillips and George Bryan. The new company also included William Shakespeare and Richard Burbage. In the following Christmas season at Court, the Chamber accounts record a payment for performances 'to William Kempe, William Shakespeare and Richard Burbage, servants to the Lord Chamberlain' of £13.6.8, with Her Majesty's reward of an additional £6.13.4! In other words, Shakespeare was among the leading sharers of the new company, ranking with its chief comic and tragic actors. He had arrived. For the rest of his working life he was to stay in fellowship with these men, and after his death 'Old stuttering Heminges', by then the doyen of the group, was to collect his plays. Kempe left in 1600, Bryan took service in the royal household as an ordinary groom of the chamber, but Phillips and Pope stayed; the most successful and the longest lived of all Elizabethan acting troupes, under the title of the King's Men, persisted through fifty glorious years till the closure of the theatres during the Civil War in 1642.

Henry Carey, Lord Hunsdon, was Elizabeth's first cousin, the son of Mary Boleyn. His son Sir George Carey, Governor of the Isle of Wight, we have met as the protector of Nashe; in 1596 he succeeded his father, and the players would still wear the badge of the Hunsdons, the flying swan, on their sleeves. The Hunsdons, father and (eventually) son, were in charge of all Elizabeth's entertainments and of her household, while detailed supervision of plays was delegated to the Master of the Revels. Although the Queen had set up a troupe in 1583 (as mentioned on page 31), that plan had not worked well. 'Twelve of the best men' had been chosen from all the companies in London; but it might have been guessed that a troupe of stars would not hold together. The separate members went their ways, and the name became attached to a very second-rate body. From 1594, the new troupe of the Lord Chamberlain replaced them as the leading group of actors; they worked as a team, and they were, in effect, under royal patronage, although they did not acquire the royal title.

The Lord Chamberlain was in a much stronger position than the Queen to keep a firm hand on his players, to ask privileges for them and, by his influence or merely the power of his name, to smooth their way with all sorts of minor officials.

Alleyn headed the troupe of the Lord Admiral, Lord Charles Howard (who had at one time himself been Lord Chamberlain), afterwards created Earl of Nottingham. Alleyn had long been attached to Howard; such continued attachment doubtless brought its rewards: even when he directed the Earl of Derby's Men, he did not change his personal allegiance from the White Lion. Lord Hunsdon, it will be recalled, had been the patron of James Burbage from early days (above, p. 32). His splendid tomb in Westminster Abbey, in black and gold, with great obelisks, challenges royalty for pomp. His cheerful, bluff, countryman's face – and his son was very like him – suggests a good master of the old English type. Unlike the sensitive Italianate Ferdinando, Earl of Derby, or the rivals Ralegh and Essex, with their dark moody charm, Hunsdon looks the sort of man who drank beer rather than wine, knew the ways of hawks and hounds and kept his hair cut short. When an attorney tried to settle on the Isle of Wight, George Carey had the man hunted out of the island with a pound of lighted candles at his breech and bells fastened on his legs like a morris dancer.

Hunsdon's company used the Cross Keys for winter performances, The Theatre in Shoreditch for summer. They very seldom went on tour. It was not necessary. But they came back to London denuded of playwrights. Greene was dead, Marlowe was dead, Peele was sick, Lodge and Lyly had given up writing plays. Chapman began writing for Henslowe and the Admiral's Men – but he was a newcomer.

As Court favourites fought in their close-locked groups round the ageing Queen, the great houses became centres for party views and loyalties – Cecil House in the Strand, near Essex House, with Southampton House in Holborn, Lord Hunsdon's grander residence at Somerset House and his more modest quarters in Blackfriars – and centres of entertainment too, where plays might be commissioned. We know that on 9 December 1595 Sir Edward Hoby invited Sir Robert Cecil to supper to see a play on King Richard (i.e. *Richard II*). On New Year's Day, the players went down at the height of the season to Sir John Harington at Burley-on-the-Hill where by way of festivity they performed *Titus Andronicus*. The Inns of Court would invite the players to perform at their Christmas festivities, and on 28 December 1594 Gray's Inn enjoyed *The Comedy of Errors*.

New theatres opened; new plays were constantly needed. Shakespeare seems, because he was an actor, to have kept some control over all the plays he had written. Presumably he brought them with him as his contribution to stock, otherwise the early pieces that are included in the First Folio of 1623 would not have been the property of the King's Men. *Henry VI* and *Richard III*, which a Greene or a Peele would have sold, were kept by the Upstart Crow, evidently with some care.

The company had to be ready with something acceptable to a very varied audience; at The Theatre their audience was of all kinds. No doubt the Londoners would flock to see a play that had been given before the Queen (still, theoretically, the only reason for playing at all), and possibly the Queen would be equally influenced – through her Lord Chamberlain – by whatever had taken the fancy of the city. She prided herself on being 'mere English', and her tastes were catholic: Ascham tells us that she admired metaphors and rhetorical balance.

William Shakespeare was already well known. He was in a field virtually bare of rivals, and stimulated by new experience in two years' absence from the public theatre. He brought a new reputation with him, and perhaps he brought a new play – *Love's Labour's Lost*. Mounting like a rocket, he produced four

masterpieces in two years, each of an entirely different kind:
Romeo and Juliet, Richard II, A Midsummer Night's Dream and *The
Merchant of Venice*. Every one was a tremendous success. *Romeo
and Juliet* was piratically printed in 1597 (so perhaps was *Love's
Labour's Lost*); with *Midsummer Night's Dream* and *The Merchant
of Venice*, it remains the stand-by of all hard-pressed troupers.
A sixth play, which perhaps belongs to the very end of the old
era or the beginning of the new, offering yet another model,
is *The Taming of the Shrew*.[2]

The full splendour of the late Elizabethan drama was built
by Shakespeare on the foundations of others; but it was his personal construction. He wrote no more poems (that chapter was
closed) but proceeded in 1596 to get his coat-of-arms; and the
next year he bought the best house in Stratford – rather ruined,
but substantial, with two orchards and two gardens. He was
creating his own little demesne. The years were bad ones in
the country: crops failed, the poverty and starvation was cruel.
But the city prospered again. Shakespeare became a man with
two centres for his life – of course it was the ambition of every
tradesman to buy an estate in the country and become a
country gentleman. Later writers for the stage were to make
savage jests out of such pretensions. But Shakespeare kept in
touch with his Stratford neighbours the Quineys and such,
although we cannot know how much time he spent in his native
town. In London, he lived casually near his work.

Love's Labour's Lost has enough private jests to show it was
aimed at a small circle; but it is also a full drama and in the
last thirty years has revived wittily enough. It is written both
from the 'inside' and also from the 'outside' of high life. The
unusual number of women's parts suggests that it was first
written for private production with some co-operating boys'
group; the Southamptons looked on it as 'their' play at a later
date. All sorts of people have tried to interpret it, from Frances
Yates' theory that it satirized Walter Ralegh and John Florio
to Leslie Hotson's theory that it is about the Inns of Court
and 'his' candidate for Shakespeare's friend, one William
Hattecliffe.[3]

This delicious romp, laughing at learning and also laughing
at love, is set far from the city in a green park where a king
and three lords, vowed to three years' celibate study, are met

and defeated by the Princess of France and her three ladies – the *escadron volant*. In this pastoral world, a series of wooing games which are very largely word-games is played – almost danced; supposedly in the kingdom of Navarre – not much bigger than the Earl of Derby's kingdom of the Isle of Man – really on some English estate, where Antony Dull is constable and Costard the swain runs errands.

Yet this enchanting retreat is finally penetrated by a sombre messenger of death, recalling the Princess to duty and preventing the conventional happy ending. 'Jack hath not Jill'; the ladies impose severe penance on their foresworn lovers, Berowne the mocker-in-chief being sent 'to jest a twelvemonth in a hospital'. We are back with the plague, which has been kept outside the park; the life of artifice, whether of study or wooing, closes in a humble rustic song of the seasons which reminds everyone of time's vagaries.

All learn what their creator had learned – the educative power of what used to be called 'the best society'. Schooled by 'beauty's tutors', the gentlemen have all profited enough to justify themselves in poems, of which the King's is much the worst and young Dumain's the most charming.

> On a day – alack the day! –
> Love, whose month is ever May,
> Spied a blossom passing fair
> Playing in the wanton air . . .
> Do not call it sin in me
> That I am forsworn for thee;
> Thou for whom Jove would swear
> Juno but an Ethiope were;
> And deny himself for Jove,
> Turning mortal for thy love.
>
> (4.3.97–116)

Every character in this symmetrical play has his own style, from the stolid persistence of Constable Dull in maintaining facts ('Twas not a haud credo, 'twas a pricket') to the grandiloquent fancies of Armado the Spaniard. Since these prevented the lovers from being believed, all their fine speeches are abandoned

BEROWNE   ... wench, so God help me, law –
           My love to thee is sound, sans crack or flaw.
ROSALINE   Sans 'sans', I pray you,

(5.2.414–15)

The 'tongues of mocking wenches' are keener even than the very complex debates of Berowne with himself: 'The King he is hunting the deer: I am coursing myself. They have pitch'd a toil: I am toiling in a pitch – pitch that defiles. Defile! a foul word. Well, "set thee down, sorrow!" for so they say the fool said, and so say I, and I am the fool. Well proved, wit' (4.3.1 – 6).

Shakespeare is playing a variation on the courtly model of John Lyly, who, himself a courtier, had written his elegant comedies for the boys' companies some fifteen years before, but who now, forlorn and still without office, was asking the Queen piteously for 'any plank or rafter to waft me into the country ... where I may write prayers instead of plays – prayers for your long and prosperous life and repentence that I have played the fool so long'.

The little page Moth is nearest to Lyly's wit-comedy, in which love was a disease – but not a serious disease; his is the realm of Cupid, not of Venus – his central figure, and the only unambiguous one, being the Queen herself. The characters were formally divided into lovers, clowns and witty pages, and sometimes did not even meet; the magic transformations that occur merely switch them about, without the possibility of complex development such as Shakespeare puts into his word-games. Lyly's plays have not survived the society that bred. them; but Shakespeare's is still a favourite at the Inns of Court (the Law Dramatic Society put it on in 1967) or for under-graduates; I have seen a pretty musical version in Buda Pesth, a mixture of fantasy and romance. It is now often seen in Shake-spearean repertory and can be played in many different modes.

Armado, the Spanish fantastic, is the most likely figure to be a direct caricature (though he is modelled on Lyly's Sir Thopas); he has been variously identified as Gabriel Harvey, Sir Walter Ralegh, John Florio. But Shakespeare is not satiriz-ing the Court, as Ben Jonson was to do a few years later in *Cynthia's Revels* – he 'places' its artifice without moralizing or rancour, in its own terms. *Romeo and Juliet* is the twin of *Love's Labour's Lost* in the sense in which *Hamlet* is the twin of *Troilus and Cressida*. Universal drama sprang out of something with a strictly controlled audience, a limited code of appeal.

In *Romeo and Juliet* the park has shrunk to an orchard in a town house (there were plenty of these in London, and sometimes they became the scene of plays); the plague lurks in the confines of the city, 'swift bright things come to confusion' – in four days Romeo and Juliet have met, have wedded and are dead. The headlong speed of action is 'too like the lightning, which doth cease to be / Ere one can say, it lightens' (2.2.119–20). Images of light and darkness, the leading symbol of the play, alternate life with death, hate with love – the ultimate categories in Shakespeare's imagination.[4] Though Juliet makes the tomb 'a feasting presence [i.e. a Presence Chamber] full of light', yet Romeo fears that Death keeps her as his paramour, which is her father's thought too:

> O son, the night before thy wedding day
> Hath Death lain with thy wife.
>
> (4.5.35–6)

he tells Paris. Though these are not plague deaths, they partake of that speed, and even speedier is Mercutio's: 'No, 'tis not so deep as a well, nor so wide as a church door, but 'tis enough, 'twill serve. Ask for me tomorrow, and you shall find me a grave man' (3.1.93–6).

To jest in the face of death and to find the whole world pivoted upon one being ('It is the east, and Juliet is the sun', 2.2.3), are two ways of losing one's self to find oneself. I wish, says Juliet, I could give you more than all myself,

> My bounty is as boundless as the sea,
> My love as deep: the more I give to thee,
> The more I have, for both are infinite.
>
> (2.2.133–5)

The oceanic feeling, the sense of being lost, or lapsed, into a reciprocal life, a 'universe of two' as a modern poet termed it, was to remain for Shakespeare bound to the image of the sea.

This belongs to the absolute quality of first love; Shakespeare made the lovers younger than they were in earlier accounts. Untouched by experience, Juliet is inundated by her own feeling, and her response is unconditional, total.

Perhaps the last line of the play should have been used for its title – 'Juliet and her Romeo' – for Juliet is the more astonishing creation, a fully 'sympathized'[5] girl who replaces the idealized golden-haired Laura of Petrarch, and her obverse, Shakespeare's mistress, whose 'eyes are nothing like the sun'. Laura alive or Laura dead will serve equally for brooding sonnets (Romeo's first love was of this kind) – and the other image is likewise projective. Never before had the woman been realized as partner in the dramatic and poetic bond. Here is true mingling of flesh and blood, not as an act of amorous conquest and surrender, entailing a sweet subjection and dominance. However young the lovers, they are more mature than that. Wonder, ardour, reverence, contend at the first meeting. They end their greetings with a kiss – the most beautiful, natural, *visual* 'amen' to the pilgrim's 'prayer'.

The play was the biggest success since *Richard III*. All the young men quoted it: although there had been love tragedies – even one on this story, the situation itself had not been explored, only used for action.[6] The unhappy lovers of *Gismond of Salerne* (1568, rewritten 1591) are never shown together and are mere puppets of the gods, ruled by Cupid while a Fury from hell rules the tyrant father.

Arthur Brooke, from whose dreary verses Shakespeare took his story, comes down on the side of the parents; it was something new to condemn the parents, as Shakespeare does so strongly. How welcome this would be to every young man and woman instead of Brooke's fulminations against 'enthralling themselves to unhonest desire, neglecting the authority and advice of parents and friends, conferring their principal councils with drunken gossips and superstitious friars' (*was* Juliet's nurse ever shown the worse for drink?).

Love, flowering in isolation from society, appears for the first time in English drama in the mutuality of the orchard scene, with the lovers under threat of death in 'a world they never made'. This, projected as action, still makes the play today a true image of their plight for many teenagers, who fear society at large rather than their own families.

The level of the great scenes is not always sustained – there is something childish in the hysterical paradoxes of Juliet's lament for Tybalt or Romeo's ravings in the friar's cell. Yet there is also wonderful concentration, when Juliet dismisses the nurse for ever with the quiet, ironic, 'Well, thou hast comforted me marvellous much.'

This is also an exceptionally bawdy play, reaching its height in the exchanges of Mercutio and the nurse. On the other hand, Juliet, in the courage of her innocence, had soon followed her ardour with some quite prosaic words:

> Three words, dear Romeo and good night indeed.
> If that thy bent of love be honourable,
> Thy purpose marriage ...
>
> (2.2.142–4)

It was by no means the obvious thing to say. Eros, not Venus, is the presiding god; nowhere do we meet the erotic becoming the lascivious. The friar has an excellent piece on the sacramental quality of Nature.

> The earth that's nature's mother is her tomb;
> What is her burying grave, that is her womb ...
> For nought so vile that on the earth doth live
> But to the earth some special good doth give;
> Nor aught so good but, strain'd from that fair use,
> Revolts from true birth ...
>
> (2.3.9–20)

Mercutio, the most elegantly disgraceful jester, a young man of ducal family who knows just what tone to take with a friend, an old servant or an enemy, is dismissed by Romeo as immature ('He jests at scars that never felt a wound,' 2.2.1).

The fight and exile may have touched on a theme close to Shakespeare's noble friends, perhaps to himself,[7] for the celebrations of Southampton's coming of age, on 6 October 1594, found the Earl at Titchfield in Hampshire, giving his tenants and friends a feast but also concealing a friend who had just killed his foe in a feud. Two brothers, Sir Charles and Sir Henry Danvers, were involved in a quarrel with the family of

Sir Walter Long; in a fight at an inn, Henry Long had wounded
Sir Charles with his sword, whereupon Sir Henry Danvers had
shot Long dead. Both fled to Southampton, who concealed
them and tried to get them off by way of Calshott Castle, but
they had to return to Titchfield. John Florio, the Italian
teacher, who was in Southampton's household, met the sheriff
carrying his warrant on the ferry-boat and threatened to throw
him overboard. The next that is heard of the Danvers brothers
is their arrival at the Court of Henry IV of France, from
whence, after three years and on payment of a heavy fine, they
returned with pardons. No action was taken against Southampton, who had clearly arranged their flight. Was Shakespeare,
like Florio, down for the celebrations, and did he, so knowing
about horses, hear of the two that had been seen in the stables,
with rich saddles stained with blood? Or had the Earl behaved
like Henry v and cast off his old companion in the moment
of triumph? It could not have been from any intention to live
a better life. To the Danvers brothers at least he had proved
loyal; and one of them was to die with Essex, drawn in by 'the
great obligation of love and duty' he felt to Southampton.[8]

We have evidence that the Montagues and Capulets had
been of special interest to Southampton's family, for in George
Gascoigne's *Hundred Sundry Flowers* (1575) appears a masque
written for a double wedding in the Montague family – the
family of Southampton's mother, the Dowager Countess, from
whom he derived whatever claim to ancient blood he had. In
this masque of Gascoigne, eight gentlemen of the Italian Montagues, victors from the battle of Lepanto, were presented by
a boy who bore their badge in his cap:

This token which the Montagues did always bear for that
They covet to be known from Capels where they pass,
For ancient grudge which long ago 'tween these two houses was.[9]

By transforming the Montecchi to Montagues, Shakespeare
forged a link with the Earl of Southampton, who loved things
Italian and was, thanks to John Florio, himself a good Italian
scholar, although to his chagrin he had never been allowed to
visit the country.

Such private gestures did not appear obvious to the public

eye. This was a play for the common stages, and while the penalties of marrying in defiance of public opinion had been dramatically shown in the fall of Sir Walter Ralegh, who had married a daughter of the Throckmortons, one of the Queen's maids-of-honour, it was several years before Southampton committed the same heinous fault. His problem at the moment was rather that he still refused to get married.

Only one other love poem equalled *Romeo and Juliet* in deploying the power that passion lends. *Hero and Leander* was not yet in print but circulated widely; it is far closer to *Romeo and Juliet* than to *Venus and Adonis*, and if Shakespeare had heard it as Marlowe's rival 'offering' to Southampton, he would feel the impulse to go one better. Marlowe's history, essentially a comedy, since he omits the tragic end, shows two lovers instantly captivated by each other,

> Where both deliberate, the love is slight
> Whoever loved that loved not at first sight?
> (*First Sestiad*, 175-6)

Shakespeare quoted that in *As You Like It*.

Marlowe accepts and rejoices in the force of Nature to overwhelm the rational powers. Hero and Leander, two lovely magnets that draw the gods themselves to fall in love, are innocents; the triumph with which Hero's priestly vows of virginity are overcome is celebrated in rich jewelled lines that somehow give distance and coolness (it is partly the effect of the rhyming couplets) to the bold erotic assault.

> Love is not full of pity as men say,
> But deaf and cruel when he means to prey.
> (*Second Sestiad*, 287-8)

The writer of the Sonnets would have said Amen to that.

In Shakespeare's next two plays this artificial beauty supplies a great part of the total effect.

Of course we cannot tell the order: if *Venus and Adonis* provoked *Hero and Leander*, which led in turn to *Romeo and Juliet*, Shakespeare's *Henry VI* had provoked *Edward II* – to which Shakespeare now replied with *Richard II*.

These two tragic histories have so much in common that they have been played together in repertory for the sake of contrast or comparison. Marlowe is much more explicit about the King's homosexuality – a practice he reputedly defended in real life – whereas Shakespeare plays it down so far in *Richard II* that the presence of Bushy, Bagot and Green can seem rather pointless; but he is much more unconventional than Marlowe in that Marlowe showed instant vengeance overtaking the murderers of the King, while the deposition and murder of Richard left his opponent to rule the shattered realm (as history required).

The ceremonial beauty of Edward's Court is set out at the opening by his lover Gaveston – 'Music and poetry are his delight' – and his last memory in the filthy dungeon recalls a tournament in which he had fought gallantly. *Richard II* is full of ceremony, from the opening combat at Coventry, through Richard's elaborate ritual of self-degradation, to the final scene in the dungeon at Pomfret, where he carries on the brooding search for his identity, now he is no more than mere man. A comparison with Clarence's dream in *Richard III* will show the extraordinary range of mood; the inner debate, with conflicting religious texts, the mad hope of escape, the weak thoughts of submission, the final sense that time is past for him; it

> Runs posting on in Bolingbroke's proud joy,
> While I stand fooling here, his Jack of the clock.
>
> (5.5.59–60)

Never has he seemed less like an image than here; the playing demanded an 'inward conceit of the part' and it appealed to any frustrated, brooding mind. The Earl of Essex at his trial confessed that he had many times seen the play enacted, and his associates had paid the Lord Chamberlain's Men to stage it on the eve of his ill-fated rising, 7 February 1601, by which date it was 'an old play', not likely to draw an audience. The actors sent Augustin Phillips to the Privy Council to clear them of any complicity, but their play was made much of at the trial by Sir Edward Coke, and also in the account written by Bacon. Queen Elizabeth said angrily, 'I am Richard II, know ye not that ... this tragedy was played forty times in open streets and houses.' The night before Essex was executed, the players were summoned to Court to give her a play. They went, with the knowledge that Southampton, Blount, Danvers and a number of servants had also been condemned to death and might well follow Essex.

The deposition was not fully printed till 1623; yet Marlowe's *Edward II* had been printed in 1594, and Shakespeare could have studied the text that year. Already both Essex and Southampton were ruining themselves by extravagance, in Richard's wilful style: Richard might have been intended as a warning to them before he was used as a rallying call. The play is slow in movement at first, formal in its patterning; Richard, a 'lily that festers', is shown at his worst with old Gaunt. But his vulnerable humanity wins compassion; though Richard is cruel and can be abject, Bolingbroke says at the end, when the King's Two Bodies (his body politic and his body natural) confront each other[10] – the living and the dead:

> Though I did wish him dead,
> I hate the murderer, love him murdered.
> (5.6.39–40)

Perhaps this was what Elizabeth was to feel after the necessary examples had been made. For of course the young men had hopelessly miscast the play: Elizabeth, with her cool control, her perfect sense of timing and public relations, was a true successor to Henry IV, and they themselves were the originals of Richard, the spoiled darlings of an admiring circle as plainly their 'true-telling friend' (Sonnet 82) could see.

Richard II never enjoyed the general popularity of the earlier histories, or that which has kept *Romeo and Juliet* and *The Merchant of Venice* continually on the boards.

Venice is the one Italian city that Shakespeare really characterizes – his Verona, Padua, Messina, Milan, are interchangeable, and he always has the feeling that you can go by sea from one to the other – but Venice, at once the great seaport, *entrepôt* of trade, enlightened centre of anti-papal freedom – Venice was a greater and more glorious London, which could be worked into a day-dream. The dream offers a beautiful bride with a huge estate; fabulous gambler's luck, fortunes repaired at the expense of usurers; the law transformed from a trap to the agent of a good fairy, all ending in a beautiful country garden by moonlight, where lovers might hear the music of the spheres. Here is God's plenty, as Dryden was to say – for young lawyers, the trial; for Essex, a memory of how he wrung confessions out of the wretched Jewish physician, Dr Lopez (who was executed for attempting to poison the Queen); for Southampton, a lesson to which he paid no attention whatsoever – the lesson of Tennyson's Northern Farmer: 'Don't thee marry for money, but go where money is' (instead, as everyone saw, he was being drawn to penniless Bess Vernon). All these plays show a healthy concern with money – even *Romeo and Juliet* does not forget, as Juliet's nurse boasts, 'He that marries her shall have the chinks.'

Of late years we have heard enough about the crisis of the aristocracy in Tudor England, the growth of corruption in Court society, to know that the greatest lottery of all, presided over by the ageing Fairy Queen, was as likely to break a man as to make him. Essex was ruined when Elizabeth refused to renew his 'farming' of the tax on sweet wine. Southampton never got anything and was reduced to that last desperation of selling family estates; John Lyly's plight was reflected in the highest circles. But a rich marriage was still the favourite form of 'heavy rescue' work. In *The Merchant of Venice*, Portia is a fit object for pilgrimage, which is how her first suitor, Morocco, presents her, in words which echo Tamburlaine's praise of his divine Zenocrate:[11]

> The Hyrcanian deserts and the vasty wilds
> Of wide Arabia are as throughfares now
> For princes to come view fair Portia.
>
> (2.7.41–3)

The tale of the casket and that of the bond are both dreamlike.[12] Elizabethans had virtually no experience of Jews, for when Edward I's debts to them had become too heavy, he had expelled them (only a small colony in London persisted). It has been suggested that what is behind Shylock is the figure of the Puritan usurer, who was very ready to back his practice with scriptural quotation as Shylock does, and who maintained many Old Testament practices:

> I am a Puritan, one that will eat no pork,
> Doth use to shut his shop on Saturdays,
> And open it on Sundays; a Familist,
> And one of the arch limbs of Belzebub,
> A Jewish Christian and a Christian Jew.
>
> (Robert Davenport,
> *A New Trick To cheat the Devil*, 1639, 4.1)

There was the strong fear of the unknown, the alien, so that Turks, Moors and Jews were grouped together as infidels. In the *Croxton Play of the Sacrament* Sir Jonathas the Jew swears by 'Mahound'!

From the Gospels the Jews were treated as examples of those who rejected offered grace; so a Christian could have a 'Jewish heart' if he rejected Christ. This identification is implicit in Antonio's words, when he lists all the natural impossibilities:

> You may as well do anything most hard
> As seek to soften that – than which, what's harder? –
> His Jewish heart.   (4.1.78–80)

This application lodges the Jew within, as the 'bad self'; the identification is not racially but psychologically distinct.[13]

In stage terms, Shylock had an ancestry stretching back to a lost play on Jews and usury shown at The Bull, which we know of from Stephen Gosson; but principally of course there was Marlowe's Barabas (*The Jew of Malta* was not in print but Shakespeare may have acted in it). Shylock is related to Barabas as Richard II is to Edward II; he represents a great refinement of the role, which may be played in a great variety of ways. There have been successively Kean's full-blooded performance – he specially rehearsed the scene with Tubal lest the young man who played the part should be terrified; Irving's stately dignity and pathos; Olivier's business-magnate fighting to get into county society; a young student's performance which made him as mad as King Lear, in the trial scene sitting with his back to the court and glaring out over the auditorium; Burbage's, we may be sure, was a challenge to memories of Edward Alleyn. Gobbo's part would be Kempe's, with its parody of old plays on Jacob and Esau, to reinforce the scriptural references to Genesis (Gobbo is traceable as a family name at Titchfield, Southampton's country seat).

Barabas remained a highly ambiguous figure, introduced by the realist, Machiavelli, but equally the joy of the groundlings, who would never have heard, except on the stage, of 'Match-evil'. Yet of course he is meant to be damned: the cauldron into which he falls is the symbol of hell reserved for usurers.[14] The ingenuity of his counterplots and the treachery of the Christians can engage a modern audience by its 'savage farce', which T. S. Eliot so brilliantly discerned in his brief essay, the foundation of all modern criticism of Marlowe.[15]

Shylock, on the other hand, is drawn to human scale. He does not, like Barabas, engage in mass murder or even instruct his household in that art. His case rests upon the outburst with which he enlightens the young exquisites who naturally think a usurer wants his money back and will not trouble about a pound of human flesh – 'What's that good for?'. 'To bait fish withal', opens his torrential reply, to end with a promise of a deadly kind: 'The villainy you teach me, I will execute; and it shall go hard but I will better the instruction' (3.1.45–62). Barabas had similar sentiments:

> This is the life we Jews are used to lead:
> And reason too, for Christians do the like.
> (*Jew of Malta*, 5.3)

The Christians do not recognize either Jew as members of the human race, and so Shylock's great plea 'Hath not a Jew eyes? . . .' comes from a depth unapproached in the subsequent trial scene; it has broken the restraints of the verse; its catalogue contains the terrifying question – in view of Shylock's purpose – 'If you prick us, do we not bleed?' Like old Hieronymo he seeks revenge, driven to it by the Christian joke of the abduction of Jessica and the money.

By some inner release, which unlocks a great fund of energy along with the day-dreams, comes this figure of almost pure hatred. C. L. Barber, considering the extraordinary generosity of the *Sonnets*, once asked, 'What did Shakespeare do with his aggression?' He created Shylock, releasing resentment of un-merited injuries, blank and uncomprehending dismissals. These, he attributed to Christians. It is not difficult to locate them and to see their effect, for some sermons against players survive!

To see what reward is given to these crocodiles ... if you will learn to be false and deceive your husbands, or husbands their wives, how to play the harlot, to obtain anyone's love, how to ravish, how to beguile, how to betray, to flatter, lie, swear, foreswear, how to allure to whoredom, how to murther, how to poison, how to disobey and rebel against princes, to consume treasure prodigally, to move to lusts, to rack and despoil cities and towns, to be idle and blaspheme, to sing filthy songs of love, to speak filthy, to be proud, how to mock, scoff and deride any nations, like unto Genesius Aralatinus etc, shall you not learn then at such interludes how to practise them?

O blasphemy intolerable! are filthy plays and bawdy interludes comparable to the word of God, the food of life and life itself? The devil is equipollent with the Lord. ...

God only gave authority of public instruction and correction but to two sorts of men; to his ecclesiastical ministers and temporal magi-strates.... God requireth no such thing at their hands, that they should take it upon them; but it is the devil's craft, that will sometimes change himself into an angel of light.... God gave authority to in-struct and preach, to correct and anathematize, only to the Apostles and to their successors and not to Players; for it is unlawful to cast pearls before swine.

These pulpit pronouncements, from the Reverend John Northwood, the Reverend Philip Stubbes, and the anonymous clerical respondent to Heywood's *Apology for Actors*, belong to 1577, 1583 and 1615 respectively. Throughout his life Shake-speare would have found himself exposed to such diatribes, among the most virulent being those of the Rector of St Botolph's, Bishopsgate, not far from The Theatre. Stephen Gos-son had failed to make his living as a playwright and had taken holy orders. Of course he cringed to Edward Alleyn for a place in his charitable foundation to be given to a member of his parish; of course Henslowe and Heminges and Condell all ended as churchwardens, and Alleyn in old age married the daughter of John Donne, by then Dean of St Paul's. This in no way protected any player from a sudden onslaught; the royal troupe might find themselves confounded with the wretches who came under the Statute of Vagrancy. In the cause of controversy, as we shall see again later, no distinctions were drawn and no insults spared. The players were held guilty of 'contempt' if they responded with spirit.

What then becomes of the familiar equation between Shakespeare and Antonio, in his resigned self-sacrificing melancholy love for the younger man, Bassanio? This equation has often been made.

The antagonism between Shylock and Antonio is an antagonism within the writer himself. That part which in dignity and grace clung to an unacknowledged devotion ('I am a tainted wether of the flock') was opposed by a grotesque, protesting but very powerful voice springing out of nowhere. The emergence of such negative feelings is apt to take derisive form (a psychiatrist gives an account of how in some horror he once caught a dream glimpse of a malicious dwarf figure, cracking gleeful jokes about the opportunities provided by the possible death of his wife). To meet the thoroughly unacceptable part of oneself in a dream – or a play – is to gain some measure of recognition, and therefore of control.[16]

In *The Merchant of Venice*, Shakespeare provided a wide variety of dream worlds for other people; the play draws upon a great range of theatrical and personal experience, and yet it can hardly be placed in any of the traditional theatrical categories. It is cathartic to such a degree that when, in the last scene, the new 'gentle bond' of the rings can tolerate the bawdiness of Gratiano, deep springs of resentment and the impulse to revenge seem to have been absorbed. At this final point in his production of 1971 at the National Theatre, Jonathan Miller movingly turned the celestial music into the Kaddish.

There is evidence in the *Sonnets* that Shakespeare felt the public humiliations of the way of life that yet to him was life itself. His 'outcast state' (Sonnet 29), his 'blots' and his

'bewailed guilt' (Sonnet 36) made a different kind of challenge
to Fortune from his initial one:

> O, for my sake do you with Fortune chide,
> The guilty goddess of my harmful deeds,
> That did not better for my life provide
> Than public means which public manners breeds.
> Thence comes it that my name receives a brand,
> And almost thence my nature is subdu'd
> To what it works in, like the dyer's hand ...
>
> (Sonnet 111, 1-7)

Sufferance was the badge of all his tribe. The clergy drew cheap
morals from the death of Marlowe, altering the facts to suit their
text. Even praise might sound like insult. John Davies of Hereford was to commend the players (noting in the margin
'R.B., W.S.'):

> ... Fortune cannot be excus'd
> That hath for better uses you refus'd,
> Wit, courage, good shapes, good parts and all good
> As long as all these goods are no worse us'd;
> And, though the stage doth stain pure, gentle blood
> Yet generous ye are, in mind and mood.

With such friends, what need of enemies?

Yet the stage, evidently, was what Shakespeare chose, before
anything else, before the beauty of the beloved youth or the
beauty of the countryside.[17] 'He flowed with that facility that
we have scarce receiv'd from him a blot in his papers', was to be
the testimony of his fellow 'outcasts' in publishing his plays.

In the year that Shakespeare died, a young actor-playwright
of his company, son of the Puritan preacher John Field, knew
how to answer the preacher at St Mary Overy:

> ... Pardon me, sir, if in patience and humbleness of spirit, I ex-
> postulate a little with you.
> You waded very low with hatred against us, when you ransacked
> Hell to find the register wherein our souls are written damned.
> ... And herein is my faith the stronger because in God's whole

volume, which I have studied as my best part, I find not any trade of life except conjurors, sorcerers and witches *ipso facto* damned, nay, not expressly spoken against, but only the abuses and bad uses of them. (*State Papers, Domestic*, James I, lxxxix, 105)

Nathan Field, who, against his Puritan father's will, had been conscripted for a Royal chorister and boy player, claimed boldly that his name was written in 'the Book of Life'. He was certainly responsible for replenishing the life of the House of Lords, for his gallantries with noblewomen were extensive.

6 The Lord Chamberlain's Men

Settled in The Shoreditch Theatre, with the Lord Admiral's troupe south of the river at The Rose, the Lord Chamberlain's Men were knit together round the Burbage family. James owned the lease of the playhouse; his son Richard played leads; another son helped on the business side. Actors lived near their theatres and took their apprentices into their homes, like any other masters of their craft.

Probably they played any good pieces that had come on the market since the plague broke up the old groups. For the Lord Chamberlain's Men, there are no such accounts as survive for the Lord Admiral's Men; even Court records do not specify what plays were offered at this time. But different kinds of play evolved in response to special demands, and the different kinds of audience became distinguished. Polonius' advertisement might describe the varied bill of fare: 'The best actors in the world, either for tragedy, comedy, history, pastoral, pastoral-comical, historical-pastoral, tragical-historical, tragical-comical-historical-pastoral, scene individable or poem unlimited . . . For the law of writ and the liberty, these are the only men!' (*Hamlet*, 2.2.392 ff). 'The law of writ' was the country at large, 'the liberty' such special places as Blackfriars, an old ecclesiastical building, where the Lord Mayor's writ did not run. *Love's Labour's Lost*, designed for a privileged audience, and *A Midsummer Night's Dream*, with a more public official air about it, were both on their title pages in 1598 and 1600 claimed as 'written by William Shakespeare'. The author's name was now worth citing, and if the second play were not intended solely for some great wedding, the compliment to the Queen suggests that it was used on one such occasion when she was present – the most probable being when Burghley at last succeeded in marrying his grand-daughter to an earl – William Stanley, Earl of Derby – on 26 January 1595; or when Lord Hunsdon married off *his* grand-daughter Elizabeth at Blackfriars on 19 February 1596.

The roots of this play are very deep in English drama and poetry and in Shakespeare's own countryside; yet it is in sum total original, totally unlike anything that had appeared previously.

There are obvious links with *Romeo and Juliet* in the lovers' plight – and what amounts to a parody of both the orchard scene and the death scene in the 'lamentable tragedy of Pyramus and Thisbe'. Wide and easy reliance on popular dramatic tradition, combined with sheer power of invention, produced a play that other writers have found particularly attractive to draw on. Critics have hailed it as Shakespeare's most perfect work of art;[1] it has been freely adapted for opera and cinema; in Peter Brook's production of 1970 at Stratford, it established the basis of what is now orthodoxy for younger directors.

An open empty space and circus 'activities' provided Brook's translation into modern terms of the Elizabethan feeling of release and carnival that accompanied the 'bringing in of May', the rites of Summer Lords and Summer Queens. This had inspired the scenes in the 'wood near Athens' as surely as Bottom and Peter Quince come from London. The fairies, Shakespeare's special creation, are woodland spirits of his own Warwickshire, transformed from his earlier poetry into a role fully dramatic (though of course Oberon has a long pedigree in medieval legend, and Robin Goodfellow an equally long pedigree in folklore).

The ceremonies which were celebrated in Chaucer (in the delicious prologue to the *Legend of Good Women*, where the Collector of Customs goes out into the fields to worship the daisy) were of course part of the ceremony of the countryman's year; they had by Shakespeare's day become associated in the clerical mind with idolatry. Here is a hostile witness:

Against May, Whitsunday or other time all the young men and maids, old men and wives run gadding overnight to the woods, groves, hills and mountains where they spend all the night in pleasant

pastimes ... they have twenty or forty yoke of oxen, every ox having a sweet nosegay of flowers placed on the tip of his horns, and these oxen draw home this Maypole (this stinking idol rather) which is covered all over with flowers and herbs ... of forty, three score or a hundred maids going to the woods over night, there have scarcely the third part of them returned home again undefiled.
(Philip Stubbes, *The Anatomy of Abuses*, 1583, ed. Furnivall, p. 149)

This is the great rite that Malory celebrated in the Maying of Queen Guinevere when 'Lovers calleth to their mind old gentleness and old service': 'And therefore all yet that be lovers, call unto your remembrance the month of May, like as did Queen Guinever, for whom I make here a little mention that while she lived she was a true lover and therefore she had a good end' (Sir Thomas Malory, *Morte d'Arthur* The Book of Sir Lancelot and Queen Guinever, IV).

Chaucer and Malory are better witnesses than Stubbes of what the rites of May could mean to poets – and to lovers. King Henry VIII in youth went Maying and appeared in a quaint disguise before Catherine of Aragon. Whitsun saw pastorals. In the last years of her life, Queen Elizabeth still rode out a-Maying and told the old to stay behind and the young to follow her. In this play, as the Master of the Revels presides over royal sports, Puck presides over the re-entry of the fairies and their blessing of the bridal, bringing Maytime into the hall and complimenting the Queen (for any palace she was in became hers by that act):

> To the best bride-bed will we,
> Which by us shall bless'd be ...
> And each several chamber bless,
> Through this palace, with sweet peace;
> And the owner of it blest
> Ever shall in safety rest.
>
> (5.1.392 ff)

Oberon and Titania, a pair of country gods, half English and half Ovid, like the kings of masking, rule only at night. The play's movement is like a dance, as the lovers pair and re-unite. Lovers, fairies, tradesmen, make a larger pattern. The main

action, the enchantments, the play within the play and the fairy
epilogue, give another kind of perspective; each offers a different imaginative relation of actors and audience. Artifice
could not be more frankly displayed.

The lovers' quarrels are quite symmetrical – for Theseus and
Hippolyta in the past, in the present for the fairies, induced
for the lovers. Everywhere in Shakespeare love brings the sense
of 'enchantment'[2] and in this 'glimmering light' it can come
to Bottom. Like the poet's, his eye 'glances from heaven to
earth', and he decides to have a ballad made on his dream.

The ass's head which he wears is no other than the usual
masque for a country 'antic'; he is properly disguised for a 'rite
of May'. Rustic dancers with animal heads may still be met
in remote villages.

The dream-world of harmless mischief – though it may look
menacing – had already been presented in the previous play,
when Mercutio ran through the dreams sent by Queen Mab,

> Which are the children of an idle brain,
> Begot of nothing but vain fantasy;
> Which is as thin of substance as the air,
> And more inconstant than the wind ...
> (*Romeo and Juliet*, 1.4.97–100)

Chaucer, the poet with whom Shakespeare here felt kinship,
drew fine distinctions between 'avisions', 'dremes', 'swevenes',
'revelations', 'fantomes' and 'oracles'. In *The House of Fame* he
explores all causes from inspiration to indigestion, including the
hard life of lovers 'that hope overmuch or dreden' and the
'spirits' that

> have the myght
> To maken folk to dreme a nyght.
> (*The House of Fame*, Proem, 40–2)

though he ends (like Bottom) in concluding that the cause is
unfathomable.

With a defiant gesture to sour Puritans, Bottom recalls holy
writ – 'The eye of man hath not heard, the ear of man hath
not seen ... what my dream was' (4.1.196 ff), and though to

the lovers all seems 'like far off mountains turned into clouds', yet Hippolyta senses something more in 'the story of the night' that

> grows to something of great constancy,
> But howsoever strange and admirable.
>
> (5.1.26–7)

The magic is lasting. The use of a 'dream' as definition of a play was not uncommon. Lyly in particular had made careful use of it to keep his plays at a safe distance from a reality which might in its interpretation be thought presumptuous. The full title of *Endimion* is *The Man in the Moon*; a later play, *The Woman in the Moon*, ends: 'Remember all is but a poet's dream.' Dreams as wish-fulfilments were a means of transmitting hopes that loyalty would not breathe aloud; so the Prologue to Lyly's *Sapho and Phao* (which comes near to showing Sapho stooping to love) begins with apology: 'We all, and I on knee for all, entreat that your Highness imagine yourself to be in a deep dream, that staying the conclusion, in your rising, your Majesty vouchsafe but to say *And so you waked*.' This is precisely what Shakespeare does in the Epilogue:

> Think ...
> That you have but slumb'red here
> While these visions did appear.
> And this weak and idle theme,
> No more yielding but a dream....
>
> (5.1.414–17)

The perspective of the play is like the perspective of a dream; the lovers and the royal pair are puppet-like or remotely grand; it is the fairies and the tradesmen with their wonderful dream of 'a play' who give the substance; the others are the shadows. Titania could not have made a happier choice than to fall in love with Bottom – much more enchanting than Theseus. A more ethereal Venus (Shakespeare had learned not to make his goddesses so physically overpowering), she permeates her world in the same way – at first to its confusion for her quarrel with Oberon breaks the delicate fairy dance, and the winds in revenge distribute pestilential fogs, the rivers overflow, harvests fail and 'the seasons alter':

> ... hoary-headed frosts
> Fall in the fresh lap of the crimson rose ...
> (2.1.107-8)

The natural rhythms are counterpoised by those of the imagination. The magic early stage is revived by Bottom and his friends in their play of *Pyramus and Thisbe* (a tale told by both Ovid and Chaucer). When Shakespeare read Golding's version of Ovid, he found exactly what he needed in such 'tragic' lines as

This said, she took the sword yet warm with slaughter of her love,
And setting it beneath her breast, did to her heart it shove.

Another Elizabethan play has preserved for us the bit of stage business which the Lord Chamberlain's Men used here: 'Like Thisbe in the play h' has almost killed himself with the scabbard.' Edmund Gayton tells us of 'a passionate butcher' who could not tolerate seeing Hector killed by the Myrmidons and, climbing on the stage,

routed the Greeks and railed upon them loudly for a company of cowardly slaves to assault one man with so much odds. He struck moreover such an especial acquaintance with Hector, that for a long time Hector could not obtain leave of him to be killed, that the play might go on, and the cudgelled Myrmidons durst not enter again, till Hector, having prevailed upon his unexpected second, returned him over the stage into the yard from whence he came.

(G. E. Bentley, *The Jacobean and Caroline Stage*, 1957, 5, 1,345-6, quoting *Pleasant Notes upon Don Quixote*, 1654)

I have known a very small child emit a real belly-roar at Bottom's suggestion, 'Let him roar again'; the actors loved it.

Only in a play where such feats of constructional engineering are displayed as the different levels of the triple plot supply, could the 'game' between the actors and the audience become part of the show. It induces a rapport on quite a new level; the magic of the theatre brings in not only the bridal couples (who were presumably in the seats of honour) but everybody. That 'bank whereon the wild thyme blows' – the grubbiest of frequently-used stage properties – and 'the Man in the Moon' issue the same challenge in different ways.

The consummate unity, the deep feeling of a single vision, a timeless moment, suspended beyond the realm of ordinary life, arises from the extraordinary capacity in Shakespeare to blend his conscious art with hidden resources till the audience, like the poet, can respond with all they know they have to give, and with something more they don't know till they sense it.

The impression Shakespeare made on his contemporaries with *A Midsummer Night's Dream* was to be reflected in the fairies of Jacobean masquing. Ben Jonson did not disdain to borrow them for the welcome he wrote to greet Queen Anne and the little Prince Henry in 1603, *The Satyr*. The satyr skips among Queen Mab and her ring of fairies:

> This is Mab, the mistress fairy,
> That doth nightly rob the dairy
> And can hurt or help the churning ...
>
> FIRST FAIRY: Pug, you can anon take warning?

And soon they pinch him black and blue.

Michael Drayton sang of the battle between 'jealous Oberon' and Pigwiggin:

> Thorough brake, thorough briar,
> Thorough muck, thorough mire,
> Thorough water, thorough fire,
> And thus goes Puck about it.
> (*Nymphidia*, 309–12)

Milton, while borrowing heavily for *Comus*, could talk of

> Sweetest Shakespeare, fancy's child,
> Warbling his native woodnotes wild ...

It was the 'fancy' that charmed; but generations of acting, a good many earlier plays,[3] reading in Chaucer as well as Ovid, and ten years of toil and trouble as actor-playwright were behind this airy toy. Shakespeare had need of both gaiety and worldly wisdom in the years to follow, for they were not easy either for himself or for his company.

On 11 August 1596, Shakespeare's only son Hamnet, aged eleven years, was buried at Stratford. We do not know whether he was bright or dull, healthy or sickly, but we do have evidence of Shakespeare's intense desire to found a family, in the specific plans for inheritance that were laid down twenty years later in his Will. Early in 1597, he paid the fine which secured himself New Place and wrote his most genial history, which is full of the relations of fathers and sons – fathers by blood and by adoption. *Henry IV* in all probability belongs to the winter season of 1596–7, and if in the laments of Constance in *King John* a personal echo may be imagined ('He talks to me that never had a son', 'Grief fills the room up of my absent child'), is there not a pathos hidden in the relation of Falstaff to the 'son' who must be lost to him, perhaps in the childish dialect word 'micher', the memory of a truant schoolboy who on the paternal visits to Stratford had to stand a wigging? '... Why, being son to me, art thou so pointed at? Shall the blessed sun of heaven prove a micher and eat black berries? A question not to be ask'd' (*1 Henry IV*, 2.4.397–9). A great deal of speculation has gone on the possible reflection in Falstaff and Hal of the relationship depicted in the *Sonnets*; it should be remembered that every reflection in a good dream is loaded with multiple associations. Falstaff has so much in common with 'sweet bully Bottom' that they are almost twins – the same gusto, the same deep and animal self-confidence, which always puts him in the lead in any company, the same imaginative elation that makes everything he undertakes at once an intense drama and a grand game.

The majority have looked at Falstaff in the light of their own interests. The eighteenth century found him not a coward after all – since personal valour was still of paramount significance; the nineteenth century found his rejection tragic. The present age has compared Falstaff with the Tempters of Youth and Divine Charity; Dover Wilson and a line of scholars standing for the prosecution, while W. H. Auden goes furthest in the other direction, seeing him as an Immortal, one who is not really caught up in this world at all.

Falstaff's happiness is almost an impregnable tower, but not quite. 'I am that I am' is not a complete description; he must also add 'The young prince hath misled me. I am the fellow with the great belly, and he is my dog.'

The Christian God is not a self-sufficient being like Aristotle's first cause, but a God who creates a world which He continues to love although it refuses to love Him in return.... And the consequence is inevitable. The highest religious and temporal authorities condemn Him as a blasphemer and a Lord of Misrule, as a Bad Companion for mankind. Inevitable because, as Richelieu said, 'The salvation of States is in this world', and history has not as yet provided us with any evidence that the Prince of this world has changed His character.

The Dyer's Hand, 1948, pp. 207–8

Since there have been great pains taken to prove Falstaff's descent from the Vice of the mid-Tudor moral play, or from Riot, or the Lord of Misrule (the tempters of youth), and since society asks a 'Judgment of Carnival', Auden's dialectic is really aimed at the academic case against Falstaff, put by Dover Wilson, Tillyard and eager moralizers who have scrambled after them.

Perhaps this is partly explained by the modern habit of reading and even watching the history plays in sequence, with the consequent emphasis on the 'Tudor myth' – a fall under Richard II, a 'troublesome time' under the usurping Henry IV, a glorious interlude under Henry V and a return to troubles under Henry VI. Shakespeare, however, was not engaged merely in rewriting *Henry VI*. What he took from The Theatre was a very popular clowns' play, in which Tarlton had starred, *The Famous Victories of Henry V*. This play opens with Prince Hal (who is throughout named Henry V) robbing his father's exchequer with the aid of 'Jockey' Oldcastle, 'Ned' and other riotous noblemen. One of his followers robs a poor carrier, much to his fury, for he believes in playing the game with only his (or his father's) money. The gang start a fight in Eastcheap and are imprisoned by the Lord Mayor; later they interrupt the robbery case brought by the comic carrier, Hal boxes the ears of the judge, who commits him ... and so on. This primitive but not unskilled set of jests is played out with vulgar oaths in rough prose:

HENRY V   Come away sirs, gogswouns, Ned,
　　　　Didst thou not see what a boxe on the ears
　　　　I took my Lord Chief Justice?
TOM   By Gogsblood, it did me good to see it,
　　　It made his teeth jar in his head.

(scene vi, 1–5)

The stuff of *The Famous Victories* provides the opening acts of *1 Henry IV.* Falstaff is at his strongest in the very beginning; he is not a character who has to be built up, and the Boar's Head sequence, where he really has no connections with the outside world at all, is a prolonged game, including the highway robbery. Though a far greater refinement on the original than was Shylock on Barabas, it is this Falstaff who is the 'immortal' and, his character being fixed, he is permitted in the second half of this play to clown it at the battle of Shrewsbury, though he never appears on stage without being joined at some point by the Prince of Wales.

There is nothing of the battle in *The Famous Victories*; but in this part of his play Shakespeare was directing his intentions to an end other than gratifying the taste for farce. It has been noted that this battle might be taken to mirror the rebellion of the Northern Earls in 1569,[4] but the salient fact is that this victory over Thomas, seventh Earl of Northumberland and the Earl of Westmoreland, Charles Neville, was won by Shakespeare's master, the Lord Chamberlain. What he made Harry Monmouth achieve at Shrewsbury, had been achieved by Harry Hunsdon at Naworth. When it happened, Shakespeare had been a boy; but his father, it will be remembered, was Bailiff that year at Stratford and must have been involved in all the flurry and alarm, with men marching north. Hunsdon's battle at Naworth came in January 1570, when the two Earls had already retreated over the border to look for aid. Their follower, Dacre, remained at Naworth, and the Scots were moving south to join him. Hunsdon quickly moved out of Berwick to intercept, with a small force of 1,500, and, after 'the proudest charge upon my shot that ever I saw', Dacre's men broke against his arquebusiers. It was 'a damned close-run thing', he might have said; what he actually wrote to the Queen was, 'If we had tarried till Wednesday, as Dacre thought I should, he had been past dealing with, for he would have had four or five thousand men out of Scotland, besides increasing his own power.' To Cecil he added that, if he had 'taken the repulse, from Trent thitherward had been in great danger and Carlisle would have been gone'. His action was decisive in the only armed uprising on English soil that Queen Elizabeth ever had to face, and she applauded her cousin:

I doubt much, my Harry, whether that the victory were given more joyed me, or that you were by God appointed the instrument of my glory; and I assure you for my country's good, the first might suffice, but for my heart's contention, the second more pleased me.

Your loving kinswoman, Elizabeth R.

The course of this campaign was mirrored in Shakespeare's battle of Shrewsbury by the failure of the reinforcements to reach Percy. The presence of the Douglas family at the battle of Shrewsbury brings in the Scots, however, although the campaign is on the Welsh and not the Scottish border. If the Hunsdon family were present, the play would seem to celebrate their finest hour; everyone could see Hunsdon's Men proclaiming his honours.

One consequence of the Northern Rebellion had been a new homily, much longer than any of the others, entitled *Against Disobedience and Wilful Rebellion*, which in 1574 had been added to the existing collection. From this and from its companion, *An Exhortation concerning good order and obedience to rulers and magistrates*, Shakespeare drew much of his doctrine of kingship and the consequences of civil war. The homilies, heard year in, year out (for few preachers had a licence to express their own sentiments), would become part of the memory in the most inattentive listeners. They denounce rebellion as violating all ten commandments, including all seven deadly sins entailing famine, war and pestilence. Shakespeare gilds rebellion with the magnificent figure of Harry Percy, 'the Hotspur of the North', whose speech on honour was spouted by apprentices (we can hear one doing so in *The Knight of the Burning Pestle*). In 'imagination of some great exploit' he cries:

By heaven, methinks it were an easy leap
To pluck bright honour from the pale-fac'd moon ...

(1.3.201–2)

The heroic fighting border lord is made the same age as the Prince of Wales to point the contrast between them, and the King wishes that the two had been changed in their cradles by fairies – 'then should he have my Harry and I his'. But the Prince of Wales mocks at Percy's valour ('he that kills me a dozen Scots before breakfast') and, at the battle of Shrewsbury, snatches his honour from him like a boxer's belt, so that all Percy's glories go to augment the reputation of Harry Monmouth – if Falstaff does not get away with his claim that it was he who finished off Percy after fighting an hour by Shrewsbury clock. The degradation of the loser, we remember from Bosworth, could be brutal.

The doctrine of the homilies had been used by Shakespeare before, of course; but he had not given it the kind of perspective he gave it now, more especially by setting it against the Falstaffian world of comedy and the ironic treatment of heroism in the character of Harry Percy. It has been observed that the voice and echo in this play transmit images and phrases from one group to another; throne, tavern and rebels alternate, jostling the story along; each claims the audience's sympathy in turn.[5] The element of artifice is introduced in that play within the play where Falstaff and the Prince play at father and son together, Falstaff promising to 'do it in Cambyses' vein' and the Hostess interjecting, 'O Jesu he doth it as like one of these harlotry players as ever I see!' (2.4.385). Another Boar's Head had been the earliest playhouse in London; Falstaff excels at improvising playlets or verbal games.

It is in these early scenes that Falstaff appears to have no need to do anything except to be his expansive self, as in his opening words: 'Now Hal, what time of day is it, lad?' – most improperly worded to the heir apparent, but very properly answered: 'What the devil hast thou to do with the time of the day?' (1.2.8). Where Hal's true father laments his own sleepless cares, Falstaff, when sought by the sheriff, is found 'fast asleep behind the arras and snorting like a horse' (*I Henry IV*, 2.4.510). As all forces converge towards Shrewsbury, the word 'honour' begins to echo and re-echo, and here Falstaff deflates Hotspur's passion.

Honour pricks me on ... yea, but how if honour prick me off when

I come on? [i.e. puts me in the casualty list] How then? Can honour set to a leg? No. Or an arm? No. Or take away the grief of a wound? No. Honour hath no skill in surgery, then? No. What is honour? A word. What is in that word? Honour. What is that honour? Air.... Who hath it? He that died o' Wednesday.... Honour is a mere scutcheon. And so ends my catechism.

(5.1.130 ff)

In a play setting out to honour his lord, these are words that might be taken as ironically deflating if it were not Falstaff, the clown on the battlefield, who speaks them, who afterwards claims to have killed Percy, giving him euphemistically a wound in 'the thigh' (a clown's joke indeed).

The prologue to the second part is given by 'Rumour, painted full of tongues', and a little later the King is told,

> Rumour doth double, like the voice and echo
> The numbers of the feared.
> (*2 Henry IV*, 3.1.97–8)

And rumour indeed took a part in this play, for Shakespeare was to enjoy no greater success than by the creation of Falstaff, but at the same time, his company never miscalculated more calamitously than by putting him on under the original name of Sir John Oldcastle. When, on 26 July 1596, Henry, Lord Hunsdon died, he was succeeded as Lord Chamberlain not by his son but by William Brooke, seventh Lord Cobham. The players became merely 'Lord Hunsdon's Men', and what advantage they had from their semi-official position as part of the royal household disappeared. They would have lost their licence and incorporation if the new Lord Hunsdon had not taken them on; and the power of the Act against vagabonds caught all such masterless men.

The new play, designed to glorify the House of Hunsdon, unfortunately, by sheer ill luck, might be held to defame the family of the new Lord Chamberlain, for Sir John Oldcastle had been the first Lord Cobham. Shakespeare had taken the name from the leading character of *The Famous Victories*, along with 'Ned' (Poins), but the more successful his outrageous 'Oldcastle', the greater the infamy and insult to Cobham.

Sir John Oldcastle had led a riotous youth, and this is why perhaps his name was used in the first place;[6] he then had reformed. Unfortunately he had also reformed in religion; he was outlawed by Henry v, a very pious king, who in 1417 hanged him as a traitor and burned him as a heretic. In Elizabethan times he had become one of the Morning Stars of the Reformation, his life written by the propagandist Bishop Bale; it was then convenient to forget that he had also been a jailbreaker and highway robber.

Perhaps there was still some feeling that players, like heralds, ought to proclaim good deeds and bad (it was a dignified role to be, in Hamlet's phrase, 'the abstract and brief chronicles of the time'). To glorify Hunsdon, everything except the rebellion had been left out of the reign of Henry iv (though religion would have been risky anyway). A more unfortunate piece of mistiming would be difficult to imagine. The Master of the Revels, Edmund Tilney, was related to the Lord Admiral, so now *his* men might get favour; the Lord Chamberlain was normally too grand to concern himself with this one department of the vast household over which he presided. (The Master of Revels perhaps drew his attention to this insult, to curry favour.) Certainly patronage counted for much in the royal circle.[7] 'Oldcastle' was changed to 'Falstaff' and subsequently, on a later plea, the alias of Ford, in *The Merry Wives of Windsor*, from Brook to Broome. This must have occurred in the years after 1602 (the first printing) and shows that the cause rankled even with the eighth Lord Cobham.

The death of the first Lord Hunsdon was a blow in other ways. On 4 February 1596, James Burbage acquired the lease of the Great Parliament Chamber in Blackfriars and began to set it up as an indoor theatre. The Liberty of the Blackfriars, just below St Paul's, was also a residence of Lord Hunsdon, and it is inconceivable that Burbage would have done this without consultation. He had been Lord Hunsdon's servant for longer than any of the others, for as we have seen in 1584[8] he had defied the Recorder of London in those terms, saying, 'he was my Lord Hunsdon's man and he would not come at me, but he would in the morning ride to my Lord' – with a complaint, of course. So he had really a personal connection and was not just a nominal bearer of the licence.

Unfortunately Hunsdon's death left other residents in Black-friars free to object that a playhouse would destroy their ameni-ties, and they petitioned the Privy Council in November 1596 against the use of the building in this way. So James Burbage's plan of a fine indoor playhouse fell through, and in February 1597 he died, leaving the property to his son Richard (The Shoreditch Theatre went to his elder son Cuthbert).

Most fortunately for the players, on 5 March Lord Cobham too died, and the second Lord Hunsdon, who had not been quick enough off the mark before, now obtained his father's office and became the new Lord Chamberlain. So the company were again the Lord Chamberlain's Men, restored to their rank, not least with the Master of the Revels. In so far as his father's military honours were 'mirrored' in *1 Henry IV*, the new Lord Chamberlain would accept the tribute to his family as to himself; a soldier also, he had stood in the front rank against the Armada as Captain-General of the Isle of Wight. The Master of the Revels, an old courtier, would easily adjust himself.

Meanwhile Alleyn and the Admiral's Men at The Rose Theatre had smugly put on a rival show announced as 'The first part of the TRUE and honourable history of the Life of Sir John Oldcastle, the good Lord Cobham'.[9] One edition of 1600 added insult to injury by bearing the words 'Written By William Shakespeare'.

George, Lord Hunsdon became Lord Chamberlain on 17 March 1597 and none too soon, for in July 1597, moved by a very scandalous play written by Thomas Nashe and per-formed by Lord Pembroke's Men at a new theatre, The Swan, the Lord Mayor wrote to the Privy Council to ask to have all players banned from the city. The Privy Council agreed and ordered that all scaffolds be torn down. This meant that the players lost their winter quarters at the Cross Keys Inn, within the city walls. (No Blackfriars, either.)

It meant also that anything like allusions to particular noble persons would have become even more risky. An epilogue was appended to the second part of *Henry IV*, promising *Henry V* to follow, where 'Falstaff shall die of a sweat, unless already 'a be kill'd with your hard opinions [pause for laughter]; for Old-castle died a martyr and this is not the man' (Epilogue, 30–33).

Yet people went on talking about 'Oldcastle' for the name had been used on stage and still remains in the text, when Prince Hal terms Falstaff 'my old Lad of the Castle' in the robbery sequence. Worse still, the new name, Falstaff, was applied to Lord Cobham by his opponents, the Southampton–Essex party (another reason for disliking Shakespeare if he knew of the personal connection), and to his successor, Henry, eighth Lord Cobham, a most unpleasant character, who subsequently betrayed his friend Ralegh under King James. Southampton heard from his wife in 1599: 'All the news I can send you that I think will make you merry is that I read in a letter from London that Sir John Falstaff is by his mistress Dame Pintpot made father of a goodly miller's thumb, a boy that's all head and very little body, but this is a secret.' A 'miller's thumb' was a name for a *cob* (or herring);[10] this refers to some scandal about Henry, Lord Cobham.

The story goes that Sir John Falstaff, after being dismissed in *Henry IV*, was revived at the request of Queen Elizabeth. John Dennis the critic declared in 1702 that *The Merry Wives of Windsor* had been written in a fortnight at her command, and in the *Life of Shakespeare* prefixed to Rowe's edition of 1709, she is said to have expressed a wish to see Sir John in love.

Nothing could have been more gratifying or better calculated to scotch the notion that Falstaff was a libellous creation. Of course plays written for public showing must be viable; but for the Queen to set a theme was common in private entertainments, and it is probable that any new reference would confer pleasure and spread his name in public. So, for instance, Sir Charles Percy, who lived down in Gloucestershire and belonged to the Southampton–Essex group, jestingly pretended to be Mr Justice Shallow. He was probably flattered by the praise of Hotspur. (It was Sir Charles who later was to pay for the production of *Richard II* on the eve of the Essex rebellion.)

Shakespeare went on creating new parts for the characters round Falstaff; in *Henry V* the lament for his death in the mouth of Mistress Quickly is more moving than the lament for the despoilment of France which in the same play is given to the Duke of Burgundy. The dead Falstaff conquers in a new way. Shakespeare tried to keep him in bounds. He had been

dismissed by phrases which a monarch would use on arising
from a play or game that did not please:

> I have long dreamt of such a kind of man,
> So surfeit-swell'd, so old, and so profane,
> But being awake'd, I do despise my dream.
>
> (*2 Henry IV*, 5.4.50–52)

Pistol was created as a parody of that liberated Falstaff, whose
power of words frees him from every tight corner. With his mad
scraps of play language he is a tatterdemalion scarecrow of a
player's nightmare; but even Falstaff hesitates to cross him
when he is in full cry, answering instead in the same kind:

> O base Assyrian knight, what is thy news?
> Let King Cophetua know the truth thereof.
>
> (*2 Henry IV*, 5.3.100–101)

The plays on *Henry IV* are the culmination of Shakespeare's
Elizabethan achievement in building a complex open form.
This is still the world of chivalry and heraldry, of the nation being
run as a family affair, of a society close to the knights of Malory
(Hotspur indeed might be a descendant of Malory's Knight of
Northumberland) – but this world is subject to the devastating
double onslaught of Falstaff's parodies and Hal's appraisal. He
has taken Hotspur's measure as his father took Richard II's.

It is impossible to imagine Falstaff coming to birth on the
Jacobean stage – a stage that was largely made by Shakespeare
but no longer as the unchallenged leader of the playwrights.
His very comprehensiveness seems to put him at the summit
of what can be achieved by the union of the popular and the
grand styles, the familiar and the heroic.

7 Enter, fighting, at several doors...

Around the year 1597 a new phase of theatrical life, and a new temper in society, began to be felt. Like the recent shifts which we have experienced in the sixties and seventies, it is easy to feel but hard to define: while one or two events serve as markers, it can be sniffed on the air of literary London, besides exploding into 'The War of the Theatres' (1599–1601).

Slowly, the old organization of players round the traditional pageantry of the Court had given way to a firmly-based London trade or profession. This was parallel to the transformation of medieval government, by officers of the royal household, into government by state departments which had, in official terms, 'gone out of court'. The old Office of the Revels, split off from its partner, the Tents and Toils (the royal hunting equipment), had become a minor bureaucracy, once the Master of the Revels saw that he could make money out of taxing the players' profits; this was 'protection' of a new sort! If Shakespeare fulfilled the old expectation of proclaiming his lord's greatness, like a herald, he also worked prudently and shrewdly as a member of that new estate, the Players of London, who had become conscious of their identity and role in society. They were a leading attraction for foreign visitors. They had become an institution. The number of theatres was growing.

A wealthy goldsmith, Francis Langley, saw a chance for investment here; his brother-in-law, the Clerk of the Privy Council, could help him get past the authorities. He built a splendid new theatre on the Bankside, The Swan – so splendid that a visiting foreigner made a sketch of it, thereby preserving the interior for posterity. It opened in the summer of 1597 with a new troupe to which some of Alleyn's best players had been enticed, in a play by that expert mischief-maker Tom Nashe, and a young actor from the new company, a cockney born and bred; his name, Ben Jonson.

As we have seen, the play contained 'very slanderous and seditious matter', and so efficient were the Privy Council in suppressing it that not a single trace of *The Isle of Dogs* survives. Nashe fled to his native East Anglia, where he settled down at Yarmouth to write *In Praise of the Red Herring*; Ben Jonson, with two other actors, went to jail in the Marshalsea. While there, he borrowed four pounds of the obliging Henslowe. He came out and joined Henslowe's team of playwrights. In August of the next year, he killed in a duel one of the men who had gone to jail with him. This time he went to Newgate and was charged with murder, saved himself by pleading 'benefit of clergy' (i.e. the ability to read) and emerged with a brand on his thumb – T for Tyburn – which meant that next time he would not get off. He also emerged a convert to Rome – a choice calculated to please neither the authorities nor Churchwarden Henslowe.

So began the stormy dramatic career of the man who was to be to Shakespeare's maturity what Marlowe had been to his early years – a constant provocation, a stimulus, rival and friend.

The Privy Council now tried to impose closer regulations on the number of playhouses in London and to permit only one south, one north of the river. Like most attempts at enforcement, it failed; Langley immediately invested in a Whitechapel theatre, The Boar's Head, and took his company, now 'Worcester's Men', there; he persuaded Kempe, the leading clown of the Chamberlain's Men, to defect to him. In spite of his influence, The Swan never saw any more plays; minor places and all City Inns disappeared; but the pruning only strengthened the stronger troupes, and within a few years the city saw a new form of theatrical enterprise, in the re-starting of the privileged choristers' theatres at Blackfriars and St Paul's. They disseminated a new mood, a satiric, mocking, self-conscious analysis of London society around them. The temper was quite different from earlier moral rebuke.[1] The young lawyers from the Inns of Court now took the lead in forming literary coteries, distinct from the Court though connected with it, based on gentry, professionalism, theatrical and literary centres. These now included clubs like the Mermaid, the Society of Antiquaries, the

men who gathered round scholars such as William Camden or
the historian Sir Robert Cotton, rather than courtiers like
Sidney and Ralegh, for the Court was becoming a suspicious and
unhappy place as Elizabeth aged and intrigues multiplied.

The sharper and more self-critical note with which society
examined itself was heard at its most venomous in the outburst
of social satire which began in 1597 and from which the new
plays, including Ben Jonson's, took their lead. It was heard in
1597 again at its most powerful and penetrating in the first
twelve *Essays* of a middle-aged lawyer earnestly in search of
preferment, Francis Bacon of Gray's Inn. The 'character', the
essay and the epigram, close to the best conversation, yet
pointed and polished, replaced older forms of wit, the repeti-
tions and 'figures' of Quintillian or John Lyly. Spreading and
voluminous eloquence shrank into 'stabbing similes'. (Compare
Richard II's eloquence on Death with the opening of Bacon's
essay, 'Men fear death as children fear to go into the dark.')
Even when discursive, Bacon imposes an order and a single
point of view, that in a similar fashion distinguishes all the new
plays. This was Art, displaying Judgment.

Ben Jonson's first comedy of this kind was given not to Henslowe but to Shakespeare's company, and when Jonson
published it, he put the names of all the actors before the play,
beginning with Shakespeare and Burbage. The legend that
Shakespeare was instrumental in the company's accepting
Every Man in His Humour is one of the older stories; it is certain
that his veto would have weighed heavily against the wild colt
from Henslowe's stable. The play was put on at The Curtain
Theatre in the autumn of 1598; on 20 September, a visiting
German who went there had his pocket picked of 300 crowns at
'a new play called *Every Man's Humour*'. It was clearly a success!
It ends as these comedies tend to do, with a judgment scene.

The scene was Italy, but Jonson later revised the perspective
and made his 'humours' what they were from the beginning,
Cockneys; he also added a Prologue which made plain his
original reforming intentions: he will not

> make a child, now swaddled, to proceed
> Man . . . or with three rusty swords
> And help of some few foot-and-half-foot words,

> Fight over York and Lancaster's long jars,
> And in the tiring house bring wounds to scars . . .

So much for Master Shakespeare! Instead, we are to have

> Deeds and language such as men do use,
> And persons such as comedy would choose,
> When she would show an image of the times . . .

His aim, like Bacon's, was to enquire, 'What actually occurs? Do not give me a textbook answer; do not produce a formula.' Jonson's hero was his schoolmaster, the historian William Camden, who had trained him so well at Westminster School that, although Fortune had destined him to be a bricklayer (and his enemies did not let him forget it), he was given honorary degrees by both universities. Jonson would have made a severe schoolmaster, and he went on treating his audience as if he were one. He was always looking for the ideal audience, addressing it, being puzzled that the people before him did not react as he expected.

Bacon opens his essay *On Love*:

> The stage is more beholding to love than the life of man; for as to the stage, love is ever a matter of comedies and now and then of tragedies. . . . They do best who, if they cannot but admit love, yet make it keep quarter, and sever it wholly from their serious affairs and actions of life . . . I know not how, but martial men are given to love; I think it is, but as they are given to wine . . .

The young lawyers who formed the new audience were not all Francis Bacons; but they shared inquisitive youth, social assurance (most were of good family) and the general anxiety of clever young people to be shown the works, given the inside information on the world of London society. This was exactly what the new bitter comedy appeared to do. At the same time, it was not devoid of horseplay. At the end of *Every Man in his Humour*, the justice who metes out rewards and punishments challenges the city fool to a rhyme competition, opening with:

Mount thee my Phlegon Muse, and testify
How Saturn, sitting in an ebon cloud,
Disrobed his podex,* white as ivory,
And through the welkin thunder'd all aloud.

* his buttocks

Jonson's central character, the clever servant, by the contrasts of his different disguises, satirizes the originals from which they are taken. The whine of the pretended discharged soldier (Jonson had been one himself) is set against the grander bragging of 'real' Captain Bobadill; the young men whose wits triumph in the end are keenly alive to all the varieties of 'character' that they dissect.

Every Man in His Humour was revived in immense zest by Charles Dickens, for Jonson's caricatures have something Dickensian about them. He loved London as Dickens did and knew it street by street. He loved oddities; he had the keenest ear for the speech that defines the speaker; and to the energy that made him so quarrelsome – and so attractive – he joined a passion for order. T. S. Eliot said: 'Whereas in Shakespeare the effect is due to the way in which the characters *act upon* each other, in Jonson it is given by the way in which the characters *fit in* with each other . . . their combination into a whole' ('Ben Jonson', *The Sacred Wood*, 1920, pp. 112–13).

While he went on with hack work for Henslowe, Ben Jonson produced a second play, *Every Man out of His Humour*, where virtually all the interest lies in close analysis of crazy behaviour. There are two critical characters who comment on the witty conversation of some and the parade of foolishness by others. Jonson takes much the same view of love as Francis Bacon, and he likes it in plays no better, especially when it seems to him conventional: '. . . the argument of his comedy might have been of some other nature, as of a duke to be in love with a countess, and that countess to be in love with the duke's son; and the son to love the lady's waiting maid; some such cross-wooing, with a clown to their serving man, better than to be thus near and familiar allied to the time' (Critical commentary at end of 3.1). The play is dedicated to the Inns of Court, for their reading at such time 'when the gown and cap is off and the lord of liberty reigneth'; but obviously Jonson thought it educative, and it would certainly have helped the lawyers to sharpen their claws for disputes at their Moots.

One of the Inns of Court youths became Jonson's rival and enemy. Young John Marston of the Middle Temple was the son of a distinguished and wealthy lawyer, who, mournfully admitting that he had produced a prodigal, in 1599 left him in his Will a good fortune and law books 'whom I hoped would have profitted by them in the study of the law, but man proposeth and God disposeth etc.' Marston attacked Hall the satirist abrasively: God's local representative, the Archbishop of Canterbury, that same year ordered Marston's satires to be burned, together with those of his opponent. (This did not stop Marston's later entering holy orders, while Hall became a bishop.) His immediate recourse was to write a mocking play for the new companies of children, in which Ben Jonson conceived himself slighted. He retorted in kind, and their brisk exchange of parody and insults occupied the London stages for two years. *The Player Whipt*, *Poetaster*, *The Untrussing of the Humourous Poet*, revived Greene's quarrel between Learning and Playing and made slighting remarks about popular actors. Ben Jonson concluded his epilogue to *Cynthia's Revels* (a satire on the Court):

> To crave your favour with a begging knee
> Were to distrust the writer's faculty.
> I'll only speak what I have heard him say,
> 'By God, 'tis good, and if you like't, you may.'

Jonson wrote for the boys' theatre *Poetaster or his Arraignement*, correcting young John Marston most magisterially. The poet is given an emetic on the orders of his judge, Horace (Jonson), and vomits up such notable phrases of Marston as 'reciprocal Incubus', 'conscious damp' and 'quaking custard'. (In *The Scourge of Villainy* he had written, 'Let Custards quake, my rage must freely run.') His last effort as he leans over the basin is 'O! obstupefact!', and he is then put on a diet of selected classics. But for a short period he is to be kept in a dark room, which was the accepted treatment for lunatics. The mixture of lofty judgment and horseplay here was no doubt known in the Inns of Court, as it might be among undergraduates today.

The students of St John's College, Cambridge, took up the whole controversy in their *Pilgrimage to Parnassus* (1598–1601).

The fact that the scene is set in Rome, however, seemed to Jonson to guarantee that no reference is intended to any living person; notwithstanding he had used many peculiar terms from Marston. But 'authority' restrained the publication of the *Apology*, in which, in his own person, 'Author' defends himself against other imputations on the law, the army and the stage.

> Now for the Players, it is true I tax'd 'em
> And yet, but some . . . What th'have done 'gainst me,
> I am not moved with. If it gave 'em meat
> Or got 'em clothes, 'tis well. That was their end.
> Only amongst them, I am sorry for
> Some better natures, by the rest so drawn,
> To run in that vile line.

According to the Cambridge undergraduates, who were following the controversy from afar, Shakespeare then intervened. They wrote a scene where Burbage and Kempe give an audition to graduates:

KEMPE Few of the university men pen plays well, they smell too much of that writer *Ovid* and that writer *Metamorphosis*, and talk too much of Proserpina and Jupiter. Why, here's our fellow Shakespeare puts them all down, ay and Ben Jonson too. O that Ben Jonson is a pestilent fellow, he brought up Horace giving the poets a pill, but our fellow Shakespeare hath given him a purge that made him bewray his credit.

> (3 *Parnassus*, 4.3.1806 ff)

The references in *Hamlet* are very cool and not personal at all ('O there has been much throwing about of brains'). Surely once was enough for Shakespeare to intervene? Ben Jonson was roaring:

> It is the happiest thing, this not to be
> Within the reach of malice. . . .
> Ay, now but think how poor their spite sets off
> Who, after all their waste of sulphurous terms,

> And burst-out thunder of their charged mouths,
> Have nothing left but the unsavoury smoke
> Of their black vomit, to upbraid themselves ...
> (Apologetic Dialogue appended to *Poetaster*, 19 ff)

while he compared the audience to the bears ready 'to swallow up the garbage of the time'. The Cambridge students did not know that Kempe had left the Lord Chamberlain's Company, and they may well have assumed that Shakespeare, the chief writer for the Chamberlain's Men, was the author of *Satiromastix*, which his company had put on. It was a great success, and the rival boys' company at St Paul's staged it against the Chapel boys at Blackfriars. But *Satiromastix* is the work of Thomas Dekker, Jonson's old collaborator, whom he had also attacked in *Poetaster*.

This is a good-natured, crazy patchwork; no one would have put Horace at the Court of William Rufus if Jonson had not treated Rome as a complete alibi. The mix-up was intended to ridicule his transparent disguise. The 'serious' plot is brought into the fun by the bride's father (Sir Quintillian Shorthose) and by a comic Welshman. To emphasize the libellous attempt of Jonson, not only the characters of the rival poets are brought into *Satiromastix* but also the soldier whom Jonson had named Tucca, founded on a certain Captain Hannam.

Horace's double punishment is first to be tossed in a blanket and then to be crowned with stinging nettles. The rough stuff is not ill-natured, though at times highly personal; Jonson's first trade as a bricklayer, his life as a strolling player, his branded thumb, his pockmarked face, his habits in the theatre, are hurled at 'Horace'. A final oath administered for his reform pledges him

not to bumbast a new play, with the old linings of jests stolen from the Temple Revels ... you shall not sit in a gallery, when your comedies and interludes have entered their actions, and there make vile and bad faces at every line ... you must foresweare to venture on the stage, when your play is ended, and to exchange courtesies and compliments with gallants in the lord's rooms, to make all the house rise up in arms and cry that's Horace, that's he, that's he, that's he, that pens and purges humours and diseases.

(5.2.298–307)

If Jonson had introduced this malicious style of characterization, his victims were showing that they could repay him. The actor who played Horace would be made up as Jonson.

Different sorts of fools and knaves were sorted out in the new bitter comedy. The individual theatres each evolved their own style. These were based on public demand, not on literary rules or code. Noisy 'spectaculars', with sword fighting, fireworks and traditional themes, prevailed at The Boar's Head east of Aldgate and were also found at The Rose; first-rate declamation and some of the best singing in Europe, with abrasive comedy and blue jokes, were found at the choristers' theatres. The nest of singing boys had been transformed into a cageful of young hawks or 'little eyasses', as Shakespeare observed in *Hamlet*; and it was to these children – not to the playwrights – that Shakespeare, through the mouth of Hamlet, put his query. He merely asked what would happen to them if they grew up to be actors themselves: 'Will they maintain the quality no longer than they can sing?' He also enquired rather pointedly, 'How are they escoted?' (i.e. who pays the rent?). Not her Majesty whose servants they nominally were. Someone's making a pile out of this, is the *sotto voce* comment; and ironically he conceded the victory to them:

> Do the boys carry it away?
> Ay, that they do, my lord – Hercules and his load too.
> > (*Hamlet*, 2.2.356–8)

Hercules bearing the world on his shoulders was the sign of The Globe, the Lord Chamberlain's Men's new theatre on the Bankside, where they had opened in the spring of 1599; and this as the result of yet another piece of in-fighting in which Shakespeare was undoubtedly involved.

The ground-lease of The Shoreditch Theatre was held by the Burbages from Giles Allen (no connection of the player) who, seeing what a profitable concern it had become, when the lease expired on 13 April 1597 raised the rent and demanded eventual possession of the building after five years. It was then that the Burbages tried to move to Blackfriars; foiled in this, they transferred to the little Curtain Theatre (where Ben Jonson's play was staged), abandoning their old house.

But see yonder,
One like the unfrequented Theatre
Walks in dark silence and vast solitude.
(E. Guilpin, *Skialethia*, 1598, sig. D6)

Cuthbert Burbage pleaded in vain, so the company acted promptly. On 28 December the Burbages, with their friends and twelve workmen, under their carpenter Peter Street, took to pieces all the wooden scaffolding that James Burbage the joiner had erected twenty-four years before. Peter Street had his own wharf. They ferried their property over the river and used it to build their new theatre on Bankside, leaving Giles Allen with the forlorn shell of an empty ring, to make what he could of an action for trespass. He did not win any of his actions – the removal had been legal enough under the expired lease. The new Globe was near The Rose, and on 21 February 1599 its lease was signed by Brand, the landlord, and by the Burbages, together with the leading members of their company – Shakespeare himself, Heminges, Phillips, Pope and Kempe. Shakespeare thus gained ten per cent of rights in The Globe, and this share could descend to his heirs.

To be a part-owner (The Globe was noted as being '*in occupatione Willielmi Shakespeare et aliorum*') gave the player an absolutely assured status, and it is likely that Shakespeare also had some form of contract for the production of plays. No other playwright was in the position that he enjoyed, and the financial harassment that plagued nearly all of them did not threaten him.

The company continued of course to play at Court, and for their patron; on 8 March 1600 'Sir John Old Castell' was given for a Burgundian emissary at the Lord Chamberlain's residence in Blackfriars. Meanwhile Edward Alleyn had prudently decided to move away from the neighbourhood of the new competitor, and transferred his men to The Fortune, in the north-west of London, which was put up by the same carpenter who had built The Globe seating and who was told to copy it in most details – except that The Fortune was square, not round. This may have been due to the adaptation of an existing courtyard, for the cost was relatively modest. The dimensions were 80 feet by 80 feet outside, 55 feet within, and the stage was 43 feet wide. The contract survives with Alleyn's papers, but the most valuable part of it – a sketch of The Globe – is lost. (The concurrent fight for the possession of The Boar's Head[2] ended only in 1603, when the plague killed off all litigants. 'Browne of the Boar's Head died very poor,' wrote Mrs Alleyn.)

The value of Shakespeare's 'share' is very difficult to calculate but was probably about £200 a year; on top of this, of course, he would get a share in extra payments for outside work, payment for his plays. Playwrights began also to attach themselves exclusively to Henslowe at about this time (one received forty shillings on 28 February 1599 as an advance on his script in return for such a promise). A little later, Henry Chettle was given £3 for the same rights, but he had to sign a bond.[3] Two plays a year seems to have been the expectation when these contractual rights became more of an institution.

Ben Jonson shot about from one company to another – which meant that he at least was not tied by any stipulations. In 1605 he wrote from prison, where yet another scandalous production had landed him and Chapman: 'The cause (would I could name some worthier) though I wish we had known none worthy our imprisonment is, a (the word irks me that our Fortunes hath necessitated us to so despised a course) a play, my Lord' (Herford and Simpson, *Ben Jonson*, 1, p. 195). The confessional lowering of the voice is quite audible.

With the development of the new theatres went a much closer identification of the adult actor with his role and with the particular 'humour' that he presented. In the old mid-Tudor theatre, it had been common enough to double parts in the small troupes of three or four men and a boy. On the other hand, it was a habit of clowns to play a one-man show, in which they took all the parts in rapid succession, perhaps clapping on a new beard or a wig or taking up a cloak. This virtuosity was considered fun and survives in plays for the quick-change artiste such as Chapman's immensely popular *Blind Beggar of Alexandria* (Henslowe, 1598). But Shakespeare's company, being particularly united and firm, developed the art of 'personation' or getting inside a complex role, for Burbage was this kind of actor and had a good 'conceit' – or general notion – of how to play a part. His collaboration with Shakespeare must have been unique on the stage of the time. Of course, those who wrote for the boys could drill the unlucky children relentlessly, but the children had only a limited range. They could be taught sharp, quick delivery and sprightly movement but they could not manage heavy parts. Moreover, the Lord Chamberlain's Men were training their own boys in a speciality for which Shakespeare provided the means.

Shakespeare's answer to the snarling satire of the children's theatre was no counter-snarl but a new imaginative delicate comedy. It can be seen in the list of plays for the years 1597–1601 – *Henry V*, *The Merry Wives of Windsor*, *Much Ado About Nothing*, *As You Like It*, *Twelfth Night*, *Julius Caesar* and *Hamlet*. He moved from history into his best love comedy, where once or twice the lead is not given to Burbage. In *As You Like It*, it is indisputably Rosalind's.

In place of the angry but very lofty line of the 'cankered Muses', he developed the love-game as a 'merry war' of wits, the total blindness and self-deception of lovers or the disguise which paradoxically allowed love to be revealed. The verbal and sometimes physical battles of his very successful early comedy *The Taming of the Shrew* are transferred to Beatrice and Benedick of *Much Ado About Nothing*. When he wrote *Much Ado About Nothing*, Shakespeare still had Kempe for the clown's part, and Dogberry has the same passion for language as the courtiers – only his weapons belong to a different kind of contest.

For *As You Like It* he had acquired the subtler, nervous, temperamental Robert Armin, a more 'bitter' fool; for him Shakespeare devised Touchstone, Feste and the Fool in *King Lear*. Armin's characteristic form of jest was the mock catechism or series of questions – he wrote a little book entitled *Quips upon Questions* – and this riddling type of wit could be bitter, disturbing, unsettling on occasion. But however he adapted the theatre's needs and opportunities – bright boys who grew up, robust clowns who drifted away, the need to meet the work of rivals with a counter-challenge – Shakespeare was secure, inwardly, in the world he had made. He could draw on his own imaginative storehouse for new and more powerful variations. Each of these comedies has its own special atmosphere, its own colouring and taste; yet throughout it is possible to see the one imagination, summoning the spirits at its command. *Much Ado About Nothing* is by its very title asserting the right to frivolity, although this is a strong play, almost as much a tragi-comedy as *The Merchant of Venice*. We hear only in a line or two ('Is this face Hero? Are our eyes our own?' or 'Kill Claudio') the depths that are to be developed later. In a mature way Shakespeare left the minor characters to carry the plot and developed his own kind of display of the world – the Ovidian world of love.

The central characters have only to be let loose to one another, and their 'merry war' generates all the action that is needed. With Katherine and Petruchio the interlude at his house marks the retreat into a dream – in this case the fantasies are all of Petruchio's creation, from which at the end both return to daylight and Padua, securely wedded. Benedick's first account of Beatrice: 'There's her cousin, and she were not possess'd with a fury, exceeds her as much in beauty as the first of May doth the last of December', betrays his love but also promises that Beatrice will live up to the first impression. In one of their latest encounters he tells Beatrice: 'Thou has frighted the word out of his right sense, so forcible is thy wit' (5.2.48). She is indeed forcible, far more free-spoken in her exchanges than the decorous ladies of other courtly plays.

'Lady Beatrice, I will get you one,' says the Prince as she cries 'Heigh Ho for a husband,' and back comes the ball: 'I would rather have one of your father's getting' (2.1.288–91). This puts the idea of really getting her a husband into the Prince's head, and the scheme of the match (which is his) is hatched before the end of the scene.

The game of insults as a form of love-play was as familiar as the bawdy game of military metaphors in which Benedick takes a bout with one of the waiting women – it could have been found in old songs.[4]

BENEDICK I give thee the bucklers.
MARGARET Give us the swords; we have bucklers of our own.
BENEDICK If you use them, Margaret, you must put in the pikes
  with a vice; and they are dangerous weapons for maids.

(5.2.16–19)

No doubt the Elizabethan lady could on occasion use surprising language, and might even be distinguished from city dames by superior invective (*1 Henry IV*, 3.4.247–59). Shakespeare's women make all their predecessors sound half awake, and most of their successors take to the lavatory jokes of satire. Marston's Crispinella is the nearest he can get to Beatrice, a lady who will 'give thoughts words, and words truth and truth boldness': 'Marry, if a nobleman or a knight with one look visit us, though his unclean goose-turd green teeth ha' the palsy, his nostrils smell worse than a putrified maribone, and his loose beard drops in our bosom, yet we must kiss him with a curtsey, a curse, for my part I would as lief they would break wind in my lips' (*Dutch Courtesan*, 1604, 3, i.19 ff). Clearly this sort of talk from angelic-faced little choirboys had its special kind of attraction. This particular lot had been discarded from the royal choir for being too impolite to King James (with the play that put Chapman and Jonson into jail). The theory that satirists had a right and even a duty to be as foul-mouthed as they pleased (with the object of curing their patients) is very similar to that of our own permissive society, except that a good lashing could be moral justification for any coarseness involved. Marston wrote an erotic poem which he defended as a satire on erotic poems, and it certainly would make present-day Soho look pretty tame. He was Italian on his mother's side and seems to have cherished a naïve belief that literary invective might open the way to political power, as it had for Aretino among the petty princes of Italy; he soon learned his mistake. Shakespeare's Italy was a land of courtesy, of wit rather than politics, Castiglione rather than Aretino. He may have learned something of the country from John Florio, the Earl of Southampton's Italian master who taught at the French embassy, and whose great translation of Montaigne was being prepared at this time.

There is something heroic in Shakespeare's transforming the old themes of courtesy, love and 'civil conversation' against the 'barking satirists', the self-appointed arbiters of true taste and learning. As ever, he reacted away from new styles by finding something different of his own.

'Much Ado about Nothing'? Perhaps. The imaginary slander, the imaginary doting, the entirely fictitious devils that Watchmen can conjure up:

BORACHIO But seest thou not what a deformed thief this fashion is?

2 WATCH I know that Deformed; 'a has been a vile thief this seven
year; 'a goes up and down like a gentleman; I remember his name.

(3.3.133–17)

The land of Shakespeare's imagination was becoming one
which was exerting its own persuasions upon society. Marston
himself, in his satire *The Scourge of Villanie*, testified to the wider
power of another tragedy:

> Luscus, what's play'd today? faith now I know,
> I set thy lips abroach, from whence doth flow
> Naught but pure *Juliet* and *Romeo*.
>
> (Satire x)

And John Weever, a young Cambridge student in 1599,
mentioned both Romeo and Richard with

> more whose names I know not,
> Their sugred tongues and power's attractive beauty
> Say they are saints, although that saints they shew not,
> For thousands vows to them subjective duty.
>
> ('Ad Guilielmum Shakespeare', *Epigrams* iv.2)

It is the characters that are remembered, not the words. This
meant that Shakespeare was getting the best out of his actors.
He created a light and airy world, and just enough dark shad-
ing to show its relation to the world of everyday. ('I made it
out of a mouthful of air', as Yeats said in one of his songs.) Critics
cannot agree about these plays: Shaw, declaring that Benedick
is 'not a wit but a blackguard', adds, 'there is only one thing
worse than the Elizabethan "merry gentleman" and that is the
Elizabethan "merry lady"'. (It might be thought that the creator of that relentlessly merry pair, the twins of *You Never Can
Tell*, laid himself open to the retort that the late Victorian version was more than a match for Shakespeare.) In comes a
modern critic to pronounce that the mature comedies are
superior to Shakespeare's final plays, another to protest that
he was writing 'only with his little finger', and yet another to
feel, 'it is as if the sensitive mind and heart sought to persuade
themselves by demonstration that life is a jest ... this is the point

at which the great clowns who are melancholic – Chaplin, Raimu, Jouvet, Fernandel – stand and abide.'[5]

The country of the mind into which Shakespeare adventured was partly a country of his own experience. In *As You Like It*, the literary world of the pastoral and his own Forest of Arden, the memory of earlier poets – such as Marlowe, whom he quotes with affection – represent a stable, secure base, from which he sets out to explore the delicate balance of gaiety and melancholy that his tough little 'leading ladies' discovered in the enchanted woodland where 'there's no clock'. All his own earlier comedies are, as it were, harnessed and put to contribute here: the light- ness of *Love's Labour's Lost*, the girl page from *Two Gentlemen of Verona*, the woodland and its magic disguises from *Midsummer Night's Dream*, and the bickering lovers from *The Merchant of Venice*. In Jacques, if anywhere, he made his comment on the satire of his contemporaries:

JACQUES Will you sit down with me? and we two will rail against our mistress the world, and all our misery.

ORLANDO I will chide no breather in the world but myself, against whom I know most faults.

(*As You Like It*, 3.2.260–64)

The alternatives of melancholy and laughter, nature and for- tune, Court and country, are endlessly debated; Rosalind holds the balance between them:

The poor world is almost six thousand years old, and in all this time there was not any man died in his own person, *videlicet*, in a love- cause . . . Leander, he would have liv'd many a fair year, though Hero had turn'd nun, if it had not been for a hot midsummer-night; for, good youth, he went but forth to wash him in the Hellespont, and, being taken with the cramp, was drown'd; and the foolish chroniclers of that age found it was – Hero of Sestos. But these are all lies; men have died from time to time and worms have eaten them, but not for love.

(4.1.83 ff)

That last phrase contradicts the gaiety, and the echo of Marlowe's death is heard elsewhere: '. . . it strikes a man more dead than a great reckoning in a little room' (3.3.11–12) is a contribution from Touchstone, of all people. Marlowe's *Hero and Leander* had been published in the previous year, and Shakespeare is now recalling him out of the past with a direct quotation – the only one in his works so clearly marked as such:

> Dead shepherd, how I find thy saw of might:
> 'Who ever lov'd that lov'd not at first sight?'
> (*As You Like It*, 3.5.80–81 ;
> *Hero and Leander*, first sestiad, 176)

It is also an oblique recollection of the sudden death in a cramped room in a Deptford tavern, during a quarrel about 'the reckoning'. Marlowe had always been for Shakespeare the poet of love as well as of conquest. The play's mood of melancholy is crowded into Act II of *As You Like It*, where Jacques appears to dominate; at the end, an old religious man converts the wicked Duke offstage, and those two conventional tinkling pastoralists, Silvius and Phoebe, join the procession of wedded couples, to beat the record of *Midsummer Night's Dream*. 'There is sure another flood toward, and these couples are coming to the ark' (5.4.34–5). Here there are four pairs, but Rosalind's wisdom and happy inconsistencies keep the delicate balance of the play together. Pastoral here is no world of escape but rather a conscious means of controlling and transforming 'hard facts' by imaginative play.

Twelfth Night, the latest of the group, offers roles of increasing subtlety for the heroine and the clown; a country even farther off, more dream-like than Italy – 'this is Illyria, lady' – and Messaline, Viola's home (Messina or Marseilles?); a blend of many, many previous plays by Shakespeare himself, and a script for varied performance mark the culmination of this particular kind of play. Only in the present century has the pathos of Feste become accepted; but Malvolio has long been a rival attraction to the lovers, and King Charles I named the play from him. John Manningham, who saw it performed for the lawyers in Middle Temple Hall during February 1602, was interested in Malvolio, and so were the general public, as a young admirer was to testify:

> The cockpit, Galleries, Boxes all are full,
> To hear Malvolio, that cross garter'd gull.
> (Leonard Digges, *Verses prefixed to Shakespeare's
> Poems*, 1640)

This play depends on its fine confusions, but the puzzle of identities ranges from the light amusement: 'No, I do not know you ... nothing that is so, is so' (4.1.5), to some metaphysical depths of 'One face, one voice, one habit and two persons', as the twins Viola and Sebastian meet.

Orsino, fixed in a conventional attitude, conventionally melancholy, is at times a sovereign duke, at times only a count; he seems like a distanced memory of Southampton. He is cured by a figure coming out of the sea, 'that can sing both high and low', a girl who is playing at being not *any* boy but specifically one she knew and loved. She tries to copy her twin but is constantly re-emerging as herself.[6]

The satiric use of disguise by the quick-change artists had nothing of this depth about it. The older use of disguise had been confined to wicked characters trying to appear as angels of light.

Shakespeare's disguised heroines are being actors. They are taking a part. Rosalind wants to be Jove's own page, loved by a god, and at the end she does call down Hymen from heaven. She seems to have liberated Shakespeare's imagination, and her two roles are constantly interweaving, as when, hearing that Orlando is come to Arden, she cries 'Alas, the day! what shall I do with my doublet and hose?' but immediately thinks of something to do with it that reveals herself to herself. The disguise or mask allows for a new form of self-discovery. In the same way, the fool shoots his shafts of wit under cover of folly.

This kind of complexity demanded much more of the actors than the satirists did and offered them a variety of possibilities for performance. Rosalind is surrounded by more conventional parts – the most conventional being the shepherd Silvius – and also by the analytic wit of Touchstone and Jacques, two characters of Shakespeare's creation. Jacques' speech on the Seven

Ages of Man had a theatrical dimension that is impossible to restore today, for it depended on the old game whereby the fool played a succession of parts, changing rapidly from one to the other. It is using not merely an old familiar literary cliché but an old piece of theatre.

Viola and her twin, because they are not of the same sex, make on others quite a different effect from the twins of *The Comedy of Errors*. Orsino has really fallen in love with the 'boy' Cesario, as he continues to call Viola even at the end; she has really tried to copy and replace her lost brother, but in her disguise she contrives in fantasy to woo Orsino, as Rosalind had done (2.4).

The page's disguise for his heroine was something so important to Shakespeare that he revived it constantly. The other device for ensuring that the woman won the 'war' was to get her with her husband into another woman's bed; but this is a mere piece of dramatic convenience – like the fact that Oliver finds Celia, and Touchstone, Audrey. The minor figures are treated as part of a pattern; they belong to the plot. But together the twins work a natural miracle. Everyone in Illyria is a little mad; the madness that is finally fastened on Malvolio is the clown's revenge, proper to the season of holiday. This revenge is brought about by invoking the victim's own powers of imagination: 'Look how imagination blows him,' says Fabian (2.5.40). Contrarywise, Sebastian, gaining Olivia's love all unexpectedly, feels himself in a new world, transformed and lifted out of everyday, yet still in his five senses.

> This is the air; that is the glorious sun;
> This pearl she gave me, I do feel't and see't;
> And though 'tis wonder that enwraps me thus,
> Yet 'tis not madness.
>
> (4.3.1–4)

The mechanics of the Plautine plot and the mechanics of Lyly's Euphuistic speech are transformed. In Lyly two girls disguised as boys have fallen in love; the scene is a model for that between Orsino and the disguised Viola:

PHYLLIDA Have you ever a sister?

GALLATHEA If I had but one, my brother must needs have two. But
  I pray you, have you ever a one?
PHYLLIDA My father had but one daughter and therefore I could
  have no sister.
GALLATHEA (*aside*) Ay me, he is as I am, for his speeches be as mine
  are.
PHYLLIDA (*aside*) What shall I do? either he is subtle or my sex
  simple.

(Gallathea, 3.2.41–9)

This covert exploration of the situation is just puzzle-solving,
whereas Shakespeare borrows the idea to reveal an undisclosed
tenderness:

ORSINO But died thy sister of her love, my boy?
VIOLA I am all the daughters of my father's house,
      And all the brothers too – and yet I know not.
      Sir, shall I to this lady?

(Twelfth Night, 2.4.118–21)

The music which the Duke favours is that of the ballads – 'Mark
it, Cesario, it is old and plain.' He does not want aristocratic
airs all the time. The admixture of the 'high' and 'low' in this
play is an example of such fine breeding that in spite of the
holiday atmosphere, there is very little bawdry. Malvolio's ima-
ginings are quite straightforward ('... come from a day bed,
where I have left Olivia sleeping' and his rapid response to her
anxious, 'Wilt thou go to bed, Malvolio?' 'Ay, sweetheart, and
I'll come to thee', 3.4.29–30). His hopes could be corroborated
from the diary of an Elizabethan serving-man.[7]
    Shakespeare's restraint in face of the outrageous indulgence
of language by the quarrelling factions is the more remarkable.
    The War of the Theatres may have been partly a simulated
quarrel, for in *Hamlet* it is said that there has been 'much ado'
on both sides – 'and the nation holds it no sin to tarre them
to controversy' (2.2.348). Before the quarrel Jonson had collaborated with Dekker; afterwards he collaborated with Marston; so differences were not irreconcilable. The nature of his
exchanges with Shakespeare must remain part of the legend

only. Thomas Fuller wrote of Shakespeare in his *Worthies* (published 1662):

Many were the wit combats between him and Ben Jonson, which two I beheld like a Spanish great galleon and an English man-of-war; Master Jonson (like the former) was built far higher in learning; solid, but slow in his performances. Shakespeare, with the English man-of-war lesser in bulk, but lighter in sailing, could turn with all tides, tack about and take advantage of all winds, by the quickness of his wit and invention.

As Fuller was born in 1608, he is unlikely to have beheld the two together literally, but the verdict is clear and does not preclude the friendliness of the encounters. Ben Jonson witnessed very simply, after Shakespeare's death, to another poet: 'I lov'd the man, and do honour his memory, on this side idolatry, as much as any.'
Ben Jonson did not bestow either love or honour lightly.

8 Hamlet, revenge!

Hamlet probably belongs to the year 1601, although it may have been started earlier, and texts were modified over the years. In February of that year, the Earls of Essex and Southampton were condemned to traitors' deaths; after Essex's execution, Southampton lay unreprieved in the Tower. On 8 September Shakespeare suffered a private grief, when the burial of John Shakespeare at Stratford was recorded.

In each of Shakespeare's tragedies, an individual world, a specific style suggests that here are particular tentacular roots reaching down to the depths of being. It would be presumptuous to be positive on psychological origins so powerfully transmuted; Shakespeare might have anticipated the ruin of his patron and certainly the death of his old father, and so done his internal mourning in advance of the events.

He took an old play, now lost but familiar for about a dozen years, in which he must have acted himself. We know that, as early as 1589, a strutting and bellowing ghost 'cried miserably' at The Theatre, 'like an oyster wife, "Hamlet, Revenge!"' In the War of the Theatres, Dekker's Captain Tucca turned on Horace with the roar, 'My name's Hamlet Revenge!' (*Satiromastix*, 4.1.121), and Shakespeare's company, who produced it, had also mocked the ghost in a prologue of 1599, given before the anonymous play *A Warning for Fair Women*:

> a filthy whining ghost,
> Lapt in some foul sheet or a leather pilch
> Comes in screaming like a pig half sticket,
> And cries *Vindicta* – Revenge, revenge!

Shakespeare's ghost makes a silent entrance – and even on his second appearance he long remains silent. He was a new kind of ghost, as Hamlet was a new kind of revenger, living not in Machiavelli's Italy but in 'a land between birth and death where three dreams cross'.

By taking an old stage play, Shakespeare could secure from his audience the memory of a firm structure of 'Senecan' verses and melodramatic action, based on the primitive, almost reflex impulse to give injury for injury. This meant that he could plant new questions and mysteries at the very heart of Hamlet the man and *Hamlet* the play.[1] He himself took such a creative leap that all his strength needed concentration for the imaginative daring and control that presented in this play of enigmas the greatest, most universal, masterpiece that the European stage had known since the Greeks. He drew back to old traditional forms now, as he was to do again in his last plays.

Hamlet encompasses every register, from grand soliloquy to brutally colloquial wit, exploiting the oral tradition of composition; the contrast of different 'voices' is emphasized by Hamlet himself ('Break my heart, for I must hold my tongue'), and each would make its special appeal to one or other temperament in the audience. Its universal appeal was attested by a humble scribbler on the passions of love who wrote in 1604 of 'friendly Shakespeare's tragedies' – and 'Faith, it should please all, like Prince Hamlet.' In another pamphlet, a gentlemanly highwayman persuaded players to give him a performance and offered to back the chief performer in London to play Hamlet against all comers. By 1607, putting a girdle half-way round the earth, *Hamlet* was being acted in a ship of the East India Company, anchored off Sierra Leone.

Today, *Hamlet* carries a load of interpretations, off and on the stage, which have made its history one with the history of the English drama itself. From Burbage's time the part has remained the summit for every tragic actor; from the critics it has drawn volumes of commentary, most of which testifies to Coleridge's confession, 'I have a smack of Hamlet myself if I may say so.'

Generous, accommodating to many different interpretations, the play for this reason is supremely dramatic. Everyone may construct his own *Hamlet*; the theatre usually has to cut the text – probably Shakespeare's own company did this. I have seen, for example, a Japanese *Hamlet* with a superb ghost (because the Japanese have many ghosts in their own classic drama), but here neither the players nor the gravedigger knew what to do. I have even seen something suggesting the crude vigour of the Old Hamlet (Albert Finney in the uncut version given at the National Theatre in 1977); and indeed, faced by this terrific text, Burbage may well have thought in despair at first, 'Let's play it the old way', and only gradually come to learn what was needed. We know that his 'mad Hamlet' appeared in his shirt; another witness testifies:

> Oft have I seen him leap into the grave
> Suiting the person which he seem'd to have
> Of a sad lover, with so true an eye,
> That there I would have sworn he meant to die ...

The actors could not really at first have grasped what they had been given. The Folio version is shorter than the Quarto version of 1604, which was issued to correct an arrant piece of nonsense of the previous year, put out by a piratical printer. He had got hold of the actor playing Marcellus. It is surprising that anyone could have been persuaded to part with sixpence to buy this 'Bad Quarto':

> To be or not to be, ay there's the point;
> To die, to sleep; is that all? Ay, all;
> No, to sleep, to dream; ay, marry, there it goes,
> For in that dream of death, when we awake
> And born before an everlasting judge,
> From which no passenger ever returned,
> The undiscover'd country at whose sight
> The happy smile and the accursed damn'd.
> But for this, the joyful hope of this ...
>
> (3.3.60 ff)

If this Bad Quarto alone had survived, what would Shakespeare's reputation have been?

If Burbage's acting was not as heavy as Alleyn's, 'what we see him personate, we think truly done before us' (as Webster said in his *Character of an Excellent Actor*). The part of 'mad

Hamlet' offered severe temptations to overact. Texts 'reported' by actors have an extraordinary number of Ahs! and Ohs! and even in the First Folio Hamlet's last words are 'The rest is silence. O, o, o, o!' In the Bad Quarto it is

> Mine eyes have lost their sight, my tongue its use.
> Farewell, Horatio. Heaven receive my soul.
>
> (5.2.106–7)

Three pivots of the action were provided by the old story. These are the Ghost, Hamlet's madness and the use of the play within the play. Shakespeare developed each of them as vital centres for his rich and complex meshing of inner and outer worlds.

Briefly to summarize his achievement, for the first time on any stage Shakespeare dramatically realized the soul of man in the daily world of Nature and Society. Hamlet is more than mind – though he is shown as intelligent, quick, sensitive to ideas; but he is also sensitive to people, to places, to the tone of words, to gesture; he can be all things to all men, moody but versatile. If the term *psyche* is used (it is appropriate to some modern contexts, such as the psychiatric, which are relevant),[2] it will serve to link him with the Ghost. The soul as the informing principle, the wholeness of body and mind and heart, was sometimes imperilled by the dichotomy of body and soul; and indeed Hamlet sometimes speaks of his 'machine' and his 'sallied flesh'; this dichotomy is part of his lamentable condition, as he himself makes plain elsewhere.

The great European portrait of the soul in time – Dante's – does not show Man in this world but follows an interior journey. Hamlet too follows an interior journey, but he is also placed precisely in a world furnished with characters like Polonius, Laertes, Rosencrantz and Guildenstern. To present a soul dramatically had been Marlowe's aim in *Faustus*, but, in order to achieve this, he had moved Faustus into such an abnormal relation to the world, and to heaven and hell, that he had to be surrounded with farce; his scholars, and the Old Man who appear at the end, have become indistinguishable voices of the humanity from which he is to part.

Hamlet keeps within our world so well that its spiritual dimension is acceptable to almost anyone who experiences an inner life at all. The mystery, the questioning, is precisely what the play is about; any critic who, like Rosencrantz and Guilden-stern, wants to get to the bottom of things, finds his answer:

HAMLET It is as easy as lying... You would play upon me; you would seem to know my stops; you would pluck out the heart of my mystery; you would sound me from my lowest note to the top of my compass... 'Sblood, do you think I am easier to be play'd on than a pipe?

(Hamlet, 3.2.348–62)

Earlier Elizabethan tragedy had sounded dark depths of treachery and supernatural evil; but the frame, the simple code, was the Rule of Nemesis. Old Hieronimo, avenging his murdered son, is led to crime, but at the end he is dismissed to felicity, for this is a thoroughly pagan play, presided over by a Ghost and by the figure of Revenge who directs the action like a god. Of course the audience knew that Revenge was wrong, and Hieronimo himself quotes the appropriate text of scripture; of course they knew too the Spanish code of honour which demanded vengeance; so here there is no simple answer. Shakespeare was soon to take another conventional, well-built old play and wreck it with ambiguities and questions. This was *King Leir.* The certitudes of the Old Revenge play were built on the punishment exacted – an eye for an eye, a tooth for a tooth; hell's darkness was lit by the torches of the Furies, snaky-haired, carrying whips smeared with blood, leading to a hell where Tantalus parched and Sisyphus toiled. Gloomy but exultant, the Revenger paid the price of his own crimes in exacting blood for blood.

> I would give all, ay and my soul to boot
> But I would see thee ride in this red pool.
> (*The Spanish Tragedy,* 4.4.205–6)

The New Revenge writers were concerned with psychology rather than ethics; their comedy was bitter and fantastic in its ironies; their model was not Seneca but the witty Lucian's *Dialogues of the Dead.* The ducal Italy of the Renaissance was witty also in crime, especially the secret wittiness of the poisoner.

Most would see providential action when the poison of Claudius and Laertes is turned against themselves. However, there are modern critics who see Hamlet as 'tainted'. He concurs: 'I could accuse me of such things that it were better my mother had not borne me: I am very proud, revengeful, ambitious; with more offences at my beck than I have thoughts to put them in, imagination to give them shape, or time to act them in. What should fellows as I do crawling between earth and heaven?' (3.1.122 ff). He does not claim to know what his own thoughts and imaginations might prompt him to. The play is about the state of being in uncertainties and doubts; about intimations from 'the undiscovered country' both without and within. Hamlet is hemmed in by circumstance, by codes of duty in conflict with each other, prompted to his revenge 'by Heaven and Hell'.

Every character in the play, except Voltimand and Cornelius, is related to Hamlet, and Hamlet responds to them all with sensitive quickness; he is the nerve-centre of all action, being in a second transformed from irony to tenderness, from rage to melancholy. The quickness, the Protean changes of temper, are not incoherent; he is always himself – 'condemned to be an individual' as a modern poet put it. Shakespeare knew, before Freud spelled it out, that jests may be a way of facing what would be otherwise intolerable, that wit and pain relieve the pressures from below; for, as Freud also knew, the poets intuitively recognized the functioning of the unconscious mind, and Hamlet could confine himself in a nutshell 'were it not that I have bad dreams'. His infinite variety, his instability, in fact lies deeper than his disguise of the 'antic disposition' which is partly, not wholly, under his control: his appearance in Ophelia's closet in mute appeal is pure grief; his later insults, verbal revenge for pain she has inflicted. Here Shakespeare is developing that art of revelation through disguise that he had explored more lightly in the comedies. Hamlet's antic disposition is a kind of second self: Shakespeare was to carry this further in the character of Edgar in *King Lear*. Madness as a form of insight had already been developed in a rudimentary way in *The Spanish Tragedy* and in his own *Titus Andronicus*; at the very nadir of misery there comes a terrible clairvoyance that leads Hieronimo and Titus to their revenge. The flashes of clairvoyance in Hamlet's part are associated with death (as they tend to be in life): the flashes of hysteria are associated with a mood from the opposite end of the emotional scale – coming immediately after his oath of consecration, at the end of the nunnery scene, and the closet scene, and in the graveyard. Dover Wilson cites the medical testimony of Robert Bridges: 'Hamlet himself would never have been aught to us, or we to Hamlet, were't not for the artful balance whereby Shakespeare so gingerly put his sanity in doubt without the while confounding his Reason.'[3] Actors had long looked on madness as giving them special opportunities: Alleyn played Orlando Furioso as well as Hieronimo, Shakespeare had given Titus, Romeo and Constance their frenzies of grief. Hamlet's intense mourning (which so endeared him to the nineteenth century) does not disguise his active intelligence. He is seen with rulers, with soldiers, with scholars, always the leader, as Ophelia testifies. It is a role to challenge any actor who strives to integrate it.

It offered an even greater refutation to those 'humourists' who thought they could analyse a character and pluck out the heart of his mystery. The play is no contribution to *that* discussion; it simply walks through and over the premises implicit in such neat little 'characters' of the 'persons' as:

Macilente: A man well parted, a sufficient scholar, and travelled; who, wanting that place in the world's account which he thinks his merit capable of, falls into such an envious apoplexy, with which his judgment is so dazzled and distasted, that he grows violently impatient of any opposite happiness in another.

(*Every Man out of His Humour: The Characters*)

Reductive accounts of Hamlet as an example of 'melancholy humour' are not wanting, of course,[4] and no doubt Shakespeare did learn something about the symptoms of that prevalent Elizabethan disease. Hamlet surmounts melancholy, as he surmounts his hysteria, for he himself turns and struggles against them, apologizes for them, defines them. His perspective on them is perceptible because in talking of himself he is absorbed in the beauty of the world, the sense of which is temporarily lost. This is what Keats called 'the feel of not to feel it'.

I have of late – but wherefore I know not – lost all my mirth, forgone all custom of exercises; and indeed it goes so heavily with my disposition that this goodly frame, the earth, seems to me a sterile promontory; this most excellent canopy the air, look you, this brave o'erhanging firmament, this majestical roof fretted with golden fire – why, it appeareth no other thing to me than a foul and pestilent congregation of vapours. What a piece of work is a man! How noble in reason! how infinite in faculties! in form and moving, how express and admirable! in action, how like an angel! in apprehension, how like a god! the beauty of the world! the paragon of animals! And yet to me, what is this quintessence of dust? Man delights not me – no, nor woman neither, though by your smiling you seem to say so.

(2.2.294–309)

This hymn to man and the earth follows on his sudden detection of falsehood in his friends Rosencrantz and Guildenstern, and ends in a jest at their expense. Not that *Hamlet* anywhere envisages absolute perfection in man; the late King, a model to his son, is undergoing the torments of Purgatory because he died without time to make his peace with heaven, and here Hamlet's doubts torment him:

'A took my father grossly, full of bread,
With all his crimes broad blown, as flush as May;
And how his audit stands who knows save heaven?
But in our circumstance and course of thought
'Tis heavy with him.

(3.3.80–4)

The elder Hamlet, a model for his son to practise kingship by, has himself told his son that he was 'cut off even in the blossom of my sins'. Ophelia, suspected of suicide, gets but scant rites from Holy Church. Hamlet is prepared to execute the conditions that were to be meted out to him and to send his schoolfellows to the block 'not shriving time allowed'. His father's imperilled soul deters the son from killing the praying Claudius when 'he is fit and seasoned for his passage' – 'Why, this is hire and salary, not revenge!' (3.3.79). That very accurate theologian Claudius soon reveals that Hamlet is mistaken; as he is unable to repent, he rises from his knees as far from grace as when he knelt.

This is a Christian play; in the opening act and the closing scenes, where such emphasis was to be expected, there is a faint echo of some celestial war between angels and devils – from Hamlet's 'Angels and ministers of grace defend us' to Horatio's committal of Hamlet's soul to flights of angels. But it is used naturally, in character, not for doctrinal effect. As he sets out for his mother's closet, Hamlet speaks with the voice of the older revengers, for he is practising the role of Lucianus, nephew to the King; there is nothing Christian about him then.

> 'Tis now the very witching time of night,
> When churchyards yawn, and hell itself breathes out
> Contagion to the world. Now could I drink hot blood,
> And do such bitter business as the day
> Would quake to look on.
>
> (3.2.378–82)

These lines would call up the dark lords of the underworld and recall also the opening scene – which, however, is one of intense beauty. Shakespeare never dreamed any setting more powerful than the moonlit battlements of the great fortress beside the sea, still and cold, with its great rows of guns, the famous guns of Elsinore, pointing out across the Sound towards Norway and Sweden.

The Ghost – who soon makes his second appearance – is an ambiguous figure. He is referred to as 'this dread sight', and Hamlet thinks some other spirit may have 'usurped' the fair and warlike form of the majesty of buried Denmark. The different theories of ghosts, Catholic theories of Purgatory, Protestant theories of diabolical spirits, some free speculation that all spirits were 'illusions', had been often canvassed on the stage and were even the subject of a little pamphlet in which the ghost of the old clown Tarlton – who was to reappear as Yorick – discusses the various possibilities.[5] Hamlet thinks that 'the spirit that I have seen may be the devil', and he tries the experiment of the play to test the Ghost.

Hamlet's own language, as Wolfgang Clemen pointed out, is close to reality, poignant and exact. His images are not lofty but they always hit the mark, they are taken from observation. Rhetorically they are in the 'low' style.

> A little month, or ere those shoes were old
> With which she followed my poor father's body,
> Like Niobe, all tears.
>
> (1.2.147-9)

This takes us back to a young man trying to walk like a prince, behind a coffin.

Ophelia's death-images are images of this world too — her white and purple flowers to which country people give gross names 'but our cold maids do dead men's fingers call them'. She is buried in a very English graveyard. Beside the one where Shakespeare in his mourning shoes had followed his father's coffin there runs a stream like the one she drowned in. In this stream a girl called Katherine Hamlett had once drowned, and only after two months had the coroner found her 'Christian burial'.[6] One death recalls another to Shakespeare, but all are worked into the fabric of the play, King Hamlet remaining a disembodied spirit, Ophelia and Polonius pitiable corpses; other deaths are suggested in images.

We have a triple sight of a man with a drawn sword standing over a kneeling figure, motionless. At first it appears in the player's speech – Pyrrhus, sword raised to strike, standing 'like a neuter' above the old King Priam;[7] then it is Hamlet, pausing with his drawn sword behind the kneeling Claudius; finally, perhaps, it is Laertes with his foil poised as Hamlet kneels before his mother (this would be the correct way to approach seated royalty) and she offers him her napkin to wipe his brow. Who knows what awful memory or dream of a public execution lies behind this image?

The modern critics who have studied the imagery of the play are no nearer agreement than those who have studied the character of the Prince.

For Caroline Spurgeon, the characteristic imagery was the hidden ulcer, 'something rotten in the state of Denmark'. As the King had died of a loathsome poison, so the country itself is undermined by the sickness that his hidden murder brings. This set of images is very powerful, but Caroline Spurgeon was herself dying of a hidden disease as she struggled to put her work in shape. Wilson Knight sees also images of death and blight, which he centres on Hamlet. Maynard Mack sees imagery of clothes, painting, all that may conceal or reveal the self; with the image of show, act or play, and of poison. These are developed by Nigel Alexander, who finds a secret war waged between Hamlet and Claudius, verbal at first but using symbolically the deadly cannon of Elsinore. For others, the question or riddle is paramount; riddles and questions reach a climax in the graveyard scene, where Armin, who loved this form of jest, would be playing opposite Burbage, displaying gruesome pride in his trade with practical calculations on the time a pocky corpse will hold out, and the advantages of having been a tanner – 'a tanner will last you nine year'.

For C. S. Lewis, the subject is the state of being dead, 'a curious groping and tapping of thoughts, about "what dream may come"'. Growth is the synthesis of change and continuity, said Lewis, defending his 'childish' view of things, against 'the straighteners of Erewhon or Vienna'. He thinks that the Prince has lost his way, and we can tell the exact moment when he finds it again: 'Not a whit, we defy the augury: there is a special providence in the fall of a sparrow. If it be now, 'tis not to come; if it be not to come, it will be now; if it be not now, yet it will come – the readiness is all. Since no man owes of aught he leaves, what is't to leave betimes?' (5.2.211 ff). This is 'a certain spiritual region though which most of us have passed'; the author of *A Grief Observed* was to pass through it himself, some time after he wrote his study of Hamlet.[8] (I would think it is rather about the Threshold – the mysterious Valley of the shadow of Death; Death's dream kingdom, Eliot termed it.)

The variety of different 'Hamlets' within the single figure of the Prince is balanced by the variety of different levels and scenes in the play. The image of the play, and its comparisons and mutual reflections between life and the theatre, help to keep the audience free from any mere 'concussion of positives on one side and negatives on the other'. These rhetorical contrasts and oppositions maintain the mystery of things: 'The experience of Hamlet culminates in a set of questions to which there are no answers.'[9]

In the second scene Hamlet disclaims his mourning as 'a part man might play'. His inky cloak might mean the whole of his part for a certain kind of actor. Later he takes up the 'antic role' of madness and dresses and acts accordingly.

The First Player shows him images both of mourning and of the avenger. The players have been introduced as 'the trage-dians of the city' and, as they come on, Hamlet – played by Burbage – greets his understudy, the First Player, who would be made up to look like Burbage himself. 'O, my old friend! Why thy face is valanc'd since I saw thee last; com'st thou to beard me in Denmark?' (2.2.418–19). While the first player is speaking, and in the soliloquy that follows, Burbage's power to respond with real tears and to lose himself in his part is pre-sented as part of the *inner* play. Later there are the jests between Polonius and Hamlet just before *The Murder of Gonzago* is put on, where Polonius confesses to acting in the university: 'I did enact Julius Caesar; I was killed i' th' Capitol; Brutus killed me.' Hamlet's rejoinder, 'It was a brute part of him to kill so capital a calf there' (3.2.100–102) sparkles with double mean-ings, one of which is that these two actors had probably played Brutus and Caesar in the last of the Lord Chamberlain's Men's tragedies, *Julius Caesar*.

The comments on acting and the holding of the 'Mirror up to Nature' by actors give a Pirandello-like reflection of how *this* Hamlet is to play, compared with the strutting and bellowing of the older version. It is an apologia for the new form. As Robert Speaight remarks, 'We are on tenterhooks to know how Claudius will stand up to *The Murder of Gonzago*, but Shake-speare is not to be hustled by an impatient audience if Hamlet has something to get off his mind, no matter when or where.' He thinks Hamlet is a character who 'answers back' to his author and insists on doing what he likes; I would prefer to say that, as a portrait of a soul, Hamlet has to be engaged with his world at every level.

The Murder of Gonzago sounds like a conventional Italianate play of the boys' theatre; it is 'writ in very choice Italian'. It will therefore have all the expected Italianate material: 'they do but jest, poison in jest,' he assures the King, having explained the alternative title, *The Mousetrap* – 'Marry how? Trapically'. 'Marry trap' was the jeer used to a plotter whose plot had recoiled on himself.[10]

The device of a play within the play, which gives both a mirror on the past and a vision of the future, shows the murderer as 'Lucianus, one nephew to the King'. To the King it shows his own crime and threatens him too with death from a nephew. The involvement of the players in *The Murder of Gonzago*, though in all innocence, may be Shakespeare's hindsight view of what it meant to the Lord Chamberlain's Men to have played *Richard II* at the plotters' request on the eve of the Essex Rebellion. (Towards the end, the deposed Richard anticipates Hamlet in bitter wit, verbal revenges, introspection and debate between his various 'selves'.)

After he has killed Polonius, Hamlet is forced back to his antic role, like the Emperor Henry iv in Pirandello. Sent on an honourable diplomatic mission as a game, or play, to conceal the King's murderous intent, Hamlet exchanges roles with his escort. Then, when he returns, he finds Laertes playing the old-fashioned avenger. The duelling match represents another play, on which the King has laid a wager, but which he also is directing from the auditorium. Hamlet improves and changes the script, involving the chief spectator finally and fatally. The design of the last scene is recognized by Laertes, by Hamlet in the jests with which he forces the poison on the King, and by Horatio in his final speech,

> ... purposes mistook
> Fall'n on th'inventors' heads.
> (5.2.376–7)

Claudius is but a player king 'of shreds and patches' to Hamlet; the sacred title is vacant, because it cannot have descended to this cutpurse of the empire, who has stolen the crown (3.4.99–101).

A further perspective is provided by those offstage actions of which we hear indirectly – the wars, the journeyings, the sea fight (which in the old play may have been staged). There are other scenes we do not witness, such as Hamlet's appearance in Ophelia's closet. The audience may note that Ophelia does not make any response to Hamlet's terror and pain. Nor, in the nunnery scene, does intuition give her insight into his pain; and she freezes when, in the play scene, he insults her in public:

'Do you think I meant country matters?' – a joke from the brothel. When in his plain seaman's garb he comes to the side of her grave, we have had the hollowness of consolations already exposed by Claudius and the value of maxims by Polonius; there will be no preaching at *this* funeral. Now, as she drops flowers into the grave, the Queen seems to be burying the future and any hope of a happy outcome for Hamlet. Like her father, Polonius' daughter is to be buried 'in hugger-mugger'; the substitution of the Queen's flowers for marriage-strewings is a powerful theme in old ballads, where the interchange of bride-bed for death-bed gives a strong climax – in modern ballads too:

> They tolled the one bell only,
> Groom there was none to see ...
> (A. E. Housman, *A Shropshire Lad* XXI)

The ridiculous humiliations, the grotesque reductions of death, bring Hamlet to his jests with the gravedigger and his discovery of Yorick – the King's jester, the original player – as an evil-smelling death's head. This scene fascinated Shakespeare's contemporaries, who used the address to the skull as the pivot for their later revenge plays: no one attempted the grotesque contrast of the gravediggers. It is Hamlet's ignorance of whose grave he is looking at that lends such irony to his 'Now, get you to my lady's chamber and tell her, let her paint an inch thick, to this favour she must come; make her laugh at that' (5.1.189). That note is heard again, in Vindice, in mocking address to the skull of his dead mistress, which he uses to effect his revenge on her murderer:

> Doth the silk worm expend her yellow labours
> For thee? for thee doth she undo herself?
> Are lordships sold to maintain ladyships
> For the poor benefit of a bewitching minute?
> (*The Revenger's Tragedy*, 3.5.75 8)

and again in the macabre jesting of the Duchess of Malfi's 'last presence chamber':

BOSOLA Thou art a box of worm seed, at best, but a salvatory of green
    mummy.

What's this flesh? a little crudded milk, fantastical puff
paste ...
DUCHESS What would it pleasure me, to have my throat cut
With diamonds? or to be smothered
With cassia? or to be shot to death with pearls? ...
Any way, for heaven's sake,
So I were out of your whispering.

(*Duchess of Malfi*, 4.2.124 ff)

Beauty, glory, the rich fountain of life as being identical with
death, so that life feeds death, makes the clown's praise of his
trade as tomb-maker a jest as lacerative as the torturers' jest
in the old Passion plays. Hamlet arrives at the transmutation
of the dust of Alexander and Caesar to ignoble uses – but he
has already meditated how a counsellor, aiming to circumvent
God, may go a progress through the guts of a beggar: 'But if,
indeed, you find him not within this month, you shall nose him
as you go up the stairs into the lobby' (4.3.36–7). Of John Shakespeare, whom his son had so recently buried, it was said: '[I]
... saw once his old father in his shop – a merry cheek'd old
man – that said – Will was a good honest fellow but he durst
have crackt a jeast with him at any time' (E. K. Chambers,
William Shakespeare, vol. 2, p. 247). This, I take it, means that
Will dared crack a jest with his father. (The sort of family
where apple-pie beds were not unknown?) I don't think John
Shakespeare stalks the battlements of Elsinore, but he may be
remembered in the graveyard, a scene that belongs to the later
strata of the play and is without precedent in earlier drama.

Meditation upon a skull was a familiar religious exercise; the
poignancy of this scene lies in its circumstantial details, setting
off Hamlet's ranging fancy. Laertes completes the death cycle
with his cry at the untimely nature of this death

And from her fair and unpolluted flesh
May violets spring!

(5.1.233–4)

Hamlet's rage and grief explode when the identity of this victim
hits him. In the various stages of mourning, an initial period
of stunned apathy is usually succeeded by rage, often directed

against the dead for having 'forsaken' the living. Hamlet passes immediately to this second stage, but his rage is undirected. He is seeking suicide ('Be buried quick with her and so will I' – 5.1.273). Laertes, whom he challenges, is his rival in revenge and is already pledged to kill him, as the audience has seen in the previous scene. So Hamlet is as good as dead, and the fight in the grave anticipates the duel which is already arranged; the grave is his – it waits him as a result of the deaths of Polonius and Ophelia. The third stage of mourning is a fanciful restitution, when the dead is restored in some way (perhaps by introjection, as part of the self), and the fourth, full adjustment or acceptance of loss. Hamlet assumes the person of his father when he uses the royal Danish signet to seal the death-warrant of Rosencrantz and Guildenstern and when he comes forward with the proclamation, 'This is I, Hamlet the Dane!' – that is, the King of Denmark. He now accepts his role but without the compulsion and the obsessiveness of the old revengers. As he dies, there is a poignant echo of the ghost's fading 'on the crowing of the cock:'

> O, I die, Horatio!
> The potent poison quite o'er-crows my spirit.
>
> (5.2.344–5)

The metaphor is that of the winning bird in a cockfight crowing over its fallen opponent. Hamlet is dying by the same secret mischief that killed his father – but like a soldier too.

Although the old *Hamlet* is lost, some measure of the distance that Shakespeare travelled may be guessed by looking at the old *Spanish Tragedy* with the additions that Ben Jonson (of all people) was asked to make to it following the success of the new *Hamlet*. The original is a finely-built piece, and its climax is the play within the play, where old Hieronimo suddenly reveals that, in the tragedy he has been staging, the deaths have been in earnest, not in jest. He then draws a curtain to reveal his own 'show', the body of his murdered son, whose death promoted his dreadful act of vengeance. The stage audience were unaware that the stage deaths were real acts; from above, a Ghost, who is the victim of an earlier murder, and the spirit of Revenge, have presided over the whole action from start to finish, to pronounce the final judgment. They consign all the avengers to Heaven, all the rest to Hell.

Ben Jonson's additions to Hieronimo's part (if those that survive are his) give depth by adding earlier to his scenes of madness, especially in his scene with a painter, whom he asks to paint the murder of his son, in the narrative technique of some Elizabethan pictures with different incidents depicted on the one canvas in perspective.[11] Hieronimo prefers to be mad because then he feels less pain; now the mere description of the painting so transports him that he fancies he has one of the murderers in his grip. He is re-enacting the night of the murder and of his discovery:

Well, sir, then bring me forth, bring me through alley and alley, still with distracted countenance going along, and let my hair heave up my nightcap. Let the clouds scowl, make the moon dark, the stars extinct, the winds blowing, the bells tolling, the owl shrieking, the toads croaking, and the clock striking twelve.

This is an attempt to create the atmosphere that accompanies the appearance of the Ghost in *Hamlet*.

And then, at last sir, starting, beholding a man hanging, and tottering as you know the wind will wave a man, and I with a trice to cut him down. And looking upon him by the advantage of my torch, find it to be my son Horatio. There you may show a passion, there you may show a passion. Draw me like old Priam of Troy, crying 'The house is afire, the house is afire, as the torch over my head.'

(*The Spanish Tragedy*, 3.12.148 ff)

Here the players' scene is evoked, and the older 'tapestry' of Troy.

Hamlet worked upon other dramatists like a stone thrown into a pool; the ripples spread out, breaking up the fixed stern code of the Rule of Nemesis. This was already, as we have seen, subject to parody, and Marston had written a tragedy of Machiavellian revenge and Italian vice for the boys' company which half exploits, half explodes the old form. Every moral assumption is undermined, the final effect being one of total insecurity.[12] The new kind of revenge tragedy grew in its own

way as conventional as the old, but in a sceptical and sophisticated mode.

Tourneur and Webster were both deeply indebted to *Hamlet*
and wrote far beyond their usual capacity when they followed
with *The Revenger's Tragedy* (1606), *The White Devil* (1611) and
The Duchess of Malfi (1612), played by Shakespeare's company.
Webster's deepest levels of uncertainty and his clearest intimations of something beyond the daily pattern of his Italian Courts
bring him very close to Shakespeare –

> I am in the way to study a long silence.
> There's nothing of so infinite vexation
> As man's own thoughts.
> (*The White Devil*, 5.6.204–7)

> O, this gloomy world!
> In what a shadow or deep pit of darkness
> Doth womanish and fearful mankind live?
> (*The Duchess of Malfi*, 5.5.99–101)

This is *Hamlet* without its revelation, for if *Hamlet* includes so
many varied scenes of the world – even some merry ones – it
does not lack the thrust towards the realm of the soul where,
in the words of a later poet, 'words, beyond speech, reach into
the silence'.

In T. S. Eliot's early view, *Hamlet* 'so far from being Shakespeare's masterpiece, is most certainly an artistic failure'. When
Eliot wrote this, he had just published a poem whose final
sequence opened,

> No, I am not Prince Hamlet, nor was meant to be;
> An attendant lord, perhaps . . .
> (*The Love Song of J. Alfred Prufrock*)

Because 'workmanship and thought are in an unstable condition' and 'the intense feeling, ecstatic or terrible, without an
object or exceeding its object, is something which every person
of sensibility has known ... we must simply admit that here
Shakespeare tackled a problem which proved too much for
him.'

He might be answered by a quotation out of Gerard Manley Hopkins:

There are, you know, some solutions to chess problems, some resolutions of suspension so lovely in music that even the feeling of interest is keenest when they are known and over.... How must it be then when the very answer is the most tantalizing statement of the problem and the solution you are to rest in the most pointed putting of the difficulty!

(*Letters to Robert Bridges*, cx, p. 187)

9 'His Majesty's poor players'

'She was born on a Lady Eve and died on a Lady Eve.' Queen Elizabeth, who died on the eve of Lady Day, 24 March 1603, had been born on the eve of the Nativity of the Virgin, 7 September 1533. The most detailed account of her last days is found in the memoirs of the Lord Chamberlain's youngest brother, Robert Carey, who on coming down from his border post was greeted by the Queen with the sad words, 'No, Robin, I am not well.' Carey, who had been on missions to Scotland, wrote at once to the Scottish King James, Elizabeth's cousin and presumed heir, telling him not to leave Edinburgh, 'for if of that sickness she should die, I would be the first man to bring him news of it'. The porter was bribed to let Carey in if called; his sister waited on the Queen in her last hours. But, as soon as Elizabeth was dead, he was seized by the Lords of the Council, who tried to prevent his departure. The Lord Chamberlain manœuvred him through the gates and he got away from London between nine and ten in the morning, reaching Doncaster that night. The next night he had James proclaimed at Morpeth and Alnwick on the border, and in spite of a fall from his horse, he reached Edinburgh by the third nightfall, where he gave James for a token 'a blue ring from a fair lady' – probably a prearranged signal from his sister. Robert Carey had won the race.

The importance of personal connections and the family network was demonstrated, for the Careys now had to exert every nerve to keep the degree of intimacy with the throne which they had enjoyed before by kinship. Though but a younger son and with little fortune, when asked what reward he would desire, Carey requested only to be admitted as Gentleman of the Bedchamber, in the closest personal attendance on the King.

Shortly afterwards, however, by the manœuvring of others, through nominal promotion Carey lost the position; a hard struggle was needed to regain it, and to secure a like position in the new Queen's household for his wife. Carey looked back sadly to the reign of Elizabeth when he set down these events.

A peaceable succession, flawlessly arranged by Burghley's son, the quiet hunchback Robert Cecil, whom the King called 'my little beagle', brought in James, whose early history was as lurid as Elizabeth's; its effects upon him were disastrous. From his father, Henry Darnley, he inherited a miserable physique, not improved by his father's assassination of his mother's Italian secretary in her presence, while she was still carrying James in her womb. Before he was a year old, his father had been murdered – as it was generally believed, with his mother's active assistance. She was deposed; so James began his regal childhood at the risk of being kidnapped by rival Scottish nobles, the certainty of being educated in the sternest precepts of the Kirk, of being well beaten by his schoolmaster, Buchanan, and with only a distant chance of succeeding to the rich prospects that lay along the highroad to the south. He made it, however; he and his raw-boned Danish wife, his ten-year-old heir, Prince Henry, and the rest of the family. However, as he moved south, the signs of the plague drove him away from the capital, where the throngs gathered to welcome him increased the danger of infection – but not before he had issued a warrant for Letters Patent under the Great Seal creating Shakespeare and eight of his fellows 'the King's Men'. The date is 17 May 1603, and the warrant passed under the Great Seal on 19 May. A royal honeymoon of bounty had begun. They, with their associates, were permitted

freely to use and exercise the art and faculty of Playing Comedies, Tragedies, Histories, Interludes, Morals, Pastorals, Stage Plays and such others like ... to show and exercise publically to their best commodity ... as well within their usual house called The Globe within our county of Surrey as also within any town halls or Moote halls or other convenient places within the liberties and freedom of any other City, University Town or Borough. ...[1]

They were also to be allowed 'such former courtesies as hath been given to men of their place and quality' and any further favour 'we shall take kindly at your hands'. The times were both foul and fair for players. Southampton, who had been set free and gone up the Great North Road as far as Huntingdon to meet the King, was rewarded with suitable honours – including the Garter and the collection of tax on sweet wines that formerly had given Essex his fortune. For James, however, someone younger and more glamorous was really needed, and his first English favourite was the nineteen-year-old Philip Herbert, nephew of Philip Sidney, whom he created Earl of Montgomery. Philip knew nothing except the ways of horses and dogs, but the King's devotion to hunting made this acceptable to him and especially to Cecil, who did not need to fear any interference from this lout. One of James's ways of rewarding his favourites was to find a good match, and next year, with royal support, the Earl of Montgomery married Lady Susan Vere, the younger sister of that Elizabeth Vere designed by Burghley for Southampton. The masquings were magnificent; the King got up early next morning and went into the bride-chamber in his nightshirt, with a great deal of merriment ensuing 'either upon the bed, or in the bed, choose you where', a courtier reported.

The King spent early December at Wilton, home of the Herberts, and the King's Men went down to give some plays. A letter, now lost, from Lady Pembroke, mentioned that the man Shakespeare was there; and the play was *As You Like It*. From 13 July 1603, when the plague orders went out (and there were eleven hundred deaths a week), the King's players had been touring (Bath, Shrewsbury, Coventry, Mortlake), but at Christmas they appeared seven times at Hampton Court. In February the King gave them a grant of £30, as times were still hard.

For their Christmas performances, they had received the handsome sum of £103 – Mrs Alleyn notes that most of the other companies had returned to the neighbourhood by the end of October, looking for private employment.

Dekker took to pamphleteering, and Shakespeare perhaps to preparing *Hamlet* for press. During the epidemic, which at its height in September cost three thousand lives every week, the law courts moved to Winchester; The Globe Theatre was closed for eleven months. It had been 'dark' from 19 March 1603 when the Queen's illness became grave, except for a couple of weeks in early May, and the players did not come back to their theatre till Easter Monday, 9 April, when all three London companies were given warrants to act 'except there shall happen weekly to die of the plague above the number of thirty within the City of London and the Liberties thereof. At which time we think it fit they shall cease and forbear any further publically to play until the Sickness be decreased again to the same number.'

The other London companies had secured royal patronage; Alleyn's company became Prince Henry's Men, and the group at The Boar's Head, who had acquired as resident poet and actor Thomas Heywood, became Queen Anne's Men. Such licensing was now confined to royalty; playing was institutionalized. As for 'the little eyasses', it was not long before their unflattering portraits of James and his Scottish followers caused that infuriated monarch to say that they should be turned loose to beg their bread. He forbade his choirboys to act, and further, in the abrupt application of clerical standards, commanded that none of the said choristers or Children of the Chapel should 'be used or employed as Comedians or stage players or to exercise or act any stage plays interludes comedies or tragedies, for that it is not fit or decent that such as sing the praise of God Almighty should be trained up or employed in such lascivious or vain exercises'. Some of them continued, however, as a separate group. The institutionalizing, as ever, was less than perfect.

If James was prepared to welcome players, Anne was devoted to the art. She was a plain woman, nearly six feet tall, sharp of tongue and deeply mortified by James's insistence that his children should be brought up away from Court, by foster mothers. She accepted James's homosexuality, and he kept up a fiction that his favourites had been presented to him by his Queen. Their separate households doubled the chance for official positions at Court; their love of display was justified by the exaggerated sense of power that the uniting of Great Britain under one king presented to the rest of Europe. For a year or two James was courted by France and Spain. He started to receive ambassadors, and in March 1604 his Men, as Grooms of the Chamber, were sent to wait on the Spanish Ambassador, the first who had been seen in England since the Armada. Peace was signed at last. From 9 to 27 August 1604 Shakespeare and

his fellows went on duty at Somerset House in their scarlet
liveries to wait on the Constable of Castile, for which service
they were paid twenty pounds. Since the Constable brought
a train of over three hundred attendants, their function was
presumably to act as couriers or guides to the city.

That winter the Tower saw a new prisoner under sentence
of death for treason – Sir Walter Ralegh. His enemies, playing
on James's fears, made use of the power shift; with Lord Cobham, he was arrested in July; at a spectacular trial, his gallant
defence convinced even his judges. His poems rang out to the
world, defying death as magnificently as ever he had defied the
Spanish ships: he who entered into competition with Marlowe's
'Come live with me and be my love' was now writing in
Hamlet's mood:

> What is our life? a play of passion,
> Our mirth the music of division,
> Our mothers' wombs the tiring houses be
> Where we are drest for this short comedy,
> Heaven the judicious sharp spectator is
> That sits and marks still who doth act amiss.
>
> Our graves that hide us from the setting sun
> Are like drawn curtains when the play is done,
> Thus march we playing to our latest rest,
> Only we die in earnest, that's no jest.

The foreigners who now came trooping into London were
to bring with them new ideas about staging; with them
returned from Elsinore a young Londoner who, after spending
his time in Italy studying painting and architecture, had taken
service with the King of Denmark. An exact contemporary of
Ben Jonson, Inigo Jones was to introduce many features of the
modern stage, including perspective scenery, a drop curtain,
sliding flats, revolves, elaborate stage lighting and transformation scenes. Anything the Medici could do, Jones could do
better. Queen Anne loosed the royal purse-strings.

His Banqueting House in Whitehall is the only theatre of the
time to survive, except of course the halls of the Inns of Court
and the royal palaces. Partnership with Ben Jonson was to

produce the new drama-form which stood at the apex of all Jacobean entertainment – the Court Masque: in the Masque, the King's Men would have a part to play, and its sumptuousness would open new worlds of art – music, poetry, spectacle in combination.

In 1604 the city was preparing its postponed grand entry for James, with triumphal arches, pageants and speeches for which a new mythology was required. The Tudor roses would serve no longer. New coins were inscribed: 'Henry united the roses, James the kingdoms.' The favoured myth was that of Troy Restored or New Troy. The ancient kingdom, founded by the grandson of Aeneas, was reborn, and the evils of a divided state replaced by a united Great Britain. Two late enemies, Jonson and Dekker, shared the honours; Dekker used the Trojan legend in his first arch; the Four Kingdoms (including France) were on the last. The green and flourishing commonwealth was represented as a happy garden, and the triumph of virtues over vices were dramatic motifs that were to be seen on the stage.

Shakespeare remained absolutely silent. He did not mourn Elizabeth; he did not join the pageantry to greet James. He presumably walked in the procession, with the other royal servants, under the seven arches. What with the speeches (Alleyn on an arch representing the Genius of the City, a boy chorister from St Paul's, hordes of gods, goddesses, virtues, Fame, Fortune, ancient kings and priests), it took from eleven o'clock till five to get from the Tower to Westminster on that March day of 1604, a twelve-month after the old Queen's death.

Shakespeare was just on forty. Ten years earlier, he had thought it old age 'When forty winters shall besiege thy brow ...' (Sonnet 2). At the turn of the century he had twice turned back to the ancient world, in the popular *Julius Caesar*, an early success at The Globe, and in *Troilus and Cressida*, caviare to the general, where he had ironically refashioned Chaucer's tenderest love story. He was experimenting.

In 1603 along had come Ben Jonson with a Roman tragedy on which he had sweated blood – a learned work, taken out of Tacitus, sharp and ruthless in its dissection of a corrupt state. This was something worthy the King's players, he told them – no absurdities like 'Caesar did never wrong but with just cause.' The company, hoping indeed to show their new status, had briefly put it on – and found themselves hissed off the stage of The Globe! They! The King's players! Their poet was charged with blasphemy and popery too. Jonson had looked for the writing of the masque at Christmas in which Queen Anne was to appear, but it had gone to the Herberts' nominee – of course. Samuel Daniel, brother-in-law of Florio, 'a good honest man but no poet' as Ben Jonson said bitterly, was in charge of the Children of the Queen's Revels too, a little later.

In December 1604 in *Gowry*, the King's Men staged the story of two young men alleged to have tried to kidnap King James and who had met a speedy end by the sword. The Privy Council again objected to shows of living royalty; *Gowry* was withdrawn.

Clearly this kind of history was not going to fit the times; Shakespeare, who was expected to write plays about love, struggled with the remaking of old forms. He drew a young nobleman, orphaned, handsome, courageous, winning, an inveterate liar, and gave him as companion an even shabbier liar as follower, named Parolles. The debased versions of Hal and Falstaff were placed in a comedy ironically titled *All's Well that Ends Well*. In a much more powerful treatment of love misplaced, adapted from a twenty-five-year-old play for Court performance in December 1604, the superior godlike discernment of a just prince ostensibly provides strict *Measure for Measure*; but in spite of the reassuring justice of the title, there are many disturbing questions in the clash between the Judge and the Nun (a crucial opposition, according to one critic).[2] One speech struggles to accept death, countered by another, which violently rejects it.

> Reason thus with life.
> If I do lose thee, I do lose a thing
> That none but fools would keep.
> (*Measure for Measure*, 3.1.6–7)

> Ay, but to die, and go we know not where,
> To lie in cold obstruction and to rot:
> This sensible warm motion to become
> A kneaded clod.... (3.1.119–22)

Measure for Measure is the last of Shakespeare's comedies. (The Christian reference in the title[3] did not prevent the whole play's being neatly cut out of the Folio by a Jesuit censor, for the ruler's masquerade as a friar must have seemed to him unpardonable.) We may infer from Sonnet 108 that Shakespeare said his prayers, and the one clause that reappears again and again in his plays is, 'Forgive us our trespasses, as we forgive those that trespass against us.' The whole of this drama is set in a city that especially needs such generosity, and there is no happy country beyond the moated grange – where, however, the grotesque solution is worked out that permits a 'happy' ending. The scheme of morality in this play is at every point contradicted – by the obstinate vitality of the prisoner who refuses to die, the ribald jester who refuses to be silenced, the appalling cat-and-mouse tactics that are practised on all sides.[4]

And then, suddenly, to Shakespeare balance returned. Gone was the imagery of disease and corruption, of the grave and the lazar house. Gone was the uncertain judgment. Perhaps he had gone back to the *Apology for Poetry*: 'Nature never set forth the earth in so rich tapestry as divers poets have done ... her world is brazen, the poets only deliver a golden ...' for at the start of the Christmas season, Hallowmas, 1604, his players put on for the King 'Hallamas Day, being the first of November, a Play in the Banqueting House at White Hall called The Moor of Venice.'

Golden it is – like the flawless jewel to which Othello compared Desdemona:

> ... another world
> Of one entire and perfect chrysolite.
>
> (5.2.146–7)

The play is complete, rounded, simple; no subplots, no metaphysical questions. Some critics have since thought the less of it for that – Bradley missed 'that element in Shakespeare which unites him with the mystic poets and the great philosophers', but Shakespeare had reached a point of mastery where his power excluded the obvious. Meditations on heaven and hell were now so fully expected in any tragedy – and in every masque – that it was a feat of strength to keep them out; he found himself presenting a story which was tragedy not of state but of two individuals in the only great power of Europe that rejected monarchy – the Republic of Venice. To frame their tale, Shakespeare too had taken all the old stage conventions and turned them upside down. It was an infallible rule of the stage that any character who was black was bound to belong to 'the left hand side'. If not the devil, he or she would be the devil's near relation. Folk plays with black men in them were known in the countryside. Atrocity plays with black men in them had provided a stereotype upon which Shakespeare had drawn for Aaron in *Titus Andronicus* ('Seeing your face, we thought of hell'). This play opens with the yell of Iago,

> Look to your house, your daughter and your bags...
> Even now, now, very now, an old black ram
> Is tupping your white ewe ...
> The devil will make a grandsire of you.
>
> (1.1.81–92)

Iago is the only mystery in this play, and Othello's final question goes unanswered:

> Will you, I pray, demand that demi-devil
> Why he hath thus ensnar'd my soul and body?
>
> (5.2.304–5)

for to Iago have been transferred all the qualities normally associated with black men on the English stage. His artistic joy in destruction for its own sake makes him equate the night of plotting which ruins Cassio with Othello's nuptials. 'Pleasure and action make the hours seem short,' he says.

The characters of Iago and Othello are so opposed, yet so inextricably bound together by the action, that they have been seen as the two halves of a single being. 'I am your own for ever,' says Iago, as they swear vengeance and Othello blows his fond love towards heaven. After Falstaff and Hamlet, they are the most discussed personages of Shakespeare's stage. Burbage played Othello; later leading men have sometimes preferred Iago. W. H. Auden found him the more interesting, pointing out that everything he set out to accomplish, he achieved, including his own self-destruction. Iago is the completely free man – 'our bodies are our gardens, to the which our wills are gardeners,' he says, and it is the business of the will to curb love – or lust, which amounts to the same thing. This cold permission is contradicted by Othello because the function of reason itself is destroyed when he loses faith in Desdemona. In the scene where he pretends to be visiting a brothel, he claims not to know her:

> I cry you mercy, then.
> I took you for that cunning whore of Venice
> That married with Othello.
>
> (4.2.89–91)

In his imagination her image is turned black (3.3.391), yet his sense aches at the 'weed who art so lovely fair' (4.2.67–9). Othello's desperation is such that at the end he in turn becomes almost unrecognizable, to the Venetians, to himself. 'That's he which was Othello,' he says. It is a new concept of character. Here, the relationships which create identity have been freely chosen. Othello has elected to serve; he and Desdemona have elected to marry in defiance of custom, so that they have become utterly dependent on each other. They live in an enclosed 'universe of two', and the price of their free choice is vulnerability.

All this was left very largely to Burbage to depict. Jealousy had hitherto been a feeling to be laughed at; the comic jealous man, whose 'chattel' showed an unexpected independence, was a social jest. Shakespeare had depicted one such in *The Merry Wives of Windsor*. Burbage as 'the grieved Moor' would be the most prominent figure on the stage; his make-up would enhance every movement, and the painful scenes of his frenzy become the more painful because at any moment the right question, the right answer, might restore what is destroyed. The brothel scene comes very near to the truth; but Desdemona does not press her challenge, 'To whom, my lord? With whom? How am I false?' (4.2.40). Her last 'lie', that she had killed herself, implicitly affirms that they are still one flesh, something Othello cannot bear to hear:

> She's like a liar gone to burning hell:
> Twas I that kill'd her.
>
> (5.2.132–3)

His retraction when he learns the truth is complete and total; he acts as his own executioner and by this gains the right to kiss his wife in death. Otherwise nothing is left of their 'downright violence and storm of Fortune'.

Shakespeare had always been acknowledged as the poet of love; here, after ten years, the sex nausea of the sonnets to the dark wanton is heard in Iago's voice, and the pangs of betrayal in Othello's:

> Lilies that fester smell far worse than weeds.
> (Sonnet 94, 14)

> For I have sworn thee fair, and thought thee bright,
> Who art as black as hell, as dark as night.
> (Sonnet 147, 13–14)

Of course the situation is turned inside out; the triangle of love and friendship is changed, but in this play, in its ease and its sheer power to penetrate, 'expert beyond experience', Shakespeare had transmuted material that he had been carrying about within himself and had once before shaped into poetry – under another form.

He had anticipated with his Noble Moor an astonishing transformation which the Court was to see on Twelfth Night. The Queen had invited Ben Jonson to write the words of a masque in which she wished to appear with eleven of her ladies, all to be disguised as blackamoors. Anne took this fancy to appear before her husband, her brother, the Duke of Holstein, and the Spanish and Venetian Ambassadors. It cost over £3,000, and was modelled by Inigo Jones upon a masque of the Medici. Each of the ladies wore jewels worth thousands of pounds. But that a queen of England should cover herself with black paint was considered very indecorous and shocking. Anne had, the previous year, appeared as a goddess, Pallas Athene, wearing the spoils of Elizabeth's wardrobe. On this second occasion, she and her ladies sat in a huge sea-shell, which was drawn forward by fishes, on which two speakers rode to present them. The theme was that twelve 'Daughters of the Niger' had floated hither in search of a clime that would bleach their skins; and the magic isle of Britannia was, of course, their destination.

The riders on the fishes could have been Shakespeare and Burbage.

The Court masque was a ritual of magnificance, intended to assert the glory of the monarch, the happiness of his kingdom, the harmony of his rule within the course of the heavenly spheres; when the masquers joined the audience for the Revels (all-night dancing), they should all be 'rapt' out of this world, 'amazed', transported. Elizabethan masques had often dramatized conflict and presented divided selves – the Queen as Woman and as Majesty. James, who had published his first poems at eighteen, was himself the author of a wedding masque, written in Scotland for the Marquis of Huntley. Now, entirely godlike, he sat to receive homage – and to foot the bill. Once, in order to impress the ambassadors, he was given a jewel of great value which he had actually purchased himself!

Blackness was praised as the most perfect beauty – because the hue never alters, even in death:

> ... how near divinity they be
> That stand from passion or decay so free.

The Queen appeared as Euphoris or Abundance (she was rather advanced in pregnancy), but she selected for the first dance the Spanish Ambassador, who gallantly kissed her black-painted hand.

All would have needed rehearsing, producing, together with three speaking parts – Niger, Oceanus and the Moon – for which duties the King's Men were available. The next night they themselves put on *Henry V* by 'Shaxberd'; while Ben Jonson, annotating his masque with all the classical footnotes he thought it deserved, was hinting at a sequel for next Christmas.

This festival turned out to need a wedding masque, and Jonson made use of the image of the King's marriage to his kingdom to enlarge the myth of Hymen beyond a personal application. In his notes he dilated pedantically on Roman marriage customs. Thenceforward, Jonson and Inigo Jones regularly made their Christmas offering, with the royal musicians and the King's Men also taking part, the musicians to sing and the Men to recite, for the royal and noble participants were confined to appearing in costumes whose splendour beggared description, and to dance. This ritual, of course, was witnessed only by the most favoured, but the players gave their humble contribution to the display of satin and gold lace, the ropes of 'choice and orient pearl'. The notion of complete harmony in a new and ideal world was turned to stage use; in his imagination Shakespeare produced 'the one entire and perfect chrysolite'.

He was never asked to write a Court masque, either by James or by anyone else. He was one of the King's servants, and Jonson was not; but his place was in the public theatre. The omission may not have been intended as a slight; yet undoubtedly Jonson, among his friends, gloried in the *réclame*; but then he committed the indiscretion of speaking with his other voice – the satiric one. At Court he was silken, bland; in the theatre, he mercilessly satirized upstart courtiers. The climax came when a Scots voice was heard in a play declaring of the most contemptible of these, 'Ah ken the man weel; he's ane of ma thirty-pund knights.' For *Eastward Ho!* (produced early in 1605) Jonson went to jail and wrote his shamefaced confession that this was about 'a play' (see above, p. 139). He was free by October and in less than a month called on to assist the government in the investigations following the discovery of the Gunpowder Plot of 5 November that year.

Today, when terrorist violence is familiar and a threat to government, it is possible to feel what the country felt on learning that the entire government was to have been assassinated at the opening of Parliament, a puppet state under the child Princess Elizabeth proclaimed, and a Catholic régime set up, with the 'bye-plot' of an invading force from the Low Countries. In this last part, the Spanish Embassy was clearly implicated.

The small 'cell' that contrived the main plot was confined to Shakespeare's Catholic neighbours, Warwickshire gentry led by Robert Catesby, whose father had held land in Stratford, in Shottery, Bishopton and Old Stratford. Like most of the others, Catesby had been involved in the Essex Rising. His cousins, the Treshams, Winters, Throckmortons, all came from the neighbourhood; John Grant, another of the inner 'cell', held land in Snitterfield where Shakespeare's cousin still farmed on his grandfather's acres. Princess Elizabeth had lived near.

They hired Clopton Hall as their headquarters, under

pretence of hunting-parties. (Shakespeare's New Place had, of course, been Clopton's property once.)

In London the conspirators met at Catesby's lodging in the Strand, but also at the Mermaid Tavern. Early in October a supper-party there included Catesby, Lord Mordant, a Percy, younger brother of the Earl of Northumberland, Francis Tresham, Thomas Winter, John Ashfield – and Ben Jonson, who was celebrating his release from jail. Catesby, Tresham and Winter were among the inner group. Anyone connected with the Court could have given them valuable news about movements (though Ben Jonson was never suspected of complicity). How Francis Tresham betrayed the 'cell' by a warning letter to his brother-in-law to stay away from Parliament; how the conspiracy fled to the country Shakespeare knew best, where at Holbeach in Worcestershire, Catesby and Percy died fighting – is all a familiar tale. Winter and Tresham and Percy's follower, Guy Fawkes – who had been found in the cellar of the House of Lords – were duly given traitors' deaths. It was found that thirty-six barrels of explosive had been laid in the cellar under piles of wood, for it had been hired 'to store fuel'.

A round-up of Catholics followed. The shock of this to the one member of the King's Men who was also a Warwickshire man must have been the most severe, the impact of these local events far stronger than the local memories attached to Bosworth Field.[5] He might well have known the conspirators (including some who escaped the net). He certainly knew many of the intended victims – among whom, of course, was Southampton.

Shakespeare had just been walking in the coronation procession as one of the King's Men. He had just acquired, with the church tithes of Stratford, the right to be buried, like a gentleman, in the chancel of the parish church. He was possibly hoping that his daughters would marry into the local squirearchy from which the conspirators were drawn.[6]

Again the fair day and the foul day rushed together in his mind to make a new world of darkness. The world he found, Shakespeare once more transformed. The result was *Macbeth*. In many ways, the ingredients are not unfamiliar, but in one respect they are quite new. The Witches are quite unlike anything that had been seen on the stage before. Shakespeare's power to create beings not of this earth – his fairies, his witches, the creatures of Prospero's island – startled and enchanted the audience. This ability to make such characters convincing and powerful contrasts with the flat presentation of gods, goddesses, fantastics, in the masque. Their powerful identities are realized with an exact, particular embodiment, yet they remain mysterious, evocative, hypnotically attractive or horrifying.

Macbeth is an intensely concentrated play, the shortest of the tragedies; like *Othello*, it has no subplots or side issues. The poetry is densely woven with powerful images; the two leading figures stand out from the society that they dominate and destroy. There used to be a theory that it is a cut-down version of a longer play; but a deep, narrow shaft seems here to be sunk into total darkness; and terror requires brevity, which carries enormous powers of suggestion:

> Light thickens, and the crow
> Makes wing to the rooky wood ...
> (3.2.50–51)

> Hell is murky. . . .
> (5.1.36)

Darkness and blood in clammy folds fasten themselves, not to be shaken off.

> Now does he feel
> His secret murders sticking on his hands.
> (5.2.16)

The old tragedy of blood had shown the horrors of hell as the end of a life's journeying:

> A darksome place and dangerous to pass ...
> Within a hugy dale of lasting night,
> That kindled with the world's iniquities
> Doth cast up filthy and detested fumes.
> (*The Spanish Tragedy*, 3.11.64 ff)

But here there is deep uncertainty and a darkness of the mind.

The journey lies within. The Witches, who open the play, establish a kind of certainty in uncertainty:

> Fair *is* foul, and foul *is* fair,
> Hover through the fog and filthy air.
>
> (1.1.10–11)

is to be echoed at once by Macbeth, 'So fair and foul a day I have not seen ...' (1.3.38). The hags' riddling prophecies slip and slither about in Macbeth's speech. But he knows 'we still have judgment here', and the image of the most august Judgment of all comes when Macduff, discovering the murdered King, calls the sleepers of the house to rise

> and see
> The great doom's image.
>
> (2.3.75–6)

Macbeth has imagined already, 'Pity, like a naked new born babe, striding the blast', or

> Heaven's cherubim, hors'd
> Upon the sightless couriers of the air. ...
>
> (1.7.22–3)

proclaiming his crime. The image of the last Judgment, which had been painted over the chancel arch of the Guild Chapel beside Shakespeare's Stratford home, had depicted this scene, and angels with their uplifted trumpets summon the dead to rise. By his treacherous murder of his king and guest, Macbeth has put himself outside the circle of human faith and fealty; his coronation banquet is attended by one vassal whom he had bound to come ('Fail not our feast,' he says to Banquo) but whom he did not expect to see.[7] Judgment is not delivered but invoked. It comes from within. Playwrights were very ready to give judgment; in the one play where he did so, Shakespeare effectively debars the merely legal aspects: 'Your brother is a forfeit of the law', is the Judge's reply to the Nun, who quickly counters,

Why, all the souls that were forfeit once;
And He that might the vantage best have took
Found out the remedy. How would you be
If He, which is the top of judgment, should
But judge you as you are?
                    (*Measure for Measure*, 2.2.73–7)

Macbeth judges himself. The condemnation comes from within
– not in the enemies' disposal of 'this dead butcher' but in

Tomorrow, and tomorrow, and tomorrow,
Creeps in this petty pace from day to day
To the last syllable of recorded time,
And all our yesterdays have lighted fools
The way to dusty death. Out, out, brief candle!
                    (*Macbeth*, 5.5.19–23)

The slow rhythms of melancholia leave the paralysed mind
clear: 'myself am hell',

Life's but a walking shadow, a poor player,
That struts and frets his hour upon the stage
And then is heard no more . . .
                    (5.5.24–6)

The role has come home to the speaker indeed: 'His Majesty's
Poor Players' was the form of petition for justice; a 'shadow'
was a minor actor, or an actor who visibly personified someone
else (as the deposed Lear was to be termed 'Lear's shadow').
Identification with the actors ends in meaningless noise, 'signi-
fying nothing'. Macbeth had been obsessed by his future of
'sovereign sway' and lifted himself out of Time by his act. Left
in a meaningless tedium, a lifeless progression, he now has
neither a vital past nor a hopeful future, only a journey to no
end. 'We still have judgment here,' he had known before the
murder, but he did not know the internal form that judgment
would take. 'What's done is done,' says Lady Macbeth but
later – 'What's done cannot be undone.'
   It is 'Pity like a naked new-born babe' that accompanies
heaven's cherubim horsed upon the sightless couriers of the air.

This is the figure of Christ as He entered time to 'find the remedy', and as He was depicted in the great vision of the martyred Jesuit Southwell, continually returning to Judgment. It is typical of the fusions of the play, and of the power required to make them, that *The Burning Babe*[8] should be reflected even in the inverted imagery of the Witches (who have the same kind of symbiosis with Macbeth that Iago has with Othello). Southwell's family was connected by marriage with the Earl of Southampton, and a distant blood relationship between Southwell and Shakespeare himself has been established through the family of Belknap. They could have been considered cousins.[9] Southwell embodies that pity which for Macbeth becomes the Accuser.

> As I in hoary winter's night stood shivering in the snow,
> Surprised I was with sudden heat which made my heart to glow,
> And lifting up a fearful eye to view what sight was near,
> A pretty Babe all burning bright did in the air appear . . .
> 'The fuel Justice layeth on, and Mercy blows the coals,
> The Metal in this furnace wrought are men's defiled souls.'

But after Duncan's murder we have learned through the drunken porter where we are; the castle of *Macbeth* has become Hell's Castle. And here we find him letting in that other famous Jesuit, Father Garnet, 'an equivocator that could swear in both the scales against either scale; who committed treason enough for God's sake, yet could not equivocate to heaven' (2.3.9–12) – hanged for his complicity in the Gunpowder Plot.

Finally the Porter sees something that chills and sobers him – we do not know what it is. 'What are you?' he asks the air. 'This place is too cold for hell.' Hell's Castle had been one of the most familiar properties of the old stage; Shakespeare is reviving these folk memories, with the old imagery of death and judgment, though not to make any doctrinal points, for James, an expert theologian, would not have tolerated it.

The King considered the discovery to have miraculous elements, not the least being his own interpretation of the letter of warning, which – a little improving the occasion – he considered the sole means of revealing what had actually been done by the plotters, in that cellar under the House of Lords which had so readily been hired out to one of them 'for storing fuel'. Besides, being himself a writer, James had soon published a *Discourse on the Powder-Treason*, and had his speech from the throne also printed.

The play was clearly directed to the King. Apart from glorifying his ancestors Banquo and Fleance – both imaginary – and showing the procession of Scottish kings, the demonology was bound to interest James, who had written a treatise on the subject. Though himself reputedly the victim in his youth of the plottings of the Witches of Berwick, he became increasingly sceptical. The holy and healing gifts of Edward the Confessor were his by descent. The canny testing of Macduff by Malcolm (4.3) fits in with James's stratagems and secret tests of his friends (a quality also shown in the Duke of *Measure for Measure*).

Macbeth registers a shock, for it uncovers the deepest centres of Shakespeare's art. This is not a political play – Shakespeare was now leaving that to Jonson and Chapman – but a drama of heaven and hell meeting on earth. 'The crisis ... is in a sense the only interior crisis worth talking about. It is that in which every nerve of the body, every consciousness of the mind, shrieks that something cannot be. Only it is....'[10] 'My fellow-countrymen cannot have planned to murder my king, my patron and my friends. But they have.' The Witches were the most spectacular part of the play and were later given some additional scenes, which included, possibly, some flying effects, inverting the familiar pattern that Hell is under the stage.

There were attempts to borrow the Witches,[11] but no one could really approach *Macbeth*, and, unlike *Hamlet*, it fathered no progeny.

10 The kingdom of fools

In *Macbeth* the deep and narrow torrent of action carried responses swiftly along; for one critic, the key lines speak of 'outrunning the pauser, reason'. *King Lear*, vast and, in its complex double-action of Lear's three daughters and Gloucester with his two sons, eddying, is blocked with uncertainty. The sequence of these two tragedies seems to me a matter of psychological fitness. In *Macbeth* the 'night's predominance' transmutes deep shock into art, which grows more diffused, though not less powerful, in *King Lear*. Both are plays that belong to the playhouse, but also to the reader in his lonely tower, as Yeats recorded:

> We think of *King Lear* less as the history of one man than as the history of a whole evil time. Lear's shadow is Gloucester ... and the mind goes on imagining other shadows, shadow beyond shadow, till it has pictured a whole world [as] a shadow upon the wall, upon one's body in the firelight.
>
> ('Emotion of Multitude', *Essays and Introduction*, p. 215)

The double image of plot and subplot came partly from an old comedy melodrama which had been reprinted in May 1605. King Leir and his three daughters belong to the world of the ballads, where Cinderella and the Ugly Sisters follow out a pattern set during the opening scene; after which, true love in disguise, murderer and victim, faithful and false servant, move to a conclusion where virtue triumphs, all the good live happily, all the bad melt away. To this, Shakespeare joins Gloucester's story taken from that elegant repository of noble artifice, Sidney's *Arcadia*: the eye that picked them out was a keen one. To turn fairytale into lyric tragedy, he added the Fool and

Edgar the Bedlam, so forming what is, above all others, the tragedy for our time. There is no doubt that, as *Hamlet* dominates the nineteenth century, *King Lear* dominates the present age.[1] In theme, in identification, it speaks to our condition. As one critic has said, it is in part about the end of the world, and we know an image of that horror. Shakespeare simply takes all standards of order and justice and removes them. The turmoil is like the 'last days' of *Revelations*. We meet again an image of Doomsday, as it has been met in *Macbeth*, but there is no such certitude that Justice will bring the guilty to punishment. Awe predominates.

KENT Is this the promis'd end?
EDGAR Or image of that horror?
ALBANY Fall and cease!

(5.3.263-5)

'The gods reward your kindness,' says Kent to Gloucester, and although we do not know that he is to be blinded by his guests, we know that something horrible awaits him in the hell-castle of his home. 'The gods defend her!' is the cue for Lear to enter with Cordelia dead in his arms. And death is final.

All things come alike to all: and the same condition is to the just and to the wicked, to the good and to the pure, and to the polluted.... There is evil among all that is done under the sun, ... there is one condition to all, and also the heart of the sons of men is full of evil, and madness is in their hearts while they live, and after that, they go to the dead.... The living know that they shall die, but the dead know nothing at all; neither have they any more a reward; for their remembrance is forgotten.

(*Ecclesiastes* 9.2-5)

King Lear offers a vision of extreme dereliction, of man at the very extremity of his being; the dereliction is complete, but judgment remains remarkably clear. No one has ever disputed that it is better to be Lear in his madness, or Gloucester, or Kent or Edgar or Cordelia, than be Goneril or Regan or Cornwall or Edmund. Not *that* they die, but *how* they die, matters. The characters can be divided almost wholly into the good and the bad. It is not a play that even needs to say 'Choose'. But neither does it afford any consolation.

The iron rations of this country, where 'Virtue's steely bones look bleak in the cold wind', are provided by the stoical texts of *Ecclesiastes* or *Job*. *Macbeth* is a Christian play; *King Lear* is set in pagan times – 'what time Joas ruled in Judah' – and Shakespeare has totally abstracted the Christian hope, though he has left the Christian ethic. Every doctrinal expectation is contradicted. Yet this is a most religious play, in the sense that it deals with ultimate suffering and finds no answer to the mystery of evil. But the solution to the problem of justice is seen in the vanishing of this problem.

Justice reasons the need; justice deals in the superficies of things. There was, of course, an acceptable answer to Jacobeans: the stoic doctrine of endurance. This is heard from time to time:

> Men must endure
> Their going hence, even as their coming hither:
> Ripeness is all.
>
> (5.2.9–11)

an echo from Edgar of what Lear tells blind Gloucester:

> Thou must be patient; we came crying hither . . .
> When we are born, we cry that we are come
> To this great stage of fools.
>
> (4.6.179–84)

'The great stage of fools' where the 'poor player' struts and frets is shown us in the central scenes upon the heath, where time stands still, action is suspended, and we pass with the uncrowned and dispossessed Lear to a new kingdom, not of this world, his kingdom of fools and bedlam beggars.

For there is in Shakespeare a fierce energy of living that cannot accommodate to the passive stoicism of some Jacobean tragic heroes – Chapman's, for instance. This energy explodes in the scenes on the heath where ordinary action stops; in the 'fable', as distinct from the 'story', the perturbations of nature and the madness of Lear are in disharmony together (a commonplace that Shakespeare had used from *Richard II* onwards. It is specially prominent in *Macbeth*). In the timeless kingdom where madman and king and fool rule, the magic surrounding fools, and the devil's voice on the madman's lips, reinforce the curses of the old King. These three divide sovereignty between them, sit in judgment together, acting out of mystic participation rather than any consciousness of each other as persons.

The relation of Hamlet with his Ghost, of Macbeth with the Witches, leads up to the relation of Lear with the fool and the bedlam beggar. The hero is in each case symbiotically attracted to figures that are partly human but partly belong to another world. The king and his fool had been traditionally joined from early times; ancient kings had a fool beside them to keep down their pride, avert ill-luck, by mockery of greatness, by providing a 'double'.² In Greene's *Friar Bacon and Friar Bungay*, the fool Ralph Simnel accompanies the Prince of Wales, changing clothes and roles, to act the Prince's part while he goes wooing. Chapman has a character speak of sitting 'like a king in an old fashioned play; having his wife, his counsel, his children and his fool about him' (*A Humourous Day's Mirth*, 1599, 1.i). Hamlet is his own fool, for Yorick is dead.

The fool is a magic, even a sinister figure; the medieval Ship of Fools, which was part of carnival at Christmas, came from beyond the known world. Marston, who also made his princes disguise as fools, says:

> Note but a fool's beatitude,
> He is not capable of passion,
> Blow east, blow west, he steers his course alike. . . .

Being outside the ordinary social order, the joker in the pack, the fool is invulnerable; therefore he is permitted licence to say what he will; and, as one who has known the worst, he gains insights peculiar to a broken and separated mind. 'He's resolute who can no lower sink,' says Marston's disguised Malevole, anticipating Edgar (*King Lear*, 4.1.1–9). Lear's Fool belongs to the older world of Folly, while Edgar, in his 'sullen and assumed humour of Tom of Bedlam' (as the Quarto terms it), is nearer to Marston and also to those false 'possessed' madmen of whom, as we shall see, Shakespeare had recently been made most painfully conscious.

At the height of the *sottie*, or congregation of fools' wisdom, Lear, when asked by his fool if a madman be a gentleman or a yeoman, had replied, 'A king, a king!' (3.6.11).

As the king's double or shadow, the fool is kept near him only because he is potentially so dangerous; for, says Willeford, 'with one word, one laugh, pitched to the exact pitch, he could destroy the kingdom as a singer will destroy a wineglass'.

In the 'trial', when Lear appears as both judge and witness for the prosecution ('I here take my oath before this honourable assembly, she kicked the poor king, her father'), the fool's obscenity marks the height of mock ritual: 'Cry you mercy, I took you for a joint stool' (3.6.46–51) – a folk jest meaning 'kiss my arse'.

Gloucester's desperate leap from Dover Cliff is in one way like a clown's trick (they are always trying to kill themselves, like Papageno in *The Magic Flute* or Beckett's clowns in *Waiting for Godot*), after which he too becomes a courtier at the Court of Lear as the mad King of Summer, crowned with weeds; in a wild mixture of the sacred power to absolve sin, and total licence of midsummer revelry, he pardons Gloucester's adultery (4.6.110–16). In this scene Lear becomes by turn a soldier, a judge and a violent sexual cynic in language that recalls, as we shall see, the language of the church.

Although the exorcism of his madness is accomplished by Cordelia and by the power of music, Lear never really returns to the world of time and space. When he recovers, Cordelia becomes his whole world; he lives in a kingdom that she by her presence creates. The play itself moves from the archaic land of the opening scenes through the timeless centre to a medieval world of knights in armour; but after Cordelia has perished on the prison straw, Lear can no longer say words to anyone. It is idle to ask what is 'this' he points to at the end, on the Threshold.

> Do you see this? Look on her. Look, her lips.
> Look there, look there.

> (5.3.310–11)

He is in death's dream kingdom, talking to himself or to her.

The end of the action, a ritual trial by combat, with formal speeches of challenge, reply, verdict, award, matches the opening scene of Lear's love-challenge, reply, comment and award.

The Kingdom of Fools is a kingdom of misrule, an alternative state, where in the songs of the fool Lear is presented as a beaten child, his daughters his mothers. Playing bo-peep, he retains only the royal title of fool – 'that thou wast born with'. Goneril endorses the fool's wit, 'Old fools are babes again,' even before the fool has appeared. The centre of the play maintains and examines this paradox, as at the end another famous paradox, 'That it is more healthful and profitable to be in prison than at liberty', is part of Lear's new-found world. In *The Defence of Contraries* (1593), where this is found, there is also a paradox sustained both by Edmund and by the mad King, 'that the Bastard is more to be esteemed, than the lawfully begotten or legitimate'.

> Let copulation thrive; for Gloucester's bastard son
> Was kinder to his father than my daughters
> Got 'tween the lawful sheets.
>
> (4.6.114–16)

In Shakespeare's tragedy, where the depth of feeling escapes from words, what can be discerned is never more than the tip of the iceberg: paradoxes become inevitable. 'Is it then an accident that Lear's incoherence should convey his insight and Kent's rudeness his nobility, Cordelia's chilly plainness her devotion, Gloucester's courtliness his dereliction?'[3] Hidden at the centre of the play, an unseen multitude of obscene and evil things contribute to its wild chaos. In his 'codpiece' song, the fool claims that every beggar carries with him an army of lice ('Beggars marry many'); the madman is possessed by legions of devils: 'Five fiends have been in poor Tom at once: of lust as Obidicut; Hobbididence prince of dumbness; Mahu, of stealing; Modo, of murder; Flibbertigibbet, of mopping and mowing, who since possesses chambermaids and waiting-women' (4.1.55 ff). It is well known to scholars that these names come from a treatise by Samuel Harsnett, chaplain to the Bishop of London and future Archbishop of York: *A Declaration of Egregious Popish Impostures ... practised by Edmunds alias Weston, a*

Jesuit.[4] What has not been observed is that the brutal jeers and savage obscenities of this most unchristian work combine insults to Papists with insults to players, and that being first issued in 1603 and immediately reissued to anticipate the drive against priests in general and Jesuits in particular that followed the Gunpowder Plot, it was calculated to hit Shakespeare particularly hard at a particularly sensitive moment. I think the origins of *King Lear* are to be found in a collision between the smug pieties and exaggerated poetic justice of the old play (*King Leir*), and the vindictive game which Samuel Harsnett plays in his mocking pamphlet. The 'popish impostures' were cases of pretended possession by devils and of their exorcism, which links with the whole character of Edgar and the scene at Dover Cliff in particular, where the 'devil' is exorcized.

As chaplain to the Bishop of London and therefore in charge of licensing books for the press on the Bishop's behalf, Harsnett would be known to the players.[5] From all accounts a violent though an able man, he had once been accused himself of popery. He had been born a baker's son at Colchester, had entered King's College, Cambridge, as a poor student (or 'sizar'), and rose in time to succeed Lancelot Andrewes as Master of Pembroke College.

In his book Harsnett tells of an incident nearly twenty years old, when Edmunds (or Weston), Superior of the Jesuits, exorcized a group of young people who appeared to be possessed by devils. Among the assistants was a seminary priest, Robert Dibdale,[6] who had been Shakespeare's schoolfellow at Stratford Grammar School. By obtaining converts they hoped to raise funds for the Babington Plot against the Queen. One of the possessed was servant to Anthony Babington, the ringleader; others were young servant girls and a youth of good family who had been backsliding. The confessions in court of four of the possessed, and one assistant priest, if accepted, constituted a sharp exposure of an unscrupulous game. The three girls (aged fifteen to sixteen) were given nauseous potions, censed with fumigations which in the words of the youth were 'enough to make a horse mad', tied in a chair and tortured. They were Protestants by birth, put out to service in Catholic households.

Harsnett describes the rites under the metaphor of a play, with the priests as tragedians, combining conjuring with rehearsed 'lines' taught to the 'victims', and he claims to have taken the details from a Latin book put out by the Jesuits.

Earlier Harsnett had exposed a Puritan, John Darrell, who in 1597 had claimed to exorcize a boy in Nottingham. Darrell graduated from Queens' College, Cambridge, a seat of witch-hunters and witch lore; Shakespeare's son-in-law, John Hall, was also a graduate of Queens', and as a physician might be expected to take some interest in diseases of the mind.

In exposing false rituals, false vestments, false relics, Harsnett presents a paradoxical double-image – true and false devils. For Harsnett, the devil is not present and physically speaking through the mouths of the youths and girls; yet in the evil of devising such horrid rites he is in fact at work in the exorcist and speaks with *his* voice, as well as in the words he has trained his victim-assistants to say. The devil may claim Queen Elizabeth as his 'darling' and, when asked of the Queen of Heaven, say 'We have another Queen', thus as a (Catholic) devil speaking (Protestant) treason. But he will also witness to the Immaculate Conception ('I had never a bit in her') and deny that the Catholic martyrs need to pass through Purgatory.

The attentive reader may find a third diabolical level in Harsnett's own gloating taunts, his jeers not only at simulation but at the relics of men like Campion. He is seduced by his own 'game', and his deviousness and violence give a mirror image of all he denounced; for a mind capable of divided sympathies, the issue would be an agonized question of the basis of Christendom itself, as in Donne's *Holy Sonnet*:

> Show me, dear Christ, thy spouse, so bright and clear ...
> Is she self truth, and errs?

(It is worth adding that in a few years *King Lear* was being privately played in the Catholic household of Sir Richard Cholmondeley in Yorkshire.)

Harsnett describes how the priests' troupes, acting in secret of course, 'removed bag and baggage as your wandering players used to do' (often to empty houses rented by servants) (p. 11). Like the players, they hoped to collect an audience and money, so the 'holy Tragedians' play 'a sort of Christmas game' but so absurdly that a child 'will dare to take the devil by the vizard and play with the fool's nose and cry away with the priest and the devil, they have marred a good play'. Edmunds, 'author and penner of the play', played three parts in one; sometimes the priest, sometimes the devil, sometimes the devil's prompter or Interlocutor (as the puppets have always a mimic prolocutor to tell what they mean; the young actors need prompting 'for many things falling better extempore, to grace the play withal, than that which was meditated and set down') (p. 104).

The girls were favourite subjects for the display of exorcism, and much of it was obscene. A great deal of groping in the girl's 'Park', the tying of a priest's stocking round her leg, the touching of menstrues with holy relics. Of course the constant assumption is that the girls were sexually exploited. Their parents, who tried to get them away, were driven off.

One of the girls, Sara, had a vision of the devil 'with a drum and seven motley vizards' (i.e. disguised followers). The priests, according to Harsnett, 'play at bo peep with almighty God', but when they departed, their juggling was known. They would 'hunt' the devil through various parts of the woman's body, in the language of the chase, usually confining him to the lower parts.[7] This seems to link up with the sexual nausea of Lear, 'But to the girdle do the gods inherit; Beneath is all the fiends'' (4.6.126–7). For the girdle of Edmund Campion allegedly was used to confine the chief fiend to the lower part of the woman's body, her 'hell'.

The departure of the devil ensures that he is seen in his own shape for the first time, but only by the possessed, who describes him to the rest. Some 'manifestations' may accompany his departure, which Harsnett considers the work of other accomplices.

Shakespeare took the names of Edgar's devils from the passage describing the final act of dispossession:

The first devil that was disseized was Smolkin ... in the form of a mouse [he went out from Twyford's right ear]. Hilcho ... like a flame of fire; the third was Habbididance, Sara's dancing devil who appeared to the patient like a whirlwind ... turning round in a flame of fire. Captain Filpot went his way in the likeness of a smoke, turning round, and so took his way up into the chimney. Lusty Dick (as it seems) did slip a button in one of his turns above ground, for he went out in a foul unsavory stench.[8] (Chapter 22, pp. 140–1.)

Sara had in her body a whole legion of devils, of whom Maho, the chief, was the last to leave her, by the vagina. Modu left one of the young men; these are the two that Edgar links together.

The devil may appear 'with ugly horns on his head, fire in his mouth, a cow's tail at his breech, eyes like a bason, fangs like a dog, claws like a bear, a skin like a negar and a voice roaring like a lion', for 'it is good decorum in a comedy to tell us of strange monsters within, where there be none'. Poets, to strike terror, present 'the three Eumenides sisters, the Furies or tormentors of hell, with black ugly visages, grisly with smoke, with whips of blood and fire in their hands, their arms gored with blood and a huge bunch of a thousand snakes crawling down their hair' but the exorcist 'will laugh the Eumenides off the stage' (p. 94). A remembrance of one of Shakespeare's plays seems to come when he mentions *Julius Caesar*, the Ghost proclaiming 'I am thine evil angel' (and he is 'a foul, ugly, monstrous shaped ghost'), with Brutus answering 'resolutely', 'I will meet thee at the fields of Philippi' (*Julius Caesar*, 4.3.279–84). Players' morals are insulted to castigate the wandering priests: 'It is the fashion of vagabond players, that coast from town to town with a truss and a cast of fiddles, to carry in their consort broken queans and Ganimedes as well for their night's pleasance as their day's pastime' (p. 149).

We have already seen one indirect reaction towards outrage, in the figure of Shylock. The insults, of course, were old and familiar, but their use in this particular context, and with the reflections of all the divided sympathies of 'foul' and 'fair' already explored in *Macbeth*, must have been particularly agonizing to any actor: by mocking these devilish rites as mere acting, acting itself became tainted with devilry.

The exorcist heard another voice on human lips ('I am afraid it is not William who speaks to me', the Puritan Darrell observes), and Albany similarly has his doubts of Goneril:

> Howe'er thou art a fiend,
> A woman's shape doth shield thee
> (4.2.66–7)

while the voice that replies, 'Marry, your manhood – mew!'

is almost beyond speech, like the devil in Dante who croaks meaninglessly or Edgar when he cries and crows like a cock:

> Pillicock sat on Pillicock-hill,
> Alow, alow, loo, loo!
>
> (3.4.75–6)

If this is obscene in a childish way, so were many of the witches' charms.[9]

Harsnett was exploiting every device to humiliate his opponents, for ends which were basically political. His allegations of bawdyness mixed with sacramental rites, and the use of actors and priests to blacken one another, all in the name of religion, provided raw material for the central scenes of *King Lear*, more especially when juxtaposed with the docile pieties of the old play on *King Leir* which was reprinted in 1605. It was the coming together of these incompatible works in the bewilderment of the divided mind that the writing of *Macbeth* evinced, which gave Shakespeare the extremes of 'the whole evil time' in *King Lear*, its union of opposites. It is these two polarized emotional starting-points rather than the conventional ones usually mentioned that I would think illuminative of the play. They do not give us the story but they give the power drive, which injected the madness of possession into a history that was a model of reassuring providential acts. Traces of Harsnett linger as late as *Pericles* (4.6.118) and *The Tempest* (2.2.5–12).

The old play is most perversely treated by Shakespeare. He took from it the opening ritual and the basis for the reconciliation of Lear and Cordelia, but elsewhere he takes so much out, puts so much in, and alters what is left so drastically that he explodes the strong, conventional, predictable melodrama.

It is a well-made old play. Leir has buried his wife and wants to betake himself to a life of prayer: the mood is very pious, the name of God being frequently invoked. Cordelia is much less brusque, even uses endearment to her father; having been disinherited, by a plot of her two sisters, she betakes herself to the life of a sempstress. Lear, a pattern of patience, instead of cursing Goneril with sterility, excuses her strong language to him:

> Alas, poor soul, she breeds young bones,
> And that it is makes her so techy, sure . . .

only to have this taken as an insult by the newly-wedded Duchess:

> What, breeds young bones already? You will make
> An honest woman of me then belike!
> O vile old wretch, who ever heard the like?
> That seeketh his own daughter to defame.

The King of France, who has crossed to England in the disguise of a pilgrim, woos Cordelia, accompanied by a merry and slightly bawdy lord; Lear is saved from death at the hands of Regan's messenger by the intervention of heavenly thunder, crosses to France and is reunited with Cordelia, the King and the merry lord, who are having a picnic (in disguise) on the coast of Normandy. All, of course, ends happily, with some comic English watchmen failing to see the French invasion because they are too drunk.

This exercise eschews madness or mystery; never a man's thought kept the highway better than the author's. The structure is efficient at its own level and far too neat to be Greene's or Peele's – Leir is a sort of male Patient Griselda.

The very triviality of *King Leir* offers a vehicle for the molten feelings of bewilderment, confusion and rage that it carried for Shakespeare – the curses and obscenities that belong to the storm, the bound figure tortured in a chair, and, underlying all, echoes of *The Book of Job*:

> Canst thou lift up thy voice to the clouds, that the abundance of waters may cover thee? Canst thou send the lightnings that they may walk, and say, lo here we are?
>
> (38.34–5)

> Better is a poor and a wise child than an old and foolish king, which will no more be admonished.
>
> (*Eccles.* 4.13)

is more in the spirit of moralizing that informs the old play.

When Cordelia offers her pledge to her father in Shakespeare's opening scene, she uses the words of the marriage service; she will 'love, honour and obey' – but the men between whom she is to choose are waiting, and indirectly the words convey a pledge to one of them, with a rebuke to Lear. Goneril and Regan's 'court holy water' of flattery is no more excessive than language that was frequently addressed to King James; but Shakespeare had not joined in the chorus of public adulation on James's accession.

The deep distrust of words, which remains after their utmost eloquence is explored, leads to the bare cries that come when language has been pushed to its limits (it sometimes goes beyond, to wordless howls). It matches the scepticism of the Kingdom of Fools. If Lear's fool is a preacher without laurels, he is obscuring and blunting home-truths to escape the blows that are the traditional reward of plain speaking.

The logic of his defenceless loyalty is that the deeper he sees into the heart of the matter, the more he must disguise it. Edgar has the last word:

> The weight of this sad time we must obey,
> Speak what we feel, not what we ought to say.
> The oldest hath borne most; we that are young
> Shall never see so much nor live so long.
>
> (5.3.323–6)

What he 'ought to say' is some praise of the dead, customary at the end of a tragedy, but he has learned Cordelia's virtue of true counsel, to 'speak what we feel, not what we ought to say'. The emptiness and exhaustion at the end of this play match the emptiness of the stage. There is no new figure such as *Hamlet*'s Fortinbras. Albany asks Kent and Edgar to serve as his counsellors (he is not, surely, after what has happened, proposing a division of the crown). There has never been any sense of ordinary daily life in this play, such as can be felt in *Hamlet* or *Othello*. There is not even a feeling of political life as in *Macbeth*, for the whole play is too archaic, too primitive in the levels it reaches.[10] The magic kingdom dissolves; the dispossessed Edgar, in his final words finds only another way of saying 'The rest is silence.'

Was there, as in *Macbeth*, a reflection of the contemporary scene, however oblique? In so far as Shakespeare was dealing with an archaic kingdom, Lear's proposed division of his land was the opposite of James's stress upon the uniting of his kingdoms. However, at this time there was a certain amount of renewed tension as it was getting clearer that a complete political union between England and Scotland was not desired by either of the parties, and James's plans for political unification were thwarted. So far the play might be taken as reflecting for the benefit of his subjects the well-known dangers of division. The miracle hailed in the coronation procession had not taken place.

This meant, however, that there would be no further exploration of the myth of state. Jonson had this same year (1606) produced his *Hymenaei*, his most complex celebration of social and cosmic order and harmony symbolized in marriage. It was followed by a contest between Truth and Opinion, 'so alike attired that they could by no note be distinguished'; eventually an Angel descends to reveal Truth and strip Opinion. These sports were in honour of the Howard–Essex marriage designed by the King, which ended later in adultery, in divorce, in murder. Fragile indeed was the basis of courtly life upon which Jonson executed his visions. His next comedy, *Volpone*, was the bitterest he had made. Shakespeare did not follow any further his design which had obliquely reflected the life of the times in his living scene. The divisions in that life, where political conflicts took religious form, were to prove irreconcilable. Rather he shared his interests between the ancient lands of his 'Roman' plays and the mythical country of his romances, in both seeking to explore the element of fantasy and to dream in the relations of his characters with each other. He had already penetrated so far below the level of ordinary appearance that in his strange final plays he emerged on 'the other side of despair' into a new country of the mind, filled with figures 'past the size of dreaming.'

The world and the dream

11 The dream of ancient lands

After *King Lear*, what was possible? The company still turned
to their fellow-actor; circumstances still produced new hazards.
In the world without, a great gain coincided with yet another
setback; within the mind of the artist, two tendencies were at
war. Once again, another poet provides the best definition.

> Now the art I long for ... is the struggle of the dream with the
> world. ... In every great play, in Shakespeare for instance – you will
> find a group of characters, Hamlet, Lear, let us say, who express the
> dream, and another group who express its antagonist and to the an-
> tagonist Shakespeare gives a speech close to daily life ... There must
> be fable and mythology that the dream and the reality may face each
> other in visible array ... Those who try to create beautiful things with-
> out the battle in the soul are merely imitators, because we can only
> become conscious of one thing by comparing it with its opposite. The
> two real things we have are our natures and the circumstances that
> surround us. ... A sudden sense of peace and power comes ... but
> we must believe in it, and if we left out a single painful fact, we would
> be unable to believe in those images.
>
> (W. B. Yeats, 'The Poet and the Actress', 1915)

In Shakespeare's last plays the struggle of the Dream and the
World expresses itself; for his company, a dream came true in
these years, but the world was with them also.

On 8 August 1608, Richard Burbage regained the lease of
The Theatre in Blackfriars. The whole area was about to come
under the City's authority, to lose its ancient religious exemp-
tions. Since 1596, when old Burbage had bought the lease and
carefully built his theatre, that indoor playing-house had been
looked at longingly by the company, while it had perforce been

let to their rivals, the Children of the Chapel, who were run by a sharp set of operators. When King James withdrew his choristers, the children's stage still continued, but when in one of his plays, Chapman showed the Queen of France boxing the ears of the King's mistress, James placated the anger of the French Ambassador by ordering an instant shut-down. The residents who had objected to the men's company could not withstand the King's players, and the twelve years' dream came true.

The building stood just below St Paul's, near the modern Mermaid Theatre; thanks to several lawsuits, a good deal is known about it.[1] A grand and dignified stone and timber structure, formerly known as the Great Parliament Chamber, it had been built as the Upper Frater of the dissolved Dominican priory; it was approached from the modern Blackfriars' Lane through a porter's lodge and by means of a grand winding stair; beneath were rooms which had formerly been used to feed pilgrim guests, above, in the roof, some attics with dormer windows. In this stately hall, the divorce proceedings between Henry VIII and Catherine of Aragon had been heard (Shakespeare was to re-stage them in his very latest play). In Henry's time his Office of the Revels had been in Blackfriars; it gave history and dignity to the players, and it had the associations of a 'private' theatre, although in fact it had been working on a purely commercial basis. Only the prices were higher, and the seating about one-quarter that of The Globe.

Two indubitably gentlemanly young playwrights gravitated towards the King's Men and were to provide a brilliantly successful partnership – Francis Beaumont, son of a Judge of the Common Pleas, and John Fletcher, son of a Bishop of London: Fletcher also, later, collaborated with Shakespeare. Some of the disbanded troupe of boy players joined the company; others moved off to a new domain in Whitefriars, not far away, where in 1609 they were performing a play that had been written for them by Ben Jonson – a send-up of Shakespeare's comedies of girl-dressed-as-boy, which presented a boy-dressed-as-girl. It must have taken all Shakespeare's charm to live on good terms with Ben, although this latest play of his, *The Silent Woman*, was a masterpiece of its kind.

Meanwhile, the men had gained their fully-equipped theatre, which had seats at the side of the stage for privileged spectators, the possibility of evening performances by artificial-light, and easy access to The Globe across the river, by way of Puddle Wharf. For of course they kept The Globe, making one their summer playhouse, the other their winterquarters.

But even before the theatre became theirs, in July 1608, plague orders had gone out and once more the playhouses were dark. It was sixteen months before they could re-open. The boys of Whitefriars who disobeyed the orders were driven away and their sponsors soon put into jail.

The theatres had been closed for plague in 1606, two years earlier; but on this later occasion, plague persisted through the winter and became ever more violent in the summer of 1609. For three and a half years, life was hard for the King's Men. They also had to contend with one very cold winter (1607–8) when the Thames froze over and there was a shortage of food. In one year there was only a two months' play season in London.[2]

By now, too, players were less welcome in the country than they had used to be; on tour, they were often given a small 'reward' and sent away from the town. (Stratford-on-Avon did not want them!) It is therefore not unlikely that from 1606 Shakespeare might have spent more of his time privately in Stratford; by February 1608 he had become a grandfather. In London his ties were being loosened; one of his oldest friends at the playhouse, Augustin Phillips, died early in 1605 and another, Will Sly, within a week of acquiring the Blackfriars' lease. Sly had been one of the original sharers in this venture, along with Shakespeare and the Burbages, Heminges and Condell.

The English actors were doing well enough abroad, and some troupes seem to have stayed there. In February 1608 there was a troupe at Graz in Austria which seems to have been connected with Queen Anne's Men of The Red Bull playhouse since it included the younger Robert Browne and was led by John Greene, who may have been a relation of Thomas Greene, the clown who now led Queen Anne's Men and who was married to the elder Robert Browne's widow. While the troupe was at Graz, where they gave a play about 'the Jew' and 'Dr Faustus', John Greene killed a Frenchman in a duel, as the young Arch-duchess Maria Magdalena excitedly wrote to her brother.[3]

Each of the theatres catered for its own type of audience;

if the citizen and his wife strayed into Blackfriars, they might treat the function as an old-fashioned entertainment in the hall of a Livery Company (the lady ascending to the seats of the stage, most improperly) and call for whatever they wanted from 'the waits of Southwark' to a big death scene. A young fool-about-town would also take a seat on the stage in full view but rise 'with a screwed face' to leave at a critical point, or try to 'heap glory on glory' by 'talking and laughing like a ploughman in a morris'.[4]

Shakespeare did not follow the style of the old Blackfriars' repertory; he never set a tragedy in their sinister Italian ducal Courts, and he never turned to satiric city comedy. Instead he developed two kinds of play: the Roman history, based on Plutarch's *Lives of the Noble Greeks and Romans*, and the Romance, for which he turned back to the theatre of his youth, while at the same time he transposed into the theatre some of the feelings and expectations that went into the Court masque.

The Roman plays dealt with the world – whether the city or the vast Empire – with the conflicts of heroic greatness and with the stern limits that the world imposes. The romances deal with a world of dreams; here, in fantastic settings, adorned with spectacular interludes, the poetic conflicts of imagination are worked out.

The basic polarities of his imagination were life and death; the World, symbolized by the city of Rome, is death-dealing; the dream offers a way back from the world of death to a *vita nuova*. After 1608, and perhaps a little before, Shakespeare would be thinking in terms of his two different stages. He had opened at The Globe in 1599 with *Julius Caesar*, a play of close political debate but set in ancient Rome, and therefore not likely to offend the censor, even though it dealt with something much worse than the deposition of *Richard II*. Plutarch's *Lives of the Noble Greeks and Romans* was again to give Shakespeare the material for plays which could work at one theatre or the other, and in which the advantages of both are displayed. The battle scenes in *Coriolanus*, the rapid shifts from Rome to Egypt in *Antony and Cleopatra* seem to belong to the great open arena stage, yet the studies of character are likely to be developed more sensitively, through alternation of heroics with ironic comedy, in the intimate atmosphere of Blackfriars.

It might have been expected that a move to an indoor theatre from the unroofed arena playhouse would have encouraged intimacy, realism, domestic drama. But for Shakespeare the indoor theatre meant the Court masque, where he assisted at Christmas, with its sudden introduction of life on another plane, with royal or noble figures translated to divinity. The masque aimed at 'rapture' or 'delight' or 'wonder', transporting the spectators beyond this world into a dream – which was seen only once and which was supported by music and dancing, light and colour. The Blackfriars plays had also made full use of musical interludes, and the King's Men now acquired a fine orchestra of their own; special airs were composed for them, such as *Bulstrode's Coranto*.

Of course, the company had often played in a hall at Court, where they now went increasingly. In Queen Elizabeth's day they had appeared on an average three times a year, during the Christmas season; afterwards, the average was thirteen times a year, more than all the other companies put together. Their theatre at Blackfriars would enable them to transfer more easily, but it does not appear that they ran two repertories, although they would doubtless try to keep both places in use all the year by sub-letting, or perhaps putting on a second troupe at times.

One very strange play seems to show Shakespeare hovering between various possibilities. This is *Timon of Athens*, which Dover Wilson termed the 'still-born twin of *Lear*'. It cannot be called a play in the ordinary sense, but it alternates between very mordant comedy satirizing the city sharks who surround Timon, and great cosmic dreams, where he exiles himself from the city and returns to dig the bare earth for roots. It is preceded by a discussion on the nature of art between a Poet and a Painter. Here it is fairly clear who the Poet represents; the Painter could be Burbage, who was skilled in that art and once combined with Shakespeare to design and paint an 'impresa' or tilting device. The Poet describes the spontaneity of his writing, how it catches impetus as it flows, and he discovers what he wants to do by doing it. What he has produced now is the word-portrait of a man (which seems very like a painting) – a man first favoured then spurned by Lady Fortune. The Painter thinks this would be a suitable subject for a picture too and says he has seen the warning given in 'a thousand moral paintings' 'more pregnantly than words'.

In the 'show' itself, Timon's godlike bounty rains down benefits in a manner undreamt of since Portia's largesse at Belmont. On the other hand, the revealing speech of the city sharks refusing him loans gives 'the facts' very accurately – 'Alas, good lord! a noble gentleman 'tis, if he would not keep so good a house. . . . Good boy, wink at me and say thou saw'st me not,' or 'What a wicked beast was I, to disfurnish myself against such a good time, when I might ha' shown myself honourable! Servilius, now before the gods, I am not able to do – the more beast, I say!' (3.1.22 ff, 3.2.44 ff).

Timon wishes all kinds of plague on Athens; having found a heap of gold, he gives it to soldiers marching to attack the city and to their whores, to spread disease; the Poet and Painter, hearing of his wealth, revisit him, and he stones them off, crying to the Poet, 'You are an alchemist – make gold of that!'

Timon is not so much a man by now as an elemental being, a figure of love turned to hate, social man turned solitary, patron of the arts turned to the archetypal Man with the Spade, the original Adam. Finally, 'a sudden sense of peace and power' comes, but it has been severely tested against 'painful facts'.

In all its symbolism of the four seasons and the four humours, through which Timon progresses, this play is very archaic;[5] though an ancient land, Athens' corruption is none the less entirely modern – so modern in fact that the young Karl Marx studied this play. Its effect depends on Timon's speeches and on the 'pictures' of his wealthy state and his final destitution. He speaks in paradoxes, and his last is scriptural: 'Nothing brings me all things.' He moves first from the City, then out of the realm of Time, to lie at last in a grave beside the sea shore.

> Timon hath made his everlasting mansion
> Upon the beached verge of the salt flood . . .
> Thither come,
> And let my gravestone be your oracle.
> Lips, let sour words go by and language end. . . .
>
> (5.1.213 ff)

The story was tucked away in Plutarch's *Lives*, but there was also a bitter comic version which could have lent some of the dark comedy to Shakespeare. In this play, at its most simplified and symbolic, can be seen the glimpse of what is to come in the greater Roman plays, tableaux and significant stage moments ('Let language end!') of silence. The mixture of lofty vision and keenly-observed, worldly satire had been a feature of the children's plays at Blackfriars, although Shakespeare's modification of it was entirely his own. Such comedies as *The Dutch Courtesan* had etched in the thieves, whores and bawds who formed the 'alternative society' of London's underworld. Society had been shown in a state of mutual exploitation, the arts of the criminals working like clockwork (as Jonson had also shown them in *Volpone*, which he wrote for the King's Men). Much turns on legalized fraud. The children had also gained a reputation for 'operatic', declaimed political tragedy, with one star part. George Chapman, in the play that shut down the children's theatre, had shown the great Marshal of France, Charles, Duke of Byron, as a magnificently aspiring spirit trapped in a Machiavellian society, led into treason and brought down by foreign plotters.

> O, of what contraries consists a man,
> Of what impossible mixture! Vice and virtue
> Corruption and eternesse, at one time
> And in one subject, let together loose!
> We have not any strength but weakens us,
> No greatness but doth crush us into air....
> *(Byron's Tragedy, 5.3.189–94)*

Destroyed by his own intransigence, as a soldier unfitted for the power-politics of peacetime, Byron conquers his own shame and in death emerges conqueror. His death speech is his gate to life, as he himself commands the headsman, like a soldier giving orders to an inferior.

> Summer succeeds the spring; autumn the summer
> The frosts of winter the fall'n leaves of autumn:
> All these and all fruits in them yearly fade,

> And every year return; yet cursed man
> Shall never more renew his vanished face …
> Strike, strike, O strike; fly, fly, commanding soul. …
> *(Byron's Tragedy,* 5.4.245–59)

Chapman's last line is a direct translation from '*Il dit au bourreau, "Boute, boute, hé boute!"*': the French historian. Chapman's Byron looks forward to those enlarging and ennobling deaths which, at the end of Shakespeare's Roman plays, enfranchise Timon or Antony. However flawed, because of the greatness of his vision, man's heroic dream 'touches the stars' in death. Such is Timon's, such is Antony's, such is Coriolanus'. They are placed almost beyond praise or blame, as objects of admiration or astonishment.

For the men of Shakespeare's time, Rome was not a tranquil imperial state imposing the *Pax Romana*; it was full of wars and what they called 'garboils' or tumult. So Shakespeare's Rome could give a mirror of the times, if less dangerous than Chapman's.

The Rome of Coriolanus was a simple city state, with every man a soldier, although the political expertise of Menenius and the Trade Union leaders who are known as Tribunes of the Plebs operate with sufficient skill. Coriolanus himself is an almost Homeric character (and Chapman was now working steadily on his translation[6]) but he does not inhabit a Homeric world, so that his fate, like Byron's, is to perish by treachery of lesser, cunning men. Shakespeare does not limit himself to political intrigue like Chapman or Jonson; his conflict of rival groups is far more mature and balanced, combining an image of the heroic with an exact sense of how the power-game is played.

Coriolanus has always achieved stage success, even if the hero, incarnation of Mars, reaches his godlike stature by the supreme quality of his physical valour, something foreign to the present age. It is very easy to dismiss him as immature, the 'boy' he is termed by his enemies. Fighting is his means of attaining ecstasy, and for him as for his enemy, Aufidius, it is at times a sacred ritual. When he advances on his ungrateful native city, he carries in his eye a 'fire' which will burn Rome.

One fire drives out one fire, one nail, one nail;
Rights by rights falter, strengths by strengths do fail.

(4.7.54–5)

The misanthropy of Coriolanus, as he had left Rome with the
superb words '*I* banish *you*', is not absolute like Timon's,
though his language is nearly as violent. Although he becomes
metamorphosed into a kind of 'engine', pursuing his personal
honour through the rags of his exile to the leadership of the
hostile army, he cannot stand (in the way Tamburlaine had
stood, for instance)

As if a man were author of himself
And knew no other kin.

(5.3.36–7)

At one word from his wife he 'melts':

Like a dull actor now
I have forgot my part and I am out,
Even to a full disgrace. Best of my flesh,
Forgive my tyranny.

(5.3.40–3)

Shakespeare added wife and child to the pleaders, who come
out to ask mercy; but Coriolanus' mother evokes an image of
especial intimacy: 'The honour'd mould wherein this trunk was
fram'd' (5.3.22–3).

On 9 September 1608, the burial of Shakespeare's mother
had laid her with his dead son in Stratford churchyard. Here
we meet the grandmother and grandchild hand in hand again;
it is the first time so complex a family group has been used in
the plays. Coriolanus' mother knows exactly how to bring him
down completely: 'This fellow had a Volscian to his mother'
and his child is 'like him by chance'. He 'holds her by the hand,
silent', turns and goes to his death among the Volsces.

The part of Volumnia, like that of Cleopatra, is too demand-
ing for a boy. Shakespeare must have written both for a man;
it was customary for men to take the parts of older women. (He
had provided a star role for Burbage and highly individualized

parts for half a dozen other players.) Critics have often wondered how a boy could be asked to take a part like Cleopatra's: I think it is clear that he didn't and that when Cleopatra feared to hear in Rome 'some squeaking Cleopatra boy my greatness / I'the posture of a whore' (5.2.219–20), the lines were spoken by a man.

Antony and Cleopatra, the two equal stars of a less theatrical, more lyric work, are so completely one flesh that they fulfil one of the great Renaissance dreams – not only of harmony but of an exchange and union between the masculine and feminine principles. Each is defined by his or her value to the other. If in *Coriolanus* the world subdues the dream, in this play the dream subdues the world, yet it is a complex dream, where Cleopatra sees Antony 'one way like a Gorgon', the other like a Mars, and he sees her as 'enchantress' but also 'a cold morsel, left on dead Caesar's trencher'. He learns Egyptian passion, she Roman constancy, steadfastness. Neither in this play nor in *Coriolanus* are there any soliloquies to give direct access to the minds of the chief characters. What is seen, is seen through interaction, a new method of writing, which makes these characters naturally ambiguous.

There is an element of fantasy in the way the two lovers see each other – a fantasy that allows for their transvestite games and for their rapid changes of mood. This element of fantasy does not avoid realities, but it transforms them. It is the imagination playing upon ironically recognized facts within the worldly sphere – the ageing warrior, the 'strumpet's fool' as the Romans term him – and the 'Egyptian dish'. Cleopatra is both queen and gipsy.

It is not irrelevant to remember that in 1609, apparently without the consent of Shakespeare or his patron, the *Sonnets* appeared in print. At all events they were virtually suppressed, for very few copies survive, and the next publication (not till 1640) tried to appear as the first. Shakespeare's name was by now a good advertisement, and one publisher had padded out a volume purporting to be his with two pieces by Thomas Heywood – who protested and declared that Shakespeare was equally annoyed. Cleopatra 'with Phoebus' amorous pinches black and wrinkled deep in time', is of course not the dark wanton, still less the original; she is the positive of that negative image. The appearance of the *Sonnets*, unexpected, unwelcome, must have touched off memories, and while Shakespeare worked very closely on Plutarch's text for his Antony, Cleopatra is a much-expanded presentation of Plutarch's figure, dramatically given, where Plutarch merely indicates that her charms were in her manner and 'converse'. The great death scene itself owes the actual details to Plutarch, but Cleopatra's words (in their triumph over Caesar especially, the triumph of the dream over the representative of the world) are Shakespeare's.

The justification of mutual fantasy was set out by Bacon in his essay *Of Truth*:

This same truth is a naked and open daylight that doth not show the masks and mummeries and triumphs of the world half so stately and daintily as candlelight. Truth may perhaps come to the price of a pearl, that showeth best by day, but it will not rise to the price of a diamond or a carbuncle, that showeth best in varied lights. A mixture of a lie doth ever add pleasure. Doth any man doubt that if there were taken out of man's minds vain opinions, flattering hopes, false valuations, imaginations as one would and the like, but it would leave the minds of a number of men poor shrunken things, full of melancholy and indisposition and unpleasing to themselves?

The 'infinite variety' of Cleopatra includes that magnificent voyage upon the Cydnus, where she was attired as Venus, and this is modelled upon the royal progresses in stately barges up and down the Thames. When she re-enacts it at her death, at once an 'eastern star' and a 'lass unparalleled', she 'shackles accident and bolts up change'; the regal image fixes their joint greatness, validates their claims.[7] It is this which gives the note of triumph to her last speeches, the mingling of regal and intimate language.

> Dost thou not see my baby at my breast
> That sucks the nurse asleep?
>
> (5.2.307–8)

The actress is given the chance to reach this sort of height (something like Isolde's *Liebestod*) in a play where she has haled the messenger up and down, lied to Caesar, lied to Antony and frequently lied to herself. Caesar, whom she has now called 'ass unpolicied', had to content himself in his Roman triumph with a mere statue of Cleopatra, Queen of Egypt, with the asp at her breast.

In the courtly masques it was common enough to show the gods taking human form. Ronsard wrote a poem to Marguerite de Valois in which the Graces descended into her as she danced; Daniel had described Anne of Denmark embodying Pallas Athene, who entered her, being 'otherwise no spectacle for mortal eyes'. The descent of the god which comes to Coriolanus in battle, comes to Cleopatra in death. She had dreamed of a cosmic Antony whose reared arm crested the earth and whose legs bestrid the ocean, but the Roman soldiers had denied her dream. Now she validates it.

Enobarbus (a character entirely of Shakespeare's creation) is there to mock and deflate the lovers' images of their greatness, yet to give proof of how godlike Antony is, repenting his own desertion and expiating it with death. It is to this acceptably plain, blunt, worldly Roman that the description of Cleopatra sailing down the Cydnus is given. Thus Rome, even in its opposition, witnesses to Egypt's power.

In the end this magnificent poem – too large to succeed on the stage – contains both tragedy and comedy. It is like the account of the Egyptian wonders given by Antony to his Roman friends, when in his cups. 'It is shaped, sir, like itself' (2.7.43 ff).

For the groundlings, who might not know their Plutarch and his contrasted series of *Lives*, Rome stood at best for a stoic pose of constancy. It was potentially harsh and tyrannical; the only Roman name known to the simplest would be that of Pontius Pilate.[8]

Shakespeare establishes his own version of 'Rome' and criticizes it from within. Egypt's frivolity, its fierce vitality, its pranks, are powerless before Rome, but, like the poor players, or the household fool, or the Good Soldier Schweik, at lowest it achieves a disrespectful come-back. The fluid, moody variety of the lovers, their unpredictable changes, often so disastrous, put them at the opposite end of the scale from all the neat, defined people whom the King's Men had been asked to play –

in revenge tragedy like Tourneur's or in city comedy like *Volpone*. They are Protean, like the climate of the spacious world they live in.

> Sometime we see a cloud that's dragonish;
> A vapour sometime like a bear or lion,
> A tower'd citadel, a pendent rock,
> A forked mountain or blue promontory
> With trees upon't that nod unto the world
> And mock our eyes with air. Thou hast seen these signs;
> They are black vesper's pageants ...
> My good knave Eros, now thy captain is
> Even such a body. Here I am Antony,
> Yet cannot hold this visible shape, my knave.
>
> (4.14.2–14)

Yet this mutable, unpredictable Anthony is given his last words from the noble stoic phrases of Plutarch, as Shakespeare read them in North.

He earnestly prayed her and persuaded her that she would seek to save her life, if she could possibly, without reproach and dishonour, and that chiefly she should trust Proculeius above any man else about Caesar. And as for himself, that she should not lament nor sorrow for the miserable change of his fortune at the end of his days, but rather that she should think him the more fortunate for the former triumphs and honours he had received, considering that while he lived he was the noblest and greatest prince of the world, and that now he was overcome not cowardly but valiantly, a Roman by a Roman.

All is transmuted by rhythm, and by two images

> ... please your thoughts
> In *feeding them* with those my former fortunes,
> Wherein I liv'd the greatest prince o' th' world,
> The noblest; and do now not basely die,
> Not cowardly *put off my helmet* to
> My countryman – a Roman, by a Roman
> Valiantly vanquish'd.
>
> (4.15.52–8)

Plutarch's strength gave Shakespeare exactly what he needed to test his own strength upon. One of the many shapes of Antony speaks here; at his death, 'the crown o' th' earth doth melt'. If the ability to take exactly what he needed and to reject what he did not is shown up as if by a dye or stain, the texture of Shakespeare's play is absolutely unified. Coleridge pointed out the degree to which Shakespeare 'impresses the notion of giant strength ... owing to the manner in which it is sustained throughout – that he *lives* in and through the play'. The effect is one of harmony and control.

From The Globe, the plays were carried over the water some time late in 1609. Then the unpredictable Ben Jonson turned up trumps. He wrote for the King's Men a comedy, sardonic yet exuberant, about life in Blackfriars during plague time, full of so many fancies and dreams and wild hopes of Utopia that it drew in all London. Here was the City that everyone knew, with a triad of cheats, selling illusions to one and all, from the 'separated brethren' of Amsterdam to a magnificent knight and a poor little tradesman, Abel Drugger, the part Garrick chose to play. *The Alchemist* was set 'here, in the Friars'. The actors put it on in 1610. Then, of course, Jonson must needs revert to his Roman history and produce a totally unactable tragedy on *Catiline his Conspiracy*, containing whole chunks of Ciceronian oration. Once again the two rivals had tried their strengths in the arena. Jonson subordinates Dreams to the World, as Shakespeare subordinated the World to the Dream.

The two gentlemanly young lawyers, Beaumont and Fletcher, also turned up trumps, with their *Philaster*. It appeared the year before *The Alchemist*, to become one of the outstanding successes of the time.

Here the audience are no longer in the sinister Italian Courts but in an indeterminate royal scene, where the dispossessed hero, a more ineffectual Hamlet, is in love with the usurper's daughter. This tragi-comedy has a girl page and various other reminiscences of Shakespeare; it is intended as a mirror of elegant love woes modelled on *Arcadia*.

These two young gentlemen did not in the least mind plucking a feather or two from the wing of the elderly practitioner who had once been abused as an Upstart Crow. Beaumont was the age of Shakespeare's Hamnet. They were also each a

'Johannes Fac Totum', pupils of Ben Jonson and followers of courtly models. They provided a Dream, unballasted by the slightest contact with the World, with no trace of any vision of human destiny; but they knew how to borrow effective theatrical detail. Indeed, theirs are the first plays in which a theatre-goer could have recognized 'ham' – the exploitation of purely histrionic detail, the too-emphatic 'flourish'. In another of their successes, *The Maid's Tragedy*, the King's mistress, converted to virtue at the sword's point by her brother, prepares to kill the King:

> I am as foul as thou art, and can number
> As many such hells here ...
> Once I was lovely; not a blowing rose
> More chastely sweet till thou, thou, thou foul canker
> (Stir not) didst poison me ...
> I am come to kill thee.
>
> KING No!
> EVADNE I am!
>
> (*The Maid's Tragedy*, 5.1.73–81)

This is a complicated way of saying that before she was fallen she was unfallen. Evadne is an extreme example of how serpentine the 'bad' woman could become while remaining conventional. Soon another younger man – no gentleman this time, but the son of a city coachbuilder – was exercising his magpie wit on Ophelia's mad scene. John Webster wrote:

> This rosemary is wither'd; pray, get fresh
> I would have these herbs grow up in his grave
> When I am dead and rotten ...
> You're very welcome.
> There's rosemary for you and rue for you
> Heart's ease for you; pray, make much of it.
>
> (*The White Devil*, 5.4.66–78)

Shakespeare was becoming to this younger generation what Marlowe and Lyly had been to him in his own earlier days.

For five years, Beaumont and Fletcher worked for the King's Men; then Beaumont succeeded in winning a Kentish heiress and retired to the life of a country gentleman. He wrote nostalgic poems to Ben Jonson about life at The Mermaid but he did not lament the City:

> ... we want subtelty to do
> The city tricks, – lie, hate and flatter too.
> Here are none that can bear a painted show,
> Strike when you wink, and then lament the blow ...
> Methinks the little wit I have is lost
> Since I saw you; for wit is like a rest
> Set up at tennis, which men do the best
> With the best gamesters. What things have we seen
> Done at the Mermaid! heard words that have been
> So nimble and so full of subtle flame
> As if that everyone from whom they came
> Had meant to put his whole wit in a jest. ...

He did not return. About the same time (1613) Shakespeare too retired to Stratford. But in his strange last plays he had brought together the new opportunities given him by the fulfilment of that old dream, a theatre in Blackfriars, and the memories of a whole lifetime in the theatre.

12 The end of the revels

An idyllic picture of Shakespeare's last years in retirement among his orchards and vines was put forward early; this, according to his first biographer, Rowe, writing in 1709, was 'what all men of good sense will wish theirs may be'. However, it is borne out neither by such facts as can be ascertained nor by the strange, complex and continually changing form of his final Romances.

As one who had reached the status of country gentleman, it would be Shakespeare's normal ambition to mingle with the local gentry and to marry his daughters, especially his heiress, into this group. He would not desert old friends like the Saddlers, but his interests ought to attach him rather to minor gentry, like the stepsons of Thomas Russell of Alderminster, who had acquired money by marrying a wealthy London widow, known to Heminges and the parishioners of St Mary Aldermary, or perhaps to one of the Combes, the richest family in Stratford. Russell was the overseer of Shakespeare's Will, and to Thomas Combes, a young lawyer, Shakespeare left his sword – rather than to any member of his own family: not for instance, to his eldest nephew and fellow-actor, William Hart, who, with his brothers, received Shakespeare's wearing apparel – left to their mother for division. This was the sort of gift usual to a poor relation or even a servant, although it may have included some stage apparel. No Hathaway got a penny.

Just at a time when Susannah Shakespeare should have been considering matrimony, in May 1606, she was cited in the Ecclesiastical Court at Stratford, along with numerous others, for failing to attend at the Easter Communion. She did not appear, and the case was reserved to the next meeting, by which time presumably she had given satisfaction. Hamnet Saddler (and his wife), who was also cited, later asked for time to cleanse his conscience; he was given a day to receive the sacrament and promised faithfully to do so.

Was Susannah, at this time just twenty-three, leaning towards Popery or to a Papist? If so, her father would feel concern. Within twelve months she had married, on 5 June, 'John Hall, Gentleman', a strong Protestant who later, as a churchwarden, was himself to act as an officer of the same ecclesiastical court. Although in 1613 a disreputable young member of the gentry made horrid accusations of adultery and venereal disease against Susannah, she promptly sued him in the Bishop's Court, and he was excommunicated. Probably he was drunk; it was not his only offence. Susannah must have conducted herself befittingly: the verses on her tombstone record her as being witty and also 'Wise to salvation was good Mistress Hall' – rather a Puritan phrase. On her husband's tomb she was described as 'most faithful'.

John Hall, the son of a well-known physician, William Hall of Acton, Middlesex, had graduated at Queens' College, Cambridge, in 1594: he was thirty-two when he married Susannah and had been in Stratford practising physic since 1600. His degree was not in medicine but he probably learned, as many learned their profession, from his father's skill; at all events John Hall made a conscientious and skilful physician, who treated rich and poor, rode forty miles to visit a patient (admittedly a nobleman) and kept a case-book (in Latin). The first volume is missing or we might know more than we do of Shakespeare's later years and the cause of his death, for John Hall treated his family and recorded giving his daughter a purge (for fever) and his wife an enema (for colic). Twice he refused to serve on the Stratford Council by reason of his need to be on call for his patients at a distance, and if he did attend, his tongue was sharp. Clearly, if he was not actually in the squirearchy, John Hall was a solid, suitable and entirely trustworthy son-in-law.

Far otherwise was the husband of the younger daughter, Judith. She married a Quiney – but the Quineys were not what they had been. This was the twenty-five-year-old son of Shakespeare's old friend Richard Quiney, who had been killed while trying to quell a riot in the town, leaving nine small children.

Thomas was one of them and had grown up without discipline and presumably without a fortune. When Judith, at a mature thirty-one, married him, both were excommunicated since they had no licence and it was in Lent. It transpired the very next month that he had got another woman with child, and that she had died, with the infant, in childbirth. Thomas Quiney was ordered to do public penance in a white sheet and, although this was commuted to a more private acknowledgment in his ordinary clothes, it caused Shakespeare at once to alter his Will. Judith was left £150, but it was to be withheld from Thomas, and she was to get a further £150 only at such time as Thomas should make a settlement upon her, in land, of the same amount. This was in the last two months of Shakespeare's life and it has even been conjectured that the shock hastened his end. That seems a little excessive, but clearly Judith's marriage, in the words of a later expert in the social nuances, 'was not one to gratify'.

Joan Hart, Shakespeare's sister, had also married a rather unsuccessful tradesman, who died just a week before the poet; her son William acted with the King's Men (and his illegitimate son, Charles Hart, followed him). The poet's two brothers, who were unmarried (and would have lived either at New Place or at the old house in Henley Street which he left for her life to Joan), had predeceased Shakespeare.

He stood godfather to young William Walker in 1608 – thereby proving his own orthodoxy, for godfathers had to give proof of good standing – and once went up to London to testify to a lawsuit in the household where he had formerly lodged, in Silver Street. This shows him engaged in good offices about a marriage between the Huguenot landlord's daughter and his young apprentice, so that the kindly, tactful manner of his earlier years was still his. But in 1612, as all this had happened eight years earlier, Will Shakespeare of Stratford-upon-Avon, Gent., equally tactfully had forgotten what the exact conditions of the marriage settlement could have been. Or so he said. This may be taken as a tribute to his powers of mental relegation.

During his last years as playwright, Shakespeare wrote the quartet of plays that are termed his Romances or Last Plays. Although each one has its own distinctive form, there is also a family likeness between *Pericles* (which was registered by

1608), *Cymbeline* and *The Winter's Tale,* performed in the spring of 1611, and *The Tempest,* seen at Court at Hallowmas that same year.

All these plays contain the stories of two generations, and in each one the relation of fathers and daughters play an important part. The fathers range from the stupendously idiotic to the wise and careful, but the daughters are all youthful, beautiful and chaste, and they all fall in love with the right sort of people, marry and presumably live happily ever after.

In the year following her wedding, Susannah gave birth to her only child, a daughter christened Elizabeth. Grandfathers have to tell stories to grandchildren, of the kind they heard themselves when young: when he returned to the home of his youth, Shakespeare also returned to the plays of his youth – such as he might first have acted in, *The Rare Triumphs of Love and Fortune* or *Common Conditions*; one very naïve romance, *Mucedorus*, was still scoring a great success with the King's Men. There was a lifetime's experience between this old drama and the new. In his first Romance, an archaic history of the ancient world (and of his own Roman plays) was succeeded by an archaic history of Britain (with an inset of Rome). Then a tragic story of his old detractor, Robert Greene, was transformed with a happy ending (the converse of his treatment of *King Leir*), and lastly a tale of the New World and the Old blended, introduced some of those elemental beings who, like Puck and Titania and the Witches, had always been Shakespeare's particular strength.

In the Roman plays characters may dilate to cosmic proportions; here, it is rather as if we had landed on another planet where characters fully human are placed in fantastic situations and only part of them is shown. The new planet has different powers of gravity, so that one step makes a bound of fifty yards, one leap lands us at the top of the church steeple or the bottom of the ravine. The limits of common life have been suspended.

Spurts of lyric beauty or of disgust and rage may also start out; if history has been dissolved, bits of undissolved horror still float. Detached and dissociated feelings are one of the plagues of the ageing mind, as Yeats and Eliot knew; Yeats writes, 'what else have I to spur me into song?', and Eliot is mordant about these 'gifts reserved for age'.[1] The process can be seen at its most painful in *Two Noble Kinsmen*, probably Shakespeare's last work; as the revelation of a great power breaking up, this play has a special biographical relevance for the literary critic. It shows, too, Shakespeare's return to Chaucer, an author of supreme significance for him, and his nearest kinsman in English poetry. This play made use of part of the wedding masque devised by Beaumont for Gray's Inn and the Inner Temple for the wedding of Princess Elizabeth on 14 February 1613.

In the summer of 1613, the King's Men presented Shakespeare's most spectacular tribute to the special dramatic festivities of that year. At The Globe, *King Henry VIII* featured splendid processions, culminating in the christening of Elizabeth Tudor. On St Peter's Day, 29 June, during performance, the gallery's thatch caught fire and within an hour the whole of the interior was level with the earth. Sir Henry Wotton wrote to his nephew Sir Edward Bacon on 2 July:

> The King's players had a new play called All is true, representing some principal pieces of the life of King Henry VIII, which was set forth with many extraordinary circumstances of pomp and majesty, even to the matting of the stage; the Knights of the Order with their Georges and garters, the Guards with their embroidered coats, and the like; sufficient in truth within a while to make greatness very familiar if not ridiculous. Now King Henry making a masque at the Cardinal Wolsey's house, and certain chambers being shot off at his entry, some of the paper, or other stuff, wherewith one of them was stopped, did light upon the thatch, where being at first but an idle smoke, and their eyes more attentive to the show, it kindled inwardly and ran round like a train, consuming within less than an hour the whole house to the very grounds....[2]

The playbooks were saved – or about half of Shakespeare's works would have been lost to posterity: so, presumably, was the wardrobe, or the best part of it. But the theatre for which Shakespeare had worked had perished and with it many memories.

Next year it was rebuilt at a cost of £1,400 – about three times its original price and roughly equal to the debt left to Gray's Inn by their expenditure on their wedding masque. All the shareholders contributed – and the roof was tiled as a fire precaution. Shakespeare's share would be £100.

In these later years, Shakespeare may have resided at Stratford, but the life of his imagination was still centred on the London theatres. But after the burning of The Globe, perhaps he withdrew. He bought a house in Blackfriars, then sub-let it. He would certainly have been on duty for the royal wedding (in the service of the Lord Chamberlain, the Earl of Suffolk, and the new Master of the Revels, Sir George Buc, who in 1610 had succeeded his uncle Edmund Tilney and who worked at the new Revels' office in Whitefriars) – not probably as a performer, but in his scarlet livery, trying to control the very difficult situation in 'the front of the house' where such crowds had gathered that it was impossible to stage the masque in which the King's Men appeared. Sir Francis Bacon implored the King to let it go forward,

but the worst of all the King was so wearie and sleepy with sitting up almost two whole nights before, that he had no edge to it. Whereupon Sir Francis Bacon adventured to intreat his Majestie, that by this disgrace he would not as it were bury them quick; and I hear the King should answer that then they must bury him quick, for he could last no longer....

Miscalculation and disorder always threatened these visions of cosmic order; but James did his best to atone by giving a special banquet for Gray's Inn and the Inner Temple and allowing them next week to perform not in the Great Hall where the other lawyers' masque had been given but in the Banqueting House – to the 'much repining and contradiction of their emulators'.

Ben Jonson was not in attendance at any of these festivities. He was abroad, bearleading the precocious son and heir of Sir Walter Ralegh round the famous places of Italy. This young man once took occasion to make Ben dead drunk and in that condition paraded him on exhibition, making a little antimasque of his own.

The Princess Elizabeth and her brother Henry, Prince of Wales, had become the darlings of the nation; they supplied the public image that neither James nor his Queen could project. When the young Elector Palatine arrived to claim his bride, he struck up a warm friendship with the Prince of Wales. In November 1612 Henry's collapse and death (from what appears to have been typhoid fever) produced national consternation and led to the postponement of the wedding till St Valentine's Day, 1613. The martially-minded youth, whose tastes ran to shipbuilding and tough games, a friend of the imprisoned Walter Ralegh, a little martinet to his household, had promised a strong régime.

Shakespeare did not join in the flood of elegies for the young Prince nor in the congratulatory verses for the royal wedding; he kept his condolences and compliments to the distant and reflective mirror of his plays. It is seen in the mixture of funeral and wedding imagery in *Two Noble Kinsmen* (the story of which is that of Chaucer's *Knight's Tale*); here, the hymeneal opening – the wedding of Theseus and Hippolyta, revived from *A Midsummer Night's Dream* – is crossed by a black pageant of three weeping queens, mourning their husbands. The play ends with the wedding of the widowed bride, Emily, to Palamon, and with the funeral of his rival, the warlike Arcite.

> His part is played and, though it were too short,
> He did it well.
>
> (5.4.118–19)

For Jonson and for Chapman the revels now were ended. Chapman had left the stage to devote himself to his translation of Homer, in honour of the young Prince, who was his master; his appointment as Server in Ordinary had given him the kind of standing which all poets hoped for, though it had not really relieved his poverty. Ben Jonson had once made for the bright little boy of ten a 'Welcome' which drew quite heavily on his friend's *Midsummer Night's Dream*; he had drawn on it again for the masque he devised when Henry was installed Prince of Wales, *Oberon, the Fairy Prince*. He put himself into both as a playful satyr, an uncouth attendant, and with a fine touch of fantasy and lightheartedness, quite foreign to Jonson's compliments or his diatribes, he toyed with Queen Mab, a group of little fairies, or legends of King Arthur. Though at times he could not forbear to preach at Henry (the schoolmaster dominant again), he also praised him:

> He is lovelier than in May
> Is the spring, and there can stay
> As little as he can decay.
>
> (*Oberon*, 54–6)

When he led this masque, on 11 January 1611, Henry had less than two years to live; with his death and the departure of his sister for her brief reign as the 'Winter Queen' of Bohemia, the Court was left with only the weakly, sober little Prince Charles whom Henry had teasingly declared was destined to be Archbishop of Canterbury (it would have been a happier fate than the one that awaited him, outside the Banqueting Hall, upon a high stage on a cold January day of 1649).

Recently, some critics have felt that Shakespeare in his later plays was writing for the courtly circle and that he tried to reflect the fortunes of the royal family in his romances. But this is to ignore the fact that his company, who were after all the arbiters in these matters, could not have subsisted on Court payments, even though these were much more substantial than they had been in earlier days. For the wedding season they gained £93.6.8, and a further £60 for other performances following it. But they had a large company to support, two houses to maintain; Shakespeare himself as a sharer is calculated to have got about £200 a year. Once before he had thrown his lot in with the common players, and now he no more needed the precarious favour of the Court than he relied on the society of the Stratford burgesses. Thomas Russell's stepson Dudley Digges was a member of the Council for the Virginia Company (Southampton was Treasurer), and from one of these Shakespeare must have gathered the particulars of Sir Thomas Gates, who encountered adventures in the islands of the Bermudas which Shakespeare worked into his play *The Tempest*, where he used the confidential report of the Secretary to the expedition. Perhaps he read it at Russell's place, Alderminster near Stratford, perhaps with another neighbour, Lord Carew. News of Virginia was much in the air; Chapman and the other two Inns of Court were entirely topical in choosing Virginians for their masque, though to reveal them seated in a gold mine, as they did, was to confound Virginia with the Spanish conquests. Dudley Digges, in search of a north-west passage, was convinced that not more than three hundred miles separated Virginia from Drake's Nova Albion (i.e. British Columbia), and Sir Walter Ralegh was eventually to risk his life (and lose the gamble) in search of another gold mine on the Orinoco. The New World still had the character of a dream country.

In his last plays Shakespeare, coasting in the seas of his imagination, touched ancient lands first and lastly this New World, which yet somehow belongs also to the Old World. Pericles visits the ancient cities of the eastern Mediterranean; in *Cymbeline* Postumus sails away, waving his handkerchief, to a modern Italy, from which he returns with an invading force of antique Roman soldiers, who appear to have landed where Henry Tudor did (not the most strategic point for any but a Welshman). When, in *The Winter's Tale*, he exchanged the names of the kingdoms of Sicilia and Bohemia, thereby providing Bohemia with a seacoast, Shakespeare must have been well aware of what he was doing; even the Thames watermen knew better than that – and pointedly put him right! The island of *The Tempest*, emerging from its stormy seas, is partly Bermuda and partly Lampedusa, and is not to be located on any map. 'Old men should be explorers,' said T. S. Eliot: the 'undiscovered country from whose bourne / No traveller returns' looms ahead.

All these imaginary lands are inhabited by rulers erring, dispossessed or deeply evil, and by beautiful young people subjected to strange ordeals; the passions are deep and true but no part of ordinary life. They are a distillation, or concentration, of feelings produced by extremities of the kind proper to romance.

> What countrywoman?
> Here of these shores?
> No, nor of any shores.
> (*Pericles*, 5.1.101–3)

> When you do dance. I wish you
> A wave o' th'sea, that you might ever do
> Nothing but that; move still, still so . . .
> (*The Winter's Tale*, 4.4.140–2)

The beauty of these princesses has in it something indescribable, as in some glint of sunlight in a crest of foam that has itself disappeared from a changing sea; the freshness is so elemental that words like 'chastity', which relate it to the world of men, seem clumsy. Yet these are set against rage and disgust as dark as anything in Timon. Marina in the brothel defends herself from rape with language that does not sound elemental at all:

> Thou art the damned doorkeeper to every coistrel that comes
>   inquiring for his Tib;
> To the choleric fisting of every rogue
> Thy ear is liable; thy food is such
> As hath been belch'd on by infected lungs.
> BOLT What would you have me do? Go to the wars, would you?
>
> (*Pericles*, 4.6.163 ff)

And Leontes speaks in intimate physical terms of his sickness:

> There may be in the cup
> A spider steep'd, and one may drink, depart
> And yet partake no venom, for his knowledge
> Is not infected; but if one present
> Th'abhorr'd ingredient to his eye, make known
> How he hath drunk, he cracks his gorge, his sides,
> With violent hefts. I have drunk, and seen the spider.
>
> (*The Winter's Tale*, 2.1.39–45)

What Leontes *had* seen was his wife and his guest talking – as Troilus had seen Cressida and Diomede, and cried, 'If beauty have a soul, this is not she!' An image, and only an image; for there was no spider. His wife and his friend were true. The fantasy relations which he devises, spinning the spider's web himself, lead to poison and those 'dangerous lunes' that rob his Queen of any wish to live:

> My life stands in the level of your dreams,
> Which I'll lay down.
>
> (3.2.79–80)

The darkness is complete; but it is hallucination. 'I'll fill your

grave up', says Paulina to the living statue that was Hermione.
This is art, not life:

> That she is living,
> Were it but told you, should be hooted at
> Like an old tale; but it appears she lives.
>
> (5.3.115–17)

The truth is authenticated by the very absence of any ordinary
criteria.

Pericles was outstandingly successful in its own time: the
Venetian Ambassador paid twenty crowns for a special performance, inviting the French and Florentine envoys; in 1619
it was given at Court for another ambassador. This naïve tale
is told and presented by John Gower, Chaucer's contemporary,
whose tomb Shakespeare could see in the church of St Mary
Overy, where his brother was buried. Gower appeared regularly, for instance in masques, as typical of the ancient simplici-
ties of English poetry.

> To sing a song that old was sung
> From ashes Ancient Gower is come ...
>
> (*Pericles*, 1.1.1–2)

It is not straight drama but a mixture of full acting-text and
mime, with songs, dances and a tourney; unfortunately it survives only in a pirated text, which gives mere tantalizing
glimpses of Shakespeare's words. It reads in many parts like
a bad translation; the whole play seems now to exist for the
sake of one scene, where Pericles regains his daughter – just
as some of the sonnets seem to exist for the sake of one line,
like, 'Lilies that fester smell far worse than weeds.'

Humanity is here transformed into something rich and
strange – it is, yet it is not, the world we know. Characters are
raised to the seventh heaven (Pericles hears the music of the
spheres, inaudible to mortal ears) or plunged in torment; they
are 'fey' and in some way insulated from life. 'I feel the dream
within me as about me,' says Imogen, waking under her flowery
canopy to find beside her the headless corpse in her husband's
garments. *The Tempest* opens with a shipwreck where the sailors

cry 'To prayers, to prayers!', 'Farewell, my wife and children', and then in a flash a girlish voice is heard:

> If by your art, my dearest father, you have
> Put the wild waters in this roar, allay them
>
> (1.2.1–2)

and the potentially fatal is revealed as illusion. 'Sophisticated artlessness,' said Granville Barker of *Cymbeline* – but it bites deeply.

> And that most venerable man which I
> Did call my father was I know not where
> When I was stamp'd. Some coiner with his tools
> Made me a counterfeit.
>
> (*Cymbeline*, 2.5.3–6)

The brutal pun in 'tools' and the image of impressed metal combine the bracelet which was Postumus' love token and the bedrite in an act of imagination proper to the lunatic, the lover or the poet. Characters feel only love or hate – no one feels, for example, gratitude (save once, Prospero to Gonzalo). In this artificial world, strange but real tropical flowers grow under glass, protected from the outside weather; yet they are genuine organic growths, not pieces of tissue culture. The full weight of the language of experience is brought to illusions, known even to other characters as illusions. The turning-point of the action is something as grotesque as Cloten's corpse, or the bear in *The Winter's Tale* (such animals are familiar in the Court antimasques; of course this would not be a real bear, which took a lot of handling). The gods too descend: Diana and Jupiter to resolve the mysteries in *Pericles* and *Cymbeline*; Apollo in *The Winter's Tale* gives oracles, and perhaps descends in thunder as Apollo the Hunter to effect the destruction of Antigonus.[3]

Shakespeare had few of the resources of the Court masque. He had only his words and music. Yet the costly images of the Virginian knights or moors, the baroque flamboyance, the mounds of feathers, the bushels of pearls, are forgotten, and what remains of the revels are the songs of Ariel.

Full fathom five thy father lies;
Of his bones are coral made;
Those are pearls that were his eyes;
Nothing of him that doth fade
But doth suffer a sea-change
Into something rich and strange.
(*The Tempest*, 1.2.396–401)

The Tempest is Shakespeare's shortest play (but King James liked short plays, and he merely endured long masques). It is the culmination of the experiments in Romance – and of course it is not a romance in the formal sense for it observes the three unities and is in this sense Shakespeare's most classic play. It stands at the head of all the plays in the Folio, and itself culminates in Ariel. He enchanted Shakespeare's contemporaries. They did not bother, as modern writers tend to do, about Prospero and his inner conflicts; for this new kind of being, they would put down their money. Capriccio (in Chapman's wedding masque for Lincoln's Inn and the Inner Temple) is a fair example of what lesser men would offer – a too-loquacious, too-didactic substitute. Ariel appears in the two masques within this play – first as a harpy, and then as a goddess. Ariel and Caliban come out of a richly cultivated country and a barren rocky isle respectively. The King's Arcadia was a Shakespearean country, and Inigo Jones's flame-coloured spirits serve to be hunted off with dogs, as Prospero and Ariel hunt the conspiracy of Caliban, Stephano and Trinculo on the island (did Shakespeare remember how his old master, George Carey, had once hunted an intruder from the Isle of Wight?).[4]

When the King of Naples regains his son, the discovery shows a pair of lovers playing chess. This courtly game was considered a decorous pastime for noble lovers; but the whole play is a game of chess. The symmetry and balance of the contrasted conspiracies (that to kill Alonso and that to kill Prospero), the pairing-off of different groups, is all controlled by Prospero. Who then is his antagonist in the game of chess? It is, of course, himself. Vengeance against generosity.

His sudden burst of anger against Ariel, his erratic actions, are at sharpest variance with his magic powers. In some modern versions of the play, all the other characters have been seen as essentially within Prospero's mind (this was Jonathan Miller's interpretation). The condensed, enigmatic poetry almost demands expansion, proclaims itself poetry of the gaps.

There is, then, an irresistible tendency to expand this play. Dryden doubled all the characters to give a devastating series of 'mechanical beauties'. Browning extended it one way in *Caliban upon Setebos*; Auden, in *The Sea and the Mirror*, in another. Prospero here moans:

> Stay with me, Ariel, while I pack ...
> Now our partnership is dissolved, I feel so peculiar
> As if I had been on a drunk since I was born
> And suddenly now, and for the first time, am cold sober ...
> I never suspected the way of truth
> Was a way of silence ... even good music
> In shocking taste; and you, of course, never told me ...
>   (W. H. Auden, *For the Time Being*, pp. 9, 14, 15)

As in the death scene of Antony, Prospero's first epilogue is spoken with a 'beating mind' and it is not serene; the dissolving sky shapes represent that same mutability that beats in the pulse and inhales or exhales with the breath:

> Our revels now are ended. These our actors,
> As I foretold you, were all spirits, and
> Are melted into air, into thin air;
> And like the baseless fabric of this vision,
> The cloud capp'd towers, the gorgeous palaces,
> The solemn temples, the great globe itself ...
>   (4.1.148 ff)

A deep metaphysical vision rejects all dogma; indeed, it coexists with scepticism.

With the exception of *Pericles*, Shakespeare did not take a collaborator till he wrote *Two Noble Kinsmen*. The young men admired him and parodied his successes;[5] he must have heard Fletcher's verse in the playhouse, as a matter of performance; and Fletcher must have known Shakespeare in the same way, so that the Fletcherian-sounding parts of *King Henry VIII* might well have resulted from the effect on Shakespeare's always retentive ear.

Ben Jonson parodied *Two Noble Kinsmen* in his *Bartholomew Fair*, where in the Induction, he brings on the stage-keeper, an old hand and a scrivener to draw articles of agreement with the audience: 'If there be never a servant monster i' the Fair, who can help it, he says? nor a nest of antics? He is loath to make nature afraid in his plays, like those that beget Tales, Tempests and such drolleries, to mix his head with another man's heels. . . .' This has been taken as solemn censure, though in context it reads like cheerful banter; it appears that the drolleries (that is the mime without words, like the masque-element and dances) counted for a good deal.

Two Noble Kinsmen enabled the King's Men to give the general public the very successful *Anti-Masque of Country People* which had been presented by them as part of the wedding masque of Gray's Inn and the Inner Temple. It had received several encores at Court, and a little play was written round it, so that it could be publicly shown. For such a hasty piece of work, Shakespeare and Fletcher worked together. It has one passage of horrid rage and disgust (Palamon's description, in his prayer to Venus, of lust in old age). The Shakespearean verse is rich and slow and curiously stiff:

> For our crown'd heads we have no roof
> Save that which is the lion's and the bear's,
> And vault to everything,
>
> (1.1.55–7)

There is one vision more of springtime and a-Maying in the wood near Athens.

> O Queen Emilia,
> Fresher than May, sweeter
> Than her gold buttons on the boughs, or all
> Th'enamell'd knacks o' the mead and garden; yea,
> We challenge too the bank of any nymph
> That makes the stream seem flowers; thou O jewel
> O' th' wood, o' th' world . . .
>
> (*Two Noble Kinsmen*, 3.1.4–10)

The dream world is more powerful than ever before. These emblematic figures from Chaucer seem to be stiffening back from flesh and blood into statues.

In the latest plays, the conflict between the dream and the world goes on, but in some, particularly with *The Tempest*, the dream, which is the play itself, takes over from the world. As Prospero puts aside his enchantment and finally, in the last of his epilogues, appeals to his audience

> Now I want
> Spirits t'enforce, art to enchant ...
> (Epilogue, 13–14)

he is speaking in the everyday garb, as one man like themselves. This speech is customarily taken as Shakespeare's own farewell. It is modest, its fancies coming to rest in a plea for charity in judgment.

> As you from crimes would pardon'd be,
> Let your indulgence set me free.
> (Epilogue, 19–20)

As to Shakespeare's mortal end, the tradition of one unreliable cleric in Stratford is that he contracted a fever at a merry meeting with Ben Jonson and Michael Drayton. (A later and even less reliable cleric asserted 'he died a papist'.) Drayton often came to Clifford Chambers, near Stratford, but in 1616 Jonson was engaged in bringing out the Folio edition of his works, carefully edited; he would have been in attendance on the press to read proofs. There was much jesting at the presumption of terming plays *Works* and presenting them in the grand form reserved for classics or sermons.

Shakespeare was a sick man when in March he signed his Will; he pulled himself together for a firm signature. 'By me William' is steadily written, but his surname quavers. He died on 23 April, by repute his fifty-second birthday. His monument shows him holding a pen; but his lips are parted: he is declaiming. He had left his oral art to his colleagues to preserve.

Seven years later, two actors whom he had remembered in his Will, John Heminges the business manager and Henry Condell, brought out a Folio as handsome as Ben Jonson's which contained, in addition to plays already in print, as many new ones, never seen before. They were giving to the world one of their most valuable exclusive rights, 'only to keep the memory of so worthy a friend and fellow alive, as was our Shakespeare'.

Ben Jonson contributed the first of several commendatory poems, hailing a resurrection of the man he had known: 'My Shakespeare, rise ...', praising his wit and his art in unstinted terms. When, in 1632, a second edition was needed, a young Londoner, John Milton, added his tribute:

> Thou in our wonder and astonishment
> Hast built thyself a live-long Monument.

Notes

1 The cradle of security

1 In fifteen lines he invented four new words, according to F. P. Wilson (*Troilus and Cressida*, 1.3.7–21): conflux, tortive, protractive, persistive.

2 The first part of the narrative is now known to be *The Tale of the Noble King Arthur and the Emperor Lucius*, which is based on the English alliterative poem *Morte Arthure*; the extensive relations were revealed only by the discovery of the Winchester MS, which shows what printing (and Caxton) did to Malory. See *Works*, ed. E. Vinaver (Oxford, 1947), I, xxiv.

3 Mark Eccles, *Shakespeare and Warwickshire*, 9. This is the most extensive study of Shakespeare's early environment.

4 See below, chapter 3, p. 57, for the significance of the claim to 'valiant service'.

5 For the alderman's ring, see *Romeo and Juliet*, 1.4.56; *1 Henry IV*, 2.4.321. (Christopher Marlowe's father, a shoemaker, was a recognized Bondsman.)

6 At the time of her marriage, Mary Tudor was ten years older than Philip of Spain; one young Spaniard observed: 'It would take God Himself to drink of that cup!' (Christopher Morris, *The Tudors*, 1955, p. 129.)

7 Dr Peter Laslett has furnished me with information on legitimacy and on the ages customary for marriage. See also Lawrence Stone, *The Family, Sex and Marriage in England 1500–1800* (1977) pp. 50–1, 60–2, 609.

8   Our desires
        Are both too fruitful for our barren fortunes! ...
        Then 'tis the prudent'st part to check our wills

And till our state rise, make our blood lie still.
'Life, every year a child and some years two!
(Middleton, *A Chaste Maid in Cheapside*, 2.1.8–15)

9 *The Book of Sir Thomas More* was a collaborative venture; it survives in manuscript, written in five hands, of which one has been thought Shakespeare's. The full text is in *The Shakespeare Apocrypha*, and also in *The Riverside Shakespeare* (1974); extracts in Alexander's one-volume edition, and several others.
10 See Joel Hurstfield, *The Queen's Wards* (1958).

2 A challenge to fortune

1 Cited by John Dover Wilson, *Shakespeare's England* (1911), pp. 181–2. In Queen Mary's reign, assembly for Protestant worship had been carried out in London inns under pretence of assembling for a play.
2 See below, chapter 6, pp. 124–5.
3 The opening scene of Dekker's *Old Fortunatus* shows the goddess Fortune with four captive kings at her chariot, one being Bajazet, and she herself laments his fate at the hands of 'Fortune's best minion, warlike Tamburlaine'. For further examples see my *Themes and Conventions of Elizabethan Tragedy* (1935), pp. 95–6, and *Shakespeare the Craftsman* (1969), pp. 105–8.
4 See below, chapter 5, p. 105, n. 11.
5 He said that he had as good a right to coin as the Queen, tried to impress her image and found himself in Newgate jail: a characteristic insolence.
6 See L. G. Salingar, *Shakespeare and the Traditions of Comedy* (1974) for discussion of the sources. He points out that the Dromios are much more like the *zannis* of the *commedia dell' arte* than Roman slaves.
7 See Harold Brooks' 'Theory and Structure in *The Comedy of Errors*', Stratford-upon-avon Studies, number 3, ed. B. Harris and J. R. Brown (1961).

3 The upstart crow

1 *De Conscribendis Epistolis*, chapter x – studied in the upper school.
2 The most famous case, that of the Dymockes' summer play at South Kyme, is dealt with by N. J. Conor in *Godes Peace and the Quene's*,

and by C. L. Barber in *Shakespeare's Festive Comedy* (Princeton, 1959). See my *Rise of the Common Player* (1962), p. 257, and my article 'Beasts and Gods' in *Shakespeare Survey* 15 (1962), for further examples. Cf Chapter 6, p. 125.

3 See his *Francesco's Fortune* and *Greene's Groatsworth of Witte*.

4 Harvey says he died at Dowsgate, the outlet for the city sewers at the mouth of the Fleet; but the site of his burial implies that Harvey was merely being abusive. In plague time, a man would be buried hastily.

5 Robert Wilson, a player in the Queen's Men, had a show of birds and beasts presented by Folly for the marriage of Pride and Lust. Later uses of the beast fable occur in Jacobean plays (e.g. *The Changeling*, where they are presented by madmen). Spenser's *Mother Hubbard's Tale* used a beast fable to attack Leicester's enemies. The most extreme form was that of a monster with the body of one beast and the head of another; this monstrous double form is ascribed to 'Shakescene'. (For *Tamburlaine*, see above, chapter 2, p. 40.)

6 Historically neither England nor France was then clearly defined as a nation state in the modern sense; the nobles who held dominions in both would not feel the kind of patriotism which Shakespeare assumes. This matter is touched on by G. B. Shaw in *St Joan*, a play deeply in debt to Shakespeare.

7 After 1580, the King of Spain, whose right was as indisputable as his sword was sharp, claimed and annexed Portugal. The French who intervened were heavily defeated in a sea battle; in 1589 the English fared better at sea but failed to take Lisbon, as Drake would not risk his ships within range of the shore batteries.

8 *Coleridge's Shakespearean Criticism*, ed. T. H. Raysor (1930), I, p. 238. Malory provides an example when he alters the foreign campaign route of King Arthur to follow that of the victorious Henry v, in whose army he himself had served (*Works*, ed. Vinaver, I, xxv).

9 F. P. Wilson, *Shakespearean and other Essays*, p. 19.

10 This is a note to be heard again from Northumberland, mourning the death of Hotspur ('Let order die!' *2 Henry IV*, 1.1.154); it is to be heard from Albany in *King Lear*. The 'stony heart' is an image that Shakespeare continually uses, from Titus pleading with the stones, less hard than the tribunes, to Othello: 'I strike at it and it hurts my hand.'

11 Nicholas Brooke, *Shakespeare's Early Tragedies* (1968), p. 57.
12 It is Buckingham who claims to be an actor when Richard asks
him: 'Tut, I can counterfeit the deep tragedian' (3.5.5–8), giving
a full description of how an actor would present 'deep suspicion';
but Richard is the Upstart Crow *par excellence*.
13 Philip Edwards, *Thomas Kyd*, 'Writers and their Work' (1966),
p. 6.
14 Ibid., p. 40.
15 Among these are Greene's *Alphonsus of Arragon*, a bad imitation
of Marlowe, and *Selimus*, an anonymous tragedy which promises
'greater murthers' in Part II.
16 Dryden, *Essay on Dramatic Poetry* in *Shakespearean Criticism*, ed. D.
Nichol Smith (1916), p. 17.
17 See Harold Brooks' 'Marlowe and the Early Shakespeare' in *Christopher Marlowe*, ed. Brian Morris (1968).

4   The poet of the plague years

1 William Lilly on the plague of 1603, quoted by F. P. Wilson, *The
Plague in Shakespeare's London* (Oxford, 1927), p. 155. The substance of the preceding paragraphs is also indebted to Wilson.
2 *A Treatise of the Plague* (1603). Lodge died in this visitation.
3 This, the setting for *Summer's Last Will and Testament*, may have been
open to Nashe by reason of his contribution to the Marprelate
controversy. Whitgift the Archbishop enjoyed the company of
his household of young clerks. He was, like Nashe, a Cambridge
man; he had been Bishop of Worcester, Shakespeare's native diocese, and Elizabeth liked him well enough to call him 'my little
black husband'.
4 Lady Elizabeth was the wife of Sir George Carey, Governor of the
Isle of Wight and son of the Lord Chamberlain. He succeeded
his father as Lord Hunsdon in July 1596. Spenser dedicated his
Muiopotmos to this lady, who, when her husband became the
patron of Shakespeare's company, would become lady patroness
of the players.
5 See I. M., *A Health to the Gentlemanly Profession of Serving Men* (1598):
it uses the contrast between 'remuneration' and 'guerdon' of Costard in *Love's Labour's Lost* 3.1. Cf Lawrence Stone (Chapter 1,
note 7).

6 See G. P. V. Akrigg, *Shakespeare and the Earl of Southampton* (1968), p. 36.

7 See *The Autobiography of Thomas Wythorne*, ed. J. Osborne (1961).

8 This poem has gone practically unnoticed, although its significance as something to which Shakespeare was making a definite 'correction' entitles it to serious notice. It was first recognized by G. P. V. Akrigg in his *Shakespeare and the Earl of Southampton*, p. 33, as part of Burghley's campaign.

9 I have dealt with this in detail in an essay, 'No Room at the Top', in *Elizabethan Poetry*, ed. John Russell Brown and Bernard Harris (1960).

10 Rowe, in his edition of 1709, says that the story was handed down by Sir William Davenant and mentions a thousand pounds, an impossibly large sum; some scholars feel that a nought has been added.

11 His initials, W. H., are compared with the dedication to the *Sonnets*, which, however, I take to refer to the procurer not the subject of the poems.

12 For roses see 1.2, 35.2, 54.2, 67.8, 95.2, 98.10, 99.8, 109.14 and such phrases as 'summer's distillation' 5.9, 'living flowers' 16.6.

13 Guilt seems an extraordinarily strong word as used in Sonnet 36; in Sonnets 88 and 89, unjust imputations of guilt are accepted for the beloved's sake.

14 See Akrigg for an account of *The Delectable History of Clitophon and Leucippe*; and for the growth of Ovidian erotic poetry, see my *Shakespeare and Elizabethan Poetry* (1951), chapter 4; also R. A. Lanham, *The Motives of Eloquence* (Yale, 1976), chapters 1 and 2.

15 I cannot feel as confident as A. L. Rowse, who claims that between Sonnets 85 and 86 Marlowe was killed; I think both refer to one event. See *Shakespeare the Craftsman* (1969), pp. 31–2.

16 Various explanations have been offered; see S. Schoenbaum, *William Shakespeare, a Compact Documentary Life* (1977), pp. 180–2.

17 These of course were very fashionable. Daniel's *Complaint of Rosamund* (1592), in the same stanza form as Shakespeare uses, has one memorable line: 'Now did I find myself unparadis'd'. For the comparison with *Hamlet*, see p. 156.

5 The poet of love

1 See his *Shakespeare* (1964), p. 70. 'The subsequent information about this early *Hamlet* indicates that it was by Shakespeare.' This is not substantiated.

2 Discussed below, p. 141.

3 Frances Yates, *A Study of Love's Labour's Lost* (1936); Leslie Hotson, *Shakespeare by Hilliard* (1977). I had a shot myself in *The School of Night* (1936).

4 E. A. Armstrong, *Shakespeare's Imagination* (1963), chapter XI.

5 Sonnet 82.

> Thou truly fair wert truly sympathized
> In true plain words by thy truth-telling friend.

6 Arthur Brooke in the preface to *Romeus and Juliet*, Shakespeare's source, says 'I saw the same argument set forth on the stage with more commendation than I can look for' (1562). For evidence of Shakespeare's popularity at university, and the Inns of Court, see E. K. Chambers, *William Shakespeare* (1930), II, 195, 201–2; and cf below, p. 143.

7 What follows is indebted to G. V. P. Akrigg, *Shakespeare and the Earl of Southampton* (1968).

8 Sir Charles Danvers' house in London was where the conspiracy was planned. He was beheaded along with Essex's stepfather, Sir Christopher Blount, dying very bravely (though 'his cheeks trembled'). His brother Sir Henry had been Lieutenant of Horse on Essex's Irish expedition, under Southampton as Captain.

9 George Gascoigne, *A Hundreth Sundry Flowers*, ed. C. T. Prouty (Missouri, 1942), pp. 172–81. The marriages took place in November 1572, a year after Lepanto.

10 This vital distinction is essential to the play. Henry assumes the 'body politic', almost removing Richard's sense of identity, when he is deposed. Richard feels that the two cannot be severed; Edward had felt the same.

11   Now walk the angels on the walls of Heaven
       As sentinels to warn the immortal souls
       To entertain divine Zenocrate ...
                                        (*2 Tamburlaine*, 2.4.15 ff)

It is the use of the last line as a kind of refrain which they share in common: 'to view fair Portia' and 'to entertain divine Zeno-crate' are echoes. This casts a shadow of regal grief over Morocco who chooses what Tamburlaine found – death concealed in golden trophies.

12 True Venetians, who had been insuring their cargoes for genera-tions, would have had a good laugh at Antonio's expense.

13 Bach, in the chorales of the *Matthew Passion*, uses this identifica-tion, especially perhaps in '*O Bone Jesu*' ("Twas I denied Thee').

14 See G. K. Hunter, 'The theology of Marlowe's *Jew of Malta*', *Journal of the Warburg and Courtauld Institutes*, volume xxvii (1964), pp. 211–40.

15 'A note on the blank verse of Christopher Marlowe' in *The Sacred Wood* (1920).

16 It could be said, I suppose, that his hatred being directed against himself – another part of himself, i.e. Antonio – Shakespeare's aggression might lead to suicidal tendencies, if it became patho-logical.

17 John Davies of Hereford may be quoted again, from his *Scourge of Villainy* (1611): 'Some say, good Will, which I in sport do sing / Hadst thou not play'd some kingly parts in sport / Thou hadst been a companion for a king' ('To our English Terence, Mr Will Shakespeare').

6 The Lord Chamberlain's Men

1 Indeed J. M. Robertson the disintegrator went so far as to claim that it is the one play entirely written by Shakespeare.

2 Olivia sends a ring to Cesario 'after the last enchantment you did here'. Polixenes terms Perdita 'enchantment'; Ferdinand addresses Miranda, 'O you wonder'.

3 Among the plays that serve as analogues are the clumsy *John à Kent and John à Cumber* (which, however, has a good group of trades-men-players). *The Two Angry Women of Abingdon*, an excellent farce on runaway lovers lost in a wood, and *The Merry Devil of Edmonton* are later but use the same plot devices.

4 Lily B. Campbell, *Shakespeare's Histories, Mirrors of Tudor Policy* (San Marino, 1947), pp. 229–38. Neither Miss Campbell nor anyone else has seen the particular relevance of the parallel for the Lord Chamberlain's Men. Compare this with the way Malory had

adapted King Arthur's French campaigns to mirror those of his own king Henry v (see above, p. 241, n. 8).

5 Nevill Coghill, *Shakespeare's Professional Skills* (1964), pp. 64–77. This develops the contrasts of multiple plots already seen in *A Midsummer Night's Dream*.

6 'The Castle' meant the stocks, at Christmas; the 'Old Lad of the Castle' may have provided some joke for Tarlton originally.

7 See Leeds Barroll, *The Revels History of Drama in English*, volume 3, ed. Clifford Leech and T. W. Craik (1975), p. 10; compare the later efforts of the Careys to gain patronage under James (below, p. 169).

8 See above, chapter 2, p. 32.

9 Reprinted in *The Shakespeare Apocrypha*, ed. C. F. T. Brooke (Oxford, 1912). The cast includes a very weak imitation of Falstaff, Sir John of Wrotham.

10 See Ben Jonson's *Every Man in his Humour* for a character named Cobb, a water-carrier, who calls a red herring 'my princely coz'.

7 Enter, fighting, at several doors...

1 Such as the satires of Gascoyne, or even Nashe's early work. See Brian Gibbons, *The Jacobean Comedy* (1968).

2 See C. J. Sisson, ed. Stanley Wells, *The Boar's Head Theatre* (1972).

3 See G. E. Bentley, *The Profession of the Dramatist in Shakespeare's Time* (Princeton, 1971), chapter 6.

4   I laid down my arms, a buckler broad,
           But ever he smote aside.
   (Cf. *Secular lyrics of XIV and XV centuries*, ed. Robbins, p. 26.)

5 These critics are: Frank Kermode, 'Shakespeare's Mature Comedies' in *Renaissance Essays* (1971); Harold C. Goddard, *The Meaning of Shakespeare* (Chicago, 1951); A. P. Rossiter, 'Much Ado About Nothing' in *Angel with Horns* (1961).

6 As a model for more pathetic heroines of Jacobean tragi-comedy (Aspatia etc) Viola contributed to the later stage; Shakespeare's girl pages are all lucky in love, Fletcher's more melancholy. Modern critics and producers may accentuate the bitterness (see preface to the new Arden edition, ed. T. W. Craik, 1975).

7 See *The Autobiography of Thomas Whythorne*, ed. James Osborn (Oxford, 1961). Cf chapter 4 above, p. 73 (note 7).

8 Hamlet, revenge!

1 Dover Wilson deals with the significance of the lost *Hamlet* in the introduction to his New Cambridge edition of the play (1934).

2 See Victor White, *Soul and Psyche* (1958). The Freudian views on Hamlet are well known; they have been used in performance and inspired the ballet danced by Robert Helpmann.

3 Quoted Dover Wilson, *Hamlet*, p. lxv, from *The Testament of Beauty*, Book I, ll. 577–80.

4 Lily B. Campbell's *Shakespeare's Tragic Heroes: Slaves of Passion* (San Marino, 1930) initiated this approach.

5 *Tarlton's News out of Purgatorie* (1590). Tarlton's ghost appears near The Theatre, and the narrator tries to conjure him, '*Ab infernis nulla est redemptio* ... depart from me, Satan. ...' His reply is 'Why, you whoreson dunce, think you to set Dick Tarlton non plus with your aphorisms?', and he proceeds to 'defend' Purgatory.

6 See E. I. Fripp, *Shakespeare Man and Artist* (Oxford, 1938), pp. 145–6.

7 The well-known illustration by Henry Peacham to *Titus Andronicus* (1595) shows a figure in just this attitude behind the condemned man.

8 His lecture 'Hamlet, the Prince or the Poem' was given in 1942 and is reprinted in *They asked for a Paper* (1962). *A Grief Observed* was originally published under the name of N. W. Clerk in 1961.

9 Norman Rabkin, *Shakespeare and the Common Understanding* (1968), p. 9. Both these quotations are in Nigel Alexander, *Poison, Play and Duel* (1971).

10 Nym used it in *The Merry Wives of Windsor*, 1.1.150–2.

11 A well-known instance is 'The Marriage of Sir Henry Unton'. The perspective painting of Troy in *The Rape of Lucrece* was in this convention. See p. 87 above.

12 This is *Antonio's Revenge*; a new edition, by W. R. Gair, is due in the Revels Plays.

9 'His Majesty's poor players'

1 The text may be found in E. K. Chambers, *The Elizabethan Stage*, II, 208–9.

2 L. G. Salingar, *Shakespeare and the Traditions of Comedy* (1974), pp. 313–16.

3 From *Matthew* 7.1–2 (this follows the Lord's Prayer): 'Judge not that ye be not judged. For with what judgment ye judge ye shall be judged; and what measure ye mete, it shall be measured to you again.'

4 That sort of justice had been sufficiently shown on Ralegh and Cobham, brought to the verge of the scaffold, and played about with, before the King's 'especial mercy' restricted the execution to two miserable minor figures.

5 Robert Catesby was, however, the descendant of that William Catesby who was Richard III's trusted counsellor and who assists in all his plots in Shakespeare's *Richard III*. His ironic words to the doomed Hastings, 'Tis a vile thing to die, my gracious lord / When men are unprepar'd and look not for it' (3.2.63–4) might have served in 1605.

6 A full account of all Stratford connections is given in Leslie Hotson's *I, William Shakespeare* (1937), chapter 8. He makes a great deal of Sir Edward Bushell, once retainer to the Earl of Derby, whose brother married a Greville and his sister a Quiney, gentleman usher to the Earl of Essex.

7 I am indebted here to an unpublished essay by Guy Butler on 'The Great Doom's Image' and to Frederick Turner, *Shakespeare and the Nature of Time* (1971), chapter 7. For hell castle, see Glynne Wickham in *Aspects of Macbeth*, ed. K. Muir and P. Edwards (1977).

8 Robert Southwell's poem was in print by 1602; he died in 1595. Ben Jonson told Drummond that he would have given all his poetry to have written it. At the climax of the *Croxton Play of the Sacrament* an infant Christ appears to the Jew who is torturing him and effects a conversion.

9 See Peter Milward, *Shakespeare's Religious Background* (1973), p. 54, and C. Devlin, *Life of Robert Southwell* (1956), p. 15.

10 See Charles Williams, *Shakespeare Criticism, 1919–35*, ed. Anne Bradby (1936), p. 134.

11 Jonson's elaborate antimasque of witches in *The Masque of Queens* (1609) – they retreated into a traditional Hell-Mouth at the end – preluded the appearance of the Queen as herself, Bel-Anna, Queen of the Ocean, leading eleven famous queens of antiquity. There are conjurings with charms, songs and dancing round the cauldron. Marston uses a witch in *Sophronisba* (1606). *Macbeth* has, of course, been especially susceptible of translation into

other media and other cultures owing to its deep and simple intensity. Such are the Japanese film *Throne of Blood*, the Zulu *Umabatha*, etc.

10 The kingdom of fools

1 See Frank Kermode, preface to *King Lear* in the Riverside Shakespeare (Boston, 1971); Maynard Mack, *King Lear in our Time* (Berkeley, 1965).

2 See William Willeford, *The Fool and his Sceptre* (Edward Arnold, 1969).

3 Sheldon P. Zitner in *Some Facets of King Lear*, ed. R. Colie and F. T. Flahiff (Toronto, 1974).

4 Printed 1603 and reprinted 1604. I have used the Folger Library's copy of 1604. William Weston's own account in his *Autobiography* is edited by P. Caraman (1955).

5 His book was printed by James Roberts who in 1600 had printed *A Midsummer Night's Dream* and who had a special licence to print playbills for theatres. Roberts also protected players' rights by registering plays in his name, so that no one else could print them; he did this for *Troilus and Cressida*.

6 He left Stratford in 1575, returned as priest and died a martyr in 1586 (see Peter Milward, *Shakespeare's Religious Background*, pp. 39, 52).

7 'When she cries O! then the devil is there ... ever and anon they were at the holy chair and the dislodging, coursing and pinching, the devil was still in their Parks ... if they had dispatcht hastily, much good hunting sport had been lost' (pp. 76, 79).

8 A number of extracts from Harsnett are given in the Arden edition of *King Lear* edited by Kenneth Muir. He also comments on their use in *The Sources of Shakespeare's Plays* (1977), pp. 202–6.

9 Pillicock is the penis. One of the witches quoted by Darrell bewitched a boy who farted in her presence with the rhyme, 'Gip with a mischief and fart with a bell / I shall go to heaven and thou shalt go to hell' – and then, says Darrell, her Minnie entered into him.

10 'Whether one deplores or rejoices in the fact, there are still some zones in which savage thought, like savage species, is relatively protected. This is the case of art, to which our civilization accords the status of a National Park, with all the advantages and

inconveniences attending so artificial a formula' (C. Lévi
Strauss, *The Savage Mind*, quoted in Terence Hawkes, *Shakespeare's
Talking Animals*, p. 213.)

11 The dream of ancient lands

1 See *The Revels History of Drama in English*, ed. Clifford Leech and
   T. W. Craik (1975), volume 3 (1576–1613), pp. 197–220.
2 If orders were obeyed, theatres in London were closed from 16 July
   1606 to 8 January 1607, save for two weeks in late November
   and the week before Christmas; then in 1607, 5–12 February,
   12–26 March, 30 April–7 May, 9 July–26 November; from 28
   July 1608 to 7 December 1609; in 1610, 26 July–29 November,
   except for one week.
3 See the article by Orlene Murad, *Mosaic*, x, 4, summer 1977 (University of Manitoba), pp. 119–32.
4 See Francis Beaumont's *Knight of the Burning Pestle* for the first incident, and Thomas Dekker's *The Gull's Horn Book* for the second.
   Both deal with the period when the children were at Blackfriars.
5 I have dealt at length with this in chapter 8 of *Shakespeare the Craftsman* (1969) and will not expand on it here. I think *Timon* is a
   'show' or masque-like play (akin to Dekker's *The Sun's Darling*)
   which gives Timon's progress through the four seasons of the year
   (ending with Lent) and the four humours – sanguine, choleric,
   melancholy and phlegmatic, or watery, the last representing his
   death.
6 Seven books of the *Iliad* came out in 1598, and the complete work
   in 1611.
7 This point was made in a lecture by Anne Barton, entitled 'Nature's
   Piece 'gainst Fancy' with others used here.
8 Andrew Marvell has described a village play in which Moses
   appeared to Julius Caesar and forbade him to cross the Rubicon!

12 The end of the revels

1 See W. B. Yeats, *Last Poems*, 'The Spur', and T. S. Eliot, 'Little
   Gidding' in *Four Quartets*.
2 See E. K. Chambers, *William Shakespeare*, 2, pp. 343–4, for the full
   account. It is perhaps worth noting that one big scene in this
   play, the trial of the divorce between Henry and his queen, took

place in the Blackfriars, in the room used as the theatre; and that one character in this play, John Butts, the King's physician, who is introduced rather particularly, had been the owner of Shakespeare's New Place. These little hidden personal touches are like the tiny portraits of the artist found in a corner of large Renaissance paintings.

3 Leslie Hotson recently claimed that a well-known miniature by Hilliard (V & A, P21, 1942) depicts Shakespeare as Mercury! This is not how Mercury appeared in masque. Another miniature, 'Young man among roses', which he claims to be Mr W. H., is identified by Roy Strong as the Earl of Essex.

4 See above, p. 93, for how George Carey hunted an attorney from his territory. These rough country games of a mock hunt were practised in the Halls of the Inns of Court at Christmas and perhaps lay behind the antimasque at Court.

5 *Philaster* gives a neat and tidy version of Hamlet's dilemma; *The Woman's Prize* is a sequel to *The Taming of the Shrew* where Petruchio is subjugated *en seconde noces*.

A select list of sources and authorities

Shakespeare, among the most heavily studied of literary subjects, is also fortunately among the best indexed. This list supplies works to each chapter where readers may find information to support the statements made. (Place of publication London, unless otherwise given.)

General

Texts

William Shakespeare, *The Complete Works*, ed. Peter Alexander (1951): citations are from this, the most generally used of modern one-volume texts.

The Riverside Shakespeare, ed. Blakemore Evans and others (Boston, Mass., 1974). This edition contains a wide selection of secondary material; it reprints *Sir Thomas More* and *Two Noble Kinsmen*: its text is the basis of the *Harvard Concordance to Shakespeare* (1974).

A New Variorum edition is being prepared in USA; these volumes of single works give the fullest apparatus; and for the *Sonnets*, the New Variorum, ed. H. E. Rollins (Philadelphia, Pa., 1944) supplies the fullest record of biographical material and conjecture.

Christopher Marlowe was most fully edited in the annotated five volumes, ed. R. H. Case (1930–33); a convenient modern edition is in Everyman's Library ed. E. D. Pendry (1976).

Ben Jonson has been more comprehensively edited than any other Elizabethan dramatist excluding Shakespeare; the *Works*, ed. C. H. Herford, Percy and Evelyn Simpson, eleven volumes (Oxford, 1925–52). I have used the Yale edition for single plays and for the Masques (the last edited by Stephen Orgel, 1969).

Other dramatists are well represented by *Drama of the English Renaissance*, ed. Russell A. Fraser and Norman Rabkin, two volumes,

1976 (these contain *Cambyses* (see chapter I) and *Summer's Last Will and Testament* (see chapter IV).

Geoffrey Bullough, *Narrative and Dramatic Sources of Shakespeare*, eight volumes (1957–75), collects sources and analogues of the plays and poems.

Bibliography

Up to 1935 the field is covered by W. Ebisch and L. L. Schücking, *A Shakespeare Bibliography* and its supplement (Oxford, 1931, 1937).

Shakespeare, ed. Stanley Wells, *Select Bibliographical Guides* (Oxford, 1973) is the most accessible modern guide.

English Drama excluding Shakespeare, ed. Stanley Wells, *Select Bibliographical Guides* (Oxford, 1975) covers other dramatists.

Shakespeare Quarterly, ed. John Andrews (Washington DC), contains an annual bibliography of current publications, which in the last issue contained over two thousand items.

Shakespeare Survey, ed. Kenneth Muir (Cambridge), contains select annotated annual lists.

Biography

E. K. Chambers, *William Shakespeare, a Study of Facts and Problems*, two volumes (Oxford, 1930). The most fully documented life, with extracts from contemporary documents and authors.

M. M. Reese, *Shakespeare, his World and his Work* (1953). An attempt to put Shakespeare in his literary context, not as well known as it deserves to be.

S. Schoenbaum, *William Shakespeare, a Compact Documentary Life* (Oxford, 1977). This is the full and revised text of the earlier edition of 1975, but with a reduced number of illustrations and reproductions of the documents. The most authoritative of recent lives.

1 The cradle of security

Edgar I. Fripp, *Shakespeare Man and Artist*, two volumes (1938). A study of the local background.

Mark Eccles, *Shakespeare in Warwickshire* (Madison, Wis., 1961). The most detailed and scholarly exploration of the records.

E. R. C. Brinkworth, *Shakespeare and the Bawdy Court of Stratford* (1972).

New biographical material from the records of the ecclesiastical court, Holy Trinity Church, Stratford, relating to Shakespeare's family.

T. W. Baldwin, *William Shakspere's Small Latine & Less Greeke*, two volumes (Urbana, Ill., 1944). An exhaustive account of the grammar school curriculum.

Roland M. Frye, *Shakespeare and Christian Doctrine* (Princeton, NJ, 1963). A study of Shakespeare's Protestant affiliations.

Peter Milward, *Shakespeare's Religious Background* (1973). Puts the case for his Catholic affiliation.

Joel Hurstfield, *The Queen's Wards* (1958). A study of the Court of Wards under Elizabeth and Lord Burghley.

Peter Laslett, *The World We have Lost* (1965). A study of pre-industrial and more especially rural society.

Lawrence Stone, *The Crisis of the Aristocracy, 1558–1641* (abridged edition, Oxford, 1967). On the economics of the Elizabethan Court. *The Family, Sex and Marriage in England, 1500–1800* (1977).

Marie Axton, *The Queen's Two Bodies* (Royal Historical Society, 1978). Deals with the theory of the Crown and the literary image of the Queen in relation to drama.

For documents relating to the career of John Shakespeare, William Shakespeare's marriage etc, see Chambers and Schoenbaum.

2 A challenge to fortune

E. K. Chambers, *The Elizabethan Stage*, four volumes (Oxford, 1924). The basis for any study of the theatre; in spite of its title, the subject is covered to 1616, the year of Shakespeare's death.

Glynne Wickham, *Early English Stages, 1300 to 1650*, three volumes (1969; a further volume is forthcoming). An attempt to place literary drama in a wider context of other forms of social and theatrical life.

M. C. Bradbrook, *The Rise of the Common Player* (1962). A study of the acting profession in terms of society during Shakespeare's lifetime.

C. J. Sisson, ed. Stanley Wells, *The Boar's Head Theatre, an inn yard theatre of the Elizabethan age* (1972). New light from contemporary sources on the innyard stages.

Frances A. Yates, *Astraea, the Imperial Theme in the Sixteenth Century* (1975). A study of the cult of Queen Elizabeth in pageantry and drama, with extensive comparisons with events at the French Court.

Eugene M. Waith, 'The Metamorphosis of Violence in *Titus Andronicus*', *Shakespeare Survey*, No. 10 (1957). A seminal study of Shakespeare's tragic mode in this play.

3 The upstart crow

Greene's Groatsworth of Wit, ed. G. B. Harrison (Bodley Head Quartos, 1923). Relevant extracts are also printed in Chambers, II, pp. 188-9.

M. C. Bradbrook, 'Beasts and Gods; Greene's *Groatsworth of Wit* and the social purpose of *Venus and Adonis*', *Shakespeare Survey*, No. 15 (1962). A detailed study of these two works as attack and reply.

Bernard Capp, 'English Youth Groups, the Pindar of Wakefield', *Past and Present*, No. 76 (August 1977). Discusses shows of defamation and scorn in relation to the early drama.

Clifford Leech, 'The two-part play; Marlowe and the Early Shakespeare', *Jahrbuch der Deutschen Shakespeare–Gesellschaft*, XCIV, (1958). A consideration of structure.

J. P. Brockbank, 'The frame of disorder – *Henry VI*', *Early Shakespeare*, Stratford-upon-Avon Studies, III, ed. J. R. Brown and Bernard Harris (1961).

Harold Brooks, 'Marlowe and the Early Shakespeare' in *Christopher Marlowe*, ed. Brian Morris (1968).

Nicholas Brooke, *Shakespeare's Early Tragedies* (1968).

Philip Edwards, *Thomas Kyd and Early Elizabethan Tragedy*, *Writers and their Work* (1966). This study by the editor of *The Spanish Tragedy* will appear in a collected volume on Elizabethan dramatists with others from this series of booklets (see e.g. Hunter on Peele and Lyly below).

D. T. Williams, *The Battle of Bosworth* (Leicester, 1973).

4 The poet of the plague years

F. P. Wilson, *The Plague in Shakespeare's London* (Oxford, 1927). An invaluable work, from which I have drawn examples and events.

Thomas Nashe, *Works*, ed. R. B. McKerrow, five volumes, reprinted with corrections and supplementary notes by F. P. Wilson (Basil Blackwell, Oxford, 1958). A major source for knowledge of life in Shakespeare's London.

G. P. V. Akrigg, *Shakespeare and the Earl of Southampton* (1968). The most accurate biographical study of this relationship, correcting earlier misconceptions.

J. W. Lever, *The Elizabethan Love Sonnet* (1956).

W. Empson, *Seven Types of Ambiguity* (1930). Contains the analysis of several leading sonnets.

5 The poet of love

G. K. Hunter, *John Lyly, The Humanist as Courtier* (1962). A full study of Lyly and his influence. Hunter has also written a booklet, *Lyly and Peele*, in the series *Writers and their Work* (1968) – see above, under Kyd, chapter 3.

W. H. Auden, 'Brothers and Others', *The Dyer's Hand* (1948). On *The Merchant of Venice*.

M. C. Bradbrook, *Shakespeare and Elizabethan Poetry* (1951). An attempt to see the early Shakespeare in relation to the general poetic background of his time.

E. Kautorowicz, *The King's Two Bodies* (1957).

6 The Lord Chamberlain's Men

J. Dover Wilson, *The Fortunes of Falstaff* (1947). The strongest case for the influence of the Moral Play.

C. L. Barber, *Shakespeare's Festive Comedy* (Princeton, NJ, 1959). The opposing view, relating Shakespeare to folk games.

Anne Righter (Barton), *Shakespeare and the Idea of the Play* (1962). A study of the imagery of the play within Shakespeare's works.

W. H. Auden, 'The Prince's Dog', *The Dyer's Hand* (1948). On *Henry IV*.

7 Enter, fighting, at several doors . . .

Glynne Wickham, *Early English Stages, 1300–1650*, volume II, part 2, gives the most recent account of the crisis of 1597.

A. Kernan, *The Cankered Muse* (New Haven, Conn., 1959). The most comprehensive account of the satiric movement of the late nineties.

G. K. Hunter, 'English Folly and Italian Vice; the Moral Landscape of John Marston', *Jacobean Theatre*, Stratford-upon-Avon Studies, I, ed. J. R. Brown and B. Harris (1959). A wide-ranging view of the background to these plays.

P. Finkelpearl, *John Marston of the Middle Temple* (Cambridge, Mass., 1969). The drama in relation to the Inns of Court.

Thomas Dekker, *Dramatic Works*, ed. Fredson Bowers, four volumes (1953–61). This will be supplemented by 4 volumes of notes, which will include material on *Satiromastix*, by Cyrus Hoy.

Three Parnassus Plays, ed. J. B. Leishman (1949).

8   Hamlet, revenge!

Quarto 1 of *Hamlet*, ed. W. W. Greg, Quarto Facsimile Texts, No. 7 (1951).

Quarto 2 of *Hamlet*, ed. W. W. Greg, Quarto Facsimile Texts, No. 4 (1940).

The Folio Text, ed. Charlton Hinman, *The Norton Facsimile* (1961).

A. A. Raven, *A 'Hamlet' Bibliography and Reference Guide, 1877–1935* (1936).

Stanley Wells, *A Reader's Guide to Hamlet*, Stratford-upon-Avon Studies, v, ed. J. R. Brown and B. Harris (1963). This is a brief and discriminating account of the more important books on *Hamlet*.

Fredson Bowers, *The Revenge Play* (Princeton, NJ, 1940). A study of the *genre*.

Eleanor Prosser, *Hamlet and Revenge* (Stanford, Calif., 1967). A full but moralistic study.

Kenneth Muir, *The Sources of Shakespeare's Plays* (1977), chapter 24.

9   'His Majesty's poor players'

The Memoirs of Robert Carey, ed. F. H. Mares (Oxford, 1972).

Stephen Orgel and Roy Strong, *Inigo Jones, The Theatre of the Stuart Court* (1973). A full and sumptuous account of the Court Masque.

Roy Strong, *Splendour at Court* (1973). A comparative account.

David M. Bergeron, *English Civic Pageantry, 1558–1642* (1971). An account of civic welcomes, coronation processions, etc.

D. J. Gordon, ed. Stephen Orgel, *Studies in the Renaissance Imagination* (Los Angeles, 1976). A collection of Gordon's influential essays on Jonson.

Leslie Hotson, *'I, William Shakespeare...'* (1937). Deals with the Russell family and with Shakespeare's relations with other local gentry.

10 The kingdom of fools

S. Harsnett, *A Declaration of Certain Egregious Popish Impostures* (1604).
    Extracts are printed by Kenneth Muir in the New Arden edition
    of *King Lear* and his *The Sources of Shakespeare's Plays* (1977),
    chapter 28.
Some Facets of 'King Lear', ed. Rosalie Colie and F. T. Flahiff (Toronto,
    1974). I am especially indebted to the essay by Rosalie Colie in
    this volume on the biblical echoes in *King Lear*.
William Willeford, *The Fool and His Sceptre* (1969).
Grigori Kozintsev, *Hamlet* and *King Lear*; 'Stage and Film', in *Shake-
    speare, 1971*, ed. C. Leech and J. M. R. Margeson (Toronto,
    1972).

11 The dream of ancient lands

M. C. Bradbrook, *The Living Monument* (Cambridge, 1976). I have
    dealt at greater length on the plays in this chapter and chapter
    12 in this volume.
The Revels History of Drama in English, volume III, ed. C. Leech and
    T. W. Craik (1975). Contains the latest detailed account of the
    Blackfriars Theatre (by Richard Hosley, Part III, chapter 4).
Shakespeare's Plutarch, ed. T. J. B. Spencer (1964). A convenient
    reprint.
Eugene Waith, *The Herculean Hero* (New York, 1964). Deals with the
    Roman plays in relation to Chapman, and other later plays.

12 The end of the revels

Frances A. Yates, *Shakespeare's Last Plays, a new approach* (1975). The
    extreme case for taking these plays as Court drama.
Kenneth Muir, *Shakespeare as Collaborator* (1960). Deals with the early
    and late plays.
The Two Noble Kinsmen is reprinted in *The Riverside Shakespeare* and
    edited by N. W. Bawcutt for *The New Penguin Shakespeare* (1977).
For Shakespeare's Stratford connections in these years, see Chambers,
    Schoenbaum and Brinkworth, as cited in the section 'Biography'
    above and Chapter 1.

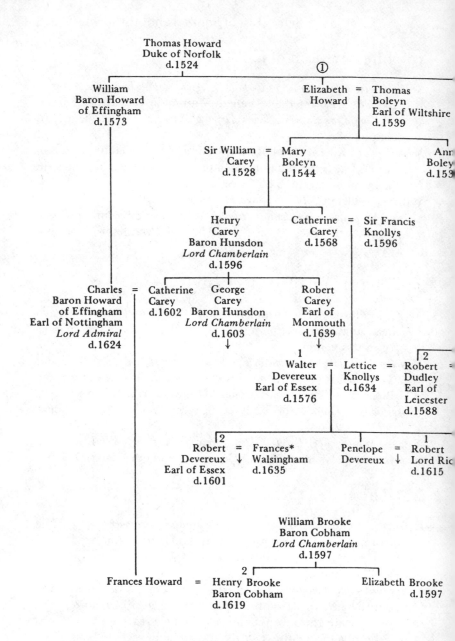

Family tree of Shakespeare's patrons

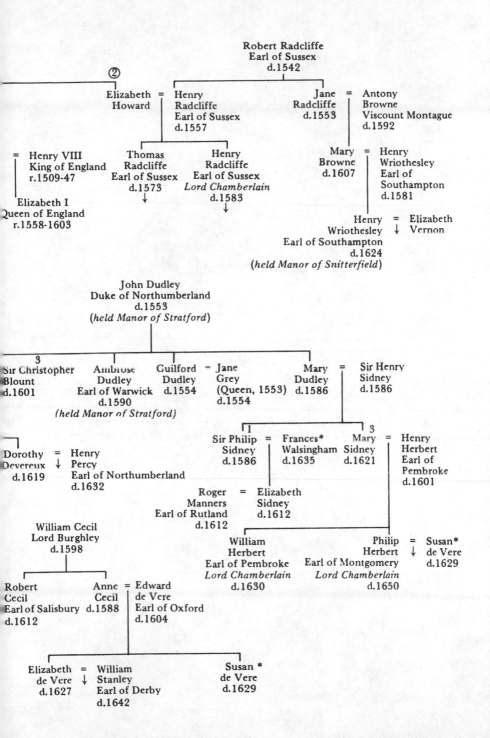

Robert Radcliffe
Earl of Sussex
d.1542

②

Elizabeth = Henry
Howard   Radcliffe
           Earl of Sussex
           d.1557

Jane = Antony
Radcliffe Browne
d.1553   Viscount Montague
           d.1592

= Henry VIII
King of England
r.1509-47

Elizabeth I
Queen of England
r.1558-1603

Thomas   Henry
Radcliffe   Radcliffe
Earl of Sussex Earl of Sussex
d.1573   *Lord Chamberlain*
↓   d.1583
                ↓

Mary = Henry
Browne   Wriothesley
d.1607   Earl of
         Southampton
         d.1581

Henry = Elizabeth
Wriothesley ↓ Vernon
Earl of Southampton
d.1624
(held Manor of Snitterfield)

John Dudley
Duke of Northumberland
d.1553
(held Manor of Stratford)

3

Sir Christopher   Ambrose   Guilford – Jane   Mary = Sir Henry
Blount   Dudley   Dudley   Grey   Dudley   Sidney
d.1601   Earl of Warwick d.1554 (Queen, 1553) d.1586   d.1586
                  d.1590   d.1554
                  (held Manor of Stratford)

                                        1
                              Sir Philip = Frances* Mary = Henry
                              Sidney   Walsingham Sidney Herbert
                              d.1586   d.1635   d.1621 Earl of
                                                              Pembroke
Dorothy = Henry   d.1601
Devereux ↓ Percy
d.1619   Earl of Northumberland
          d.1632
                              Roger = Elizabeth
                              Manners Sidney
                              Earl of Rutland d.1612
                              d.1612

William Cecil
Lord Burghley
d.1598
                              William   Philip = Susan*
                              Herbert   Herbert ↓ de Vere
                              Earl of Pembroke Earl of Montgomery d.1629
Robert   Anne = Edward   *Lord Chamberlain* *Lord Chamberlain*
Cecil   Cecil de Vere   d.1630   d.1650
Earl of Salisbury d.1588 Earl of Oxford
d.1612   d.1604

Elizabeth = William   Susan *
de Vere ↓ Stanley   de Vere
d.1627   Earl of Derby d.1629
           d.1642

Index